THE TRIPLE SOUL:
BROWNING'S THEORY OF KNOWLEDGE

"Where the heart lies, let the brain lie also."

THE TRIPLE SOUL:

BROWNING'S THEORY OF KNOWLEDGE

NORTON B. CROWELL

THE UNIVERSITY OF NEW MEXICO PRESS

THE PUBLICATION OF THIS BOOK IS MADE POSSIBLE
BY A GRANT FROM THE FORD FOUNDATION

Manufactured in the United States of America
Library of Congress Catalog Card No. 63-21031
First Edition

To Ruthmary, Larry, Dring, and Steven

CONTENTS

ACKNOWLEDGMENTS

I owe a debt of gratitude to the Administration of the University of New Mexico for their generous grant of a sabbatical leave, during which I was able to bring this book to completion. I particularly thank Dean Dudley Wynn for his wise and humane counsel and encouragement. My debt is especially heavy to Roland Dickey and to Richard C. Angell of the University of New Mexico Press, and to Professors Willis Jacobs, Katherine Simons, and Hoyt Trowbridge, who read the manuscript and who made valuable suggestions for its improvement. The grant of the Ford Foundation to the University of New Mexico Press toward the printing of this book is deeply appreciated. I also thank my wife for many services in connection with the book, not the least of which was keeping the children reasonably quiet for moments on end. I alone accept full responsibility for any faults of method or judgment the book may have. Because my thesis is in sharp variance with traditional criticism, I cannot suppose that it will escape a large measure of the resistance with which opposition to established views is commonly received. I only ask that I alone stand in the assizes.

N. B. C.

INTRODUCTION

Since the death of Robert Browning in 1889, the prevailing critical opinion of his theory of knowledge has been that set by Henry Jones in his *Browning as a Philosophical and Religious Teacher,* 1891. Jones's thesis is that Browning denigrated the mind as an instrument in the perception of truth and counseled man to trust solely to the intuitions and the heart. Since man is forced to "reject the testimony either of the heart or of the head," Jones affirms, "Browning . . . unhesitatingly adopts the latter alternative." This sundering gulf between head and heart has widened with the years. William Clyde DeVane, in his *Browning's Parleyings, the Autobiography of a Mind,* discovers that the poet "has no trust in the intellect. The faculties of the reason impeach his faith. Therefore he discounts the intellect altogether. It is his last stand on the narrow rock in pitch darkness before the sea ingulfs him."[1] In his *Browning Handbook* he finds that Browning in his later years strengthened his suspicions of the intellect.

If Browning discounted the mind, as is alleged, to support a religious faith which he feared must fall upon examination, he was both cowardly and dishonest, and his stature as a thinker, if not as a poet, must diminish with time. The purpose of this study is to examine Browning's attitude toward the mind and his theory of knowledge. I was prompted to undertake this task because my love of his poetry is inseparable from an assumption that so wise and healthy a man simply

---

1. New Haven, 1927, p. 187. See C. N. Wenger's *The Aesthetics of Robert Browning* (Ann Arbor, 1924), p. 58: "The chief criticism of Browning's philosophy has been that he degrades knowledge and vastly overrates the feelings as materials of life."

could not believe that God's gift of mind is a sort of practical joke for the discomfiture of mankind. None of his prose supports a charge of anti-intellectualism, nor do his life and conversation. Only the poetry allegedly develops the theory of nescience which everything else seems to deny. This investigation, therefore, is largely a close textual interpretation. Browning knew all too well that much error is perpetuated by "the critics reading attentively the criticisms of their brethren, and paying no attention at all to the text criticized."[2]

This study is not intended to be a history of the criticism of Browning's concept of knowledge. Such an undertaking, if added, would enormously increase its length and proportionately blur its focus. I cite only those critical opinions which seem to me most representative or most important to my thesis, by way of agreement or disagreement. I include citations here and there which, in my opinion, are remarkably wrongheaded, not because I find joy in discovering error, but because they help to explain how the myth of Browning's anti-intellectualism developed and became solidly entrenched. I omit many citations simply because they add no fresh point of view, not because their inclusion would challenge my thesis or prove embarrassing. I discuss the poems severally, under appropriate heads, even though to do so entails considerable repetition—repetition, it should be added, which is inherent in Browning. Since the sturdy misconception of Browning's attitude toward the mind arose through misreading of the individual poems, it seems reasonable to found my thesis squarely upon explication. I attempt to explicate appropriate parts of all the poems which to me seem important to my study, even though certain themes appear again and again in different settings. To omit "A Toccata of Galuppi's," for example, because the same idea appears elsewhere, is to invite a particularly damaging criticism, for the poem is widely held to be an especially effective attack upon the mind. At the risk of repetition, I have chosen to show the essential kinship of this poem

2. Robert Browning, *Letters of Robert Browning, Collected by Thomas J. Wise,* ed. Thurman L. Hood (New Haven, 1933), p. 216.

with many others in Browning, none of which is anti-intellectual in the usual sense of the word.

Whether Browning was an intellectual may possibly be debated, for the term is semantically protean; but no one could seriously doubt the thirst for knowledge that prompted him to delve into recondite studies. His abiding interest in music and musicology, history, languages—especially classical languages—art, literature, politics, philosophy, religion, and psychology is everywhere attested. His reading of the six thousand volumes in his father's library, his astonishing intellectual vitality, his quick grasp of the important issues of the day, his exuberant acceptance of life as a challenge to all of man's faculties, and, above all, the massively impressive—and often annoying—knowledge displayed throughout his poetry are evidence of an agile and inquiring, if not profound, intellect. It is true that much of his parade of little-known lore reveals erudition which is more apparent than real, and the very brevity and obscurity of his references suggest depth and breadth of learning that all too often were in reality limited to the information contained in the *Biographie universelle* (Paris, 1822), which he found in his father's library. But the fact that as a boy he read all fifty volumes of the encyclopedia in French with avid interest and retention must be admitted as significant of the bent of his mind and his love of knowledge. Could such a man distrust knowledge, fear the mind as an insidious trap, and affirm that for man there can be only illusion and lies eternally masquerading as truth? Did he really advocate as a substitute for the treacherous intellect reliance on intuition? What was his theory of knowledge?

The answer to these questions, as this study attempts to show, lies in Browning's belief in the triple soul of man: body, mind, and spirit, "Three souls which make up one soul," as St. John affirms in Browning's "A Death in the Desert." The body serves

> . . . the next soul, which, seated in the brain,
> Useth the first with its collected use,
> And feeleth, thinketh, willeth,—is what Knows:

> Which, duly tending upward in its turn,
> Grows into, and again is grown into
> By the last soul, that uses both the first,
> Subsisting whether they assist or no,
> And, constituting man's self, is what Is . . . .[3]

In short, man is the sum of his three parts: "What Does, what Knows, what Is; three souls, one man." Browning's theory of knowledge is based upon the concept of wholeness or order—the triple soul working in harmony to fulfill the divine plan. When one soul usurps the functions of another, order is disrupted and chaos ensues. Mind becomes evil only when body or spirit is atrophied through disuse or through abuse of intellect. In the harmonious functioning of the triple soul, man can find oneness with the divine purpose.

Life has a single supreme function: to test man's endurance and faith through frustration, evil, and doubt. Man is forbidden in this life to understand absolute truth, which lies beyond this world. The ultimate secrets of creation and God's inscrutable plan must not be seen by man directly, nor must he seek to tear the veil hiding the Absolute. To do so is to be guilty of hubris, the desire to become like God in knowledge and power. Life with its trials permits man to prefigure the infinite, but he can never in the flesh look steadily upon the white light of eternity. Life, this world, and all its mysteries are man's province, to study and love in wholeness and harmony. Man will never solve all the riddles of existence. But herein is precisely the test. The endless quest for truth, not absolute truth itself, is man's proper goal. Like the frog which jumps forever toward the wall, halving the distance with each leap, man is doomed never to arrive at the goal of final attainment; for if he did, life would cease to have meaning. Indeed, it would cease to be, for absolute knowledge and death are mysterious twins which man will meet in good time. Meanwhile, Browning affirmed, although ultimate knowledge is unattainable on earth, the quest for knowledge, like love and life itself, is essential to the development of the tripartite soul of man.

---

3. Ll. 90-97.

THE TRIPLE SOUL:

BROWNING'S THEORY OF KNOWLEDGE

CHAPTER I

THE DIVINE AGENCY OF IGNORANCE:
LYRICAL PERIOD

Man, therefore, thus conditioned, must expect
He could not, what he knows now, know at first;
What he considers that he knows to-day,
Come but to-morrow, he will find misknown;
Getting increase of knowledge, since he learns
Because he lives, which is to be a man. . . .

"A Death in the Desert"

I

Any revaluation of Browning must examine the validity of his "message" for our time. If the present generation finds that his massive structure of philosophic optimism is without foundation, he will rightly be discarded as a thinker, if not as a poet. It is the function of the critic to make sure that understanding and not ignorance determines whether a poet stands or falls. George Santayana, in his notorious essay "The Poetry of Barbarism,"[1] discovers Browning to be a first cousin to his own Caliban and links him with everything unwashed, hairy, and grunting. E. D. H. Johnson, in *The Alien Vision of Victorian Poetry*, finds that Browning "took over the anti-intellectualism of the Romantics and pushed it in the direction of pure primitivism."[2] The twentieth century has, perforce, seen Browning as still closer to the troglodyte than did his contemporaries.

Man's limited condition—his inability on this earth to attain perfect knowledge—lies at the heart of the charge of anti-intellectualism,

---

1. *Interpretations of Poetry and Religion*, New York, 1900.
2. Princeton, 1952, p. 92.

which is nowhere better shown than in the following statement by
William O. Raymond:

> Once convinced of the impotence of reason, Browning makes it, in a
> left-handed way, support his concept of the supreme worth of man's
> moral struggle. Truth is concealed from the eyes of the intellect in order
> that the venture and trial of faith may be the more heroic.
>
> Browning's sceptical attitude towards reason in the interests of his
> ethics and religious belief has often been represented as individual and
> unique. But it is, rather, a specialized form of the way of retreat from
> apparently insuperable problems adopted by many of the great Vic-
> torians. Newman and Tennyson exhibited it as markedly as Browning.
> Arnold dallied with it in *Dover Beach*. He too felt the lure of that escape
> to the Ages of Faith which by blinding the eyes of reason would regain
> security of belief. Yet he could not forswear allegiance to "the high,
> white star of Truth." The "Victorian Compromise," manifest in other
> spheres, is nowhere else more strikingly illustrated than in the endeavor
> to withdraw religion from the realm of knowledge in order to obtain
> spiritual peace, though at a costly price.[3]

Raymond assays a backhand explanation of "the fallacy of Browning's abnegation of reason" by citing the intellectual turmoil of the
nineteenth century: the wake of eighteenth-century Deism, the
violence done to man's beliefs by the French Revolution, Comte's
Positivism, the Higher Criticism, Darwinism, and other upsetting
developments. It is against the backdrop of such a belief that I wish
to pursue this basic problem in Browning.

"Old Pictures in Florence" develops the concept of growth, both
in this world and the next, and also the philosophy of the imperfect—
God's plan of trying man through his limitations. Perfection is the
one thing fatal in life. Unlike the Blessed Damozel, Raphael and
Michelangelo, who have passed beyond the finite into the white light
of truth, do not turn their eyes back to "the earth's old scope,/ Now
that they see God face to face. . . ." Similarly, Greek art ran and
reached the goal, stagnated, and fettered man's growth for hundreds
of years. The race of man "receives life in parts to live in a whole":

---

3. *The Infinite Moment and Other Essays in Robert Browning* (Toronto, 1950), p. 131.

> "If you knew their work you would deal your dole."
> May I take upon me to instruct you?
> When Greek Art ran and reached the goal,
> Thus much had the world to boast *in fructu*—
> The Truth of Man, as by God first spoken,
> Which the actual generations garble,
> Was re-uttered, and Soul (which Limbs betoken)
> And Limbs (Soul informs) made new in marble.[4]

The interaction of body and soul and mind is implied here. Man's truth is always garbled, but new and higher truths are the result and greater art in turn. The striving for harmonious perfection, not the gaining of it, is the true aim for man. The belief in progress through struggle to an unattainable goal explains the corollary that "The first of the new, in our race's story,/ Beats the last of the old. ...." These lines and many others like them might be cited as evidence to disprove the allegation that Browning longed to "escape to the Ages of Faith which by blinding the eyes of reason" would permit man to regain security of belief. Browning's obsessive faith in progress made it impossible for him to extol the supposed joyousness of mind and spirit of earlier peoples, for to do so would run counter to his insistence that progress is the life principle. If the long history of man since the Age of Pericles has been downhill, the conclusion is inescapable that God's plan is a failure.

Modern art, because imperfect, Browning feels is greater than Greek art, which had nowhere to go, being perfect:

> To-day's brief passion limits their range;
> It seethes with the morrow for us and more.
> They are perfect—how else? they shall never change:
> We are faulty—why not? we have time in store.
> The Artificer's hand is not arrested
> With us; we are rough-hewn, nowise polished:
> They stand for our copy, and, once invested
> With all they can teach, we shall see them abolished.

---

4. Ll. 81-88.

> 'Tis a life-long toil till our lump be leaven—
> The better! What's come to perfection perishes.
> Things learned on earth, we shall practise in heaven:
> Works done least rapidly, Art most cherishes.
> Thyself shalt afford the example, Giotto!
> Thy one work, not to decrease or diminsh,
> Done at a stroke, was just (was it not?) "O!"
> Thy great Campanile is still to finish.[5]

The famous freehand "O" of Giotto is the symbol of all dead perfection, including perfect truth. It is best that man be roughhewn and imperfect in his grasp of both art and truth.

"Saul" is a hymn to David's sudden perception of the wisdom and beauty of the divine plan. Saul, in his catatonic state, is partial, fragmentary, bent by error. David in his role of musical psychiatrist sings successively of the joys of this world and the flesh—the wine of this life. These pleasures are good, but by themselves they are not enough. Like Saul, they are parts of an incomplete whole, good, but insufficient. Saul "gives assent" to them, saying, "It is good," but these muscular delights, without "soul-wine," do not stir him from his despair. The end of the poem, beginning with the blinding vision of truth, is a marvelous fusion of mystical perception of truth and determination to report without mystical enthusiasm:

> "I have gone the whole round of creation: I saw and I spoke:
> I, a work of God's hand for that purpose, received in my brain
> And pronounced on the rest of his handwork—returned him again
> His creation's approval or censure: I spoke as I saw:
> I report, as a man may of God's work—all's love, yet all's law.
> Now I lay down the judgeship he lent me. Each faculty tasked
> To perceive him, has gained an abyss, where a dewdrop was asked.
> Have I knowledge? confounded it shrivels at Wisdom laid bare.
> Have I forethought? how purblind, how blank, to the Infinite Care!
> Do I task any faculty highest, to image success?"[6]

---

5. Ll. 121-136.
6. Ll. 238-247.

Browning has often been accused of making intuition, emotion, and love the solitary values to man, the ultimate arbiters which stand alone, unaided by the mind. Joseph E. Baker finds in "Saul" evidence that "The gush of emotion is all-sufficient in Browning's ethics. To ask the *value* of the object, the deed, or the characters involved would be an act of the critical reason, which he cannot tolerate." More serious, he indicts Browning for attacking the intellect precisely because it is a menace to man's intuitive pursuit of sin:

> His guide is Nature as it manifests itself in Man—instinct, passion, feeling. . . . Browning does indeed recognize within Man the traditional division between Reason and the natural drives; but instead of treating the latter as Original Sin, he glorifies them and deliberately attacks the Reason.[7]

It is true that in the triumvirate of body, mind, and spirit (which embraces love), "love is best." Love is to Browning always the supreme value in life, and if one should be forced to choose between the dictates of the head or the heart, the latter is always the supreme tribunal. But it does not follow therefore that there is a struggle between the two for supremacy. When David see the white light of divine revelation, each faculty responds, one no more than another, to the dazzling perception. For one moment David is wholeness, for his vision is complete. He understands with both brain and heart the submission of "man's nothing-perfect to God's all-complete. . . ." He sees in a flash the reason for man's limited state, but God's plan does not entail depreciation or abuse of the intellect. On the contrary, God's all-perfect is for our emulation, both in mind and spirit. David sees the folly of entertaining the fears of Caliban that man may overtake "God's speed in the one way of love." One should not be afraid to open the hundredth door of love because of a suspicion that man, the part, may overtake the whole, "the creature surpass the Creator." It seems reasonable to suppose that if God does not object to man's illimitable progress in love, he would

---

7. "Religious Implications in Browning's Poetry," *Philosophical Quarterly*, XXXVI, No. 4 (October, 1957), 443.

have no objection to similar progress in knowledge—and this is the theme of scores of Browning's poems. Man's divine commission is to pursue God's perfection in both love and knowledge so long as he keeps to the one road which life offers and eschews the forbidden byways that lead to forbidden knowledge of the Absolute. So far as can be told, Browning found no dividing line separating the valid from the invalid for man in "the one way of love"; but there clearly was such a line for man's mind. The reason lies in the nature of life's test: to love as fully as one may does not eliminate doubt, but knowledge of the infinite does, and thus it abrogates the validity of the test.

The concluding stanza, in which David, intoxicated with his knowledge of the coming of Christ and the reign of the new law, staggers home in the night, is one of the supremely effective passages of revelation in English. I like to believe that in making all creation come alive with the awareness of the coming rule of love and peopling the night with witnesses, cohorts, angels, powers, "the unuttered, unseen, the alive, the aware . . ." Browning was showing that Christianity does not unhaunt the air or de-gnome the mine. Far from robbing man's life of color and myth, it fills the world with magic and the new mythology wherewith the mind of the percipient might feed.

Ignorance as a test underlies the theme of man's loneliness in "Two in the Campagna." The young man, one of Browning's gallery of frustrated lovers, has brief flashes of insight into truth, but "the good minute goes." The thread of gossamer symbolizes the elusive truth which comes to man like flashes of lightning and which disappears with equal rapidity.

> Just when I seemed about to learn!
> Where is the thread now? Off again!
> The old trick! Only I discern—
> Infinite passion, and the pain
> Of finite hearts that yearn.[8]

---

8. Ll. 56-60.

Life is a test of the finite heart that yearns for infinite love and the finite brain that yearns equally for infinite knowledge. In "Love in a Life" Browning's concept of growth through frustration is again the theme as the lover endlessly pursues his unseen love through the house of life, "room after room," day after day, with never a glimpse of the beloved. The poem is humanized by a welcome note of despair at the end. The lover does not regret spending his life in a fruitless quest,

> But 't is twilight, you see,—with such suites to explore,
> Such closets to search, such alcoves to importune![9]

There is something nightmarish in the treadmill futility described here, which is hardly relieved by the companion poem, "Life in a Love," with the lover's certainty that he will never succeed:

> But what if I fail of my purpose here?
> It is but to keep the nerves at strain,
> To dry one's eyes and laugh at a fall,
> And baffled, get up and begin again,—
> So the chace takes up one's life, that's all.
> While, look but once from your farthest bound
> At me so deep in the dust and dark,
> No sooner the old hope goes to ground
> Than a new one, straight to the self-same mark,
> I shape me—
> Ever
> Removed![10]

I find it impossible to like these two illustrations of God's trial of man through uncertainty and repeated failure. The application of the principle unfortunately convinces one that the lover is deficient in spirit and moral indignation.

Another baffled person is the desolate woman in "In a Year." She

---

9. Ll. 15-16.
10. Ll. 11-22.

finds her mind quite incapable of comprehending her tragedy: "his love grown chill," although she recognizes the principle that in the mortal state man's intellect is by design inadequate to cope with life's mysteries. Their love, when in flower, was "understood" by something more subtle than the mind:

> If I spoke a word,
> First of all
> Up his cheek the color sprung,
> Then he heard.[11]

She understands neither the way love began nor "Love's decay." In reply to his request at an earlier and happier time that she reveal the depths of her love, she told him the whole truth, leaving no mystery to unravel, and he straightway chose dust instead of gold. "How perplexed/ Grows belief!" she moans, unable to understand perfectly the nature of her trial:

> Well, this cold clay clod
> Was man's heart:
> Crumble it, and what comes next?
> Is it God? [12]

"The Guardian Angel: a Picture at Fano" delves more deeply into the issue of man's trial through pain and ignorance. The Brownings were in Fano in July 1848, to spend the summer; but the weather being unbearably hot, they did little more than seek the sanctuary of the cool churches and galleries before journeying on to Ancona. In the Church of San Agostino at Fano, Browning saw on three successive days the picture *L'Angelo Custode,* by Giovanni Francesco Barbieri, known as Guercino. The picture represents an angel with outspread wings, standing by a child, who is half-kneeling on a pedestal. The angel, in prayer, looks toward heaven with clasped hands. In Browning's prayer, which DeVane describes as perhaps the

---

11. Ll. 21-24.
12. Ll. 76-80.

tenderest in the works of the poet, he says that if such supernatural care were accorded him—care and special heavenly intercession which man is granted only in the next life—

> I would not look up thither past thy head
> Because the door opes, like that child, I know,
> For I should have thy gracious face instead,
> Thou bird of God! And wilt thou bend me low
> Like him, and lay, like his, my hands together,
> And lift them up to pray, and gently tether
> Me, as thy lamb there, with thy garment's spread?
>
> If this was ever granted, I would rest
> My head beneath thine, while thy healing hands
> Close-covered both my eyes beside thy breast,
> Pressing the brain, which too much thought expands,
> Back to its proper size again, and smoothing
> Distortion down till every nerve had soothing,
> And all lay quiet, happy and suppressed.[13]

If he were granted such unearthly peace and certitude—his brain pressed and soothed back to size—"all worldly wrong would be repaired!" and he would see with "such different eyes." But this beatific condition is God's, not man's, he knows. Life is designed to expand the brain to the breaking point and to keep the nerves at stretch. If it were otherwise, man would not look up to heaven, past the head of the angel, but would look at the angel itself, the source of peace and comfort.

"Women and Roses," one of Browning's best examples of metaphysical poetry, by implication draws a parallel between man's ignorance of life and his ignorance of the future. The third rose on the rose tree symbolizes the "maidens, beauties yet unborn," and he longs for wings that will carry him into tomorrow to see the beautiful women of the future, who in turn are symbolic of the Absolute hidden from man's eyes.

---

13. Ll. 15-28.

> Wings, lend wings for the cold, the clear!
> What is far conquers what is near.
> Roses will bloom nor want beholders,
> Sprung from the dust where our flesh moulders.
> What shall arrive with the cycle's change?
> A novel grace and a beauty strange.
> I will make an Eve be the artist that began her,
> Shaped her to his mind!—Alas! in like manner
> They circle their rose on my rose tree.[14]

Man would be Godlike if he could see into the future. The reward for man's ignorance is the exercise of his mind in imagining what shall be in the next life, symbolized by the mystery of tomorrow. He becomes the artist that shapes an Eve to his own mind, as man, from the evidences of this world, shapes his vision of the world to follow.

The bluntness of man's intellectual perceptions informs "Memorabilia." The old man who saw Shelley "plain" thought nothing of it; indeed, the idea that he should have been aware of the vision of beauty that was Shelley amuses him, and another infinite moment has passed unseen, and another test has been failed. Similarly, man's obtuse refusal to distinguish between the true and the false in his rejection of Keats informs "Popularity." In "Master Hugues of Saxe-Gotha" music is lost behind the spider web of rational argument. Casuists, working "on the bone of a lie," dispute to no avail and fail to hear the music—a nice example of human disunity, a violation of man's triple soul:

> Is it your moral of Life?
> Such a web, simple and subtle,
> Weave we on earth here in impotent strife,
> Backward and forward each throwing his shuttle,
> Death ending all with a knife?
>
> Over our heads truth and nature—
> Still our life's zigzags and dodges,
> Ins and outs, weaving a new legislature—

---

14. Ll. 40-48.

> God's gold just shining its last where that lodges,
> Palled beneath man's usurpature.[15]

Truth is over our heads; "not a glimpse of the far land/ Gets through our comments and glozes." These words can easily be adduced as evidence of Browning's anti-intellectualism; but the sense is that rational argument is not the proper tool for understanding music. One should not apply the mind alone to the arts; but Browning does not deny that the mind, in conjunction with the imagination and spirit, is an aid to musical appreciation.

The rejected suitor in "The Last Ride Together," who is sustained by a durable philosophy uncommon in adversity, recognizes that the riddle of life is beyond earthly comprehension. Separated from earth by the "fleshly screen," he appeals to the poet for an interpretation: "you tell/ What we felt only . . . ," but, in contrast to Shelly's and Tennyson's view of the poet, he knows that even the poet, being mortal, is unable to pierce the veil:

> Have you yourself what's best for men?
> Are you—poor, sick, old ere your time—
> Nearer one whit your own sublime
> Than we who never have turned a rhyme?[16]

The artist and musician, likewise, are incapable of superhuman perception of truth. Man, indeed, instinctively knowing that life is greater than art, turns from the sculptor's Venus "To yonder girl that fords the burn!"

II

Christmas-Eve and Easter-Day (1850), two poems which are always linked together as expressions of Browning's religious views, have been accorded special respect as representing directly, without dramatic concealment of the author, the mature views of Browning's

---

15. Ll. 106-115.
16. Ll. 73-76.

middle years. Elizabeth Barrett Browning early discovered his un-
fitness as a dramatist and urged him to speak through his own personality and with the voice which God made with such power and
sweetness of speech. In *Christmas-Eve and Easter-Day* he follows her
advice. The two poems are of particular interest, for as DeVane suggests, they probably were prompted by the birth of Browning's son
and the death of his beloved mother, both in March 1849. The strange
juxtaposition of life and death, which would not fail to stir the poet
deeply, was intensified by his inability to return to England from
Florence for the funeral. Both the tone and substance of the poems—
his earnest probing of life's mystery and purpose, the form of worship
best suited to man, and the problems besetting belief in immortality—
suggest the stimulus of poignant experience. The two poems stand
in the fore ranks of Browning's poems of religious inquiry.

Christmas-Eve is primarily an examination, through such a dream
as befell Piers Plowman, of the three attitudes toward faith which
seemed to Browning most significant at the mid-century: the Independent, or nonconformist; the Roman Catholic, or ritualistic and
conformist; and scientific materialism, or the rationalistic. He examines these three divergent views against the basic fact of the
Christian faith: the birth of Christ. Independent Zion Chapel, to
which he pays his first visit, is life in small, with all of its ugliness,
suffering, failure, and triumph. The congregation comes through the
rain "from the road, the lanes or the common," smelling of wet wool
and unwashed humanity: a fat, weary woman, down clapping a
wreck of an umbrella: "a female something," with tuberculosis; a
gaunt cadaver of a man like the penitent thief, all of whom are led
by some inner light to come on this Christmas Eve of 1849 to the
humble little chapel. Browning sits in discomfort among the hot
smells and human noises, listening to the immense stupidity of the
minister, who fancies that he has discovered "an inkling" of truth
in the Bible and chooses to illustrate the discovery in a hell-fire sermon
of extended cliché. Browning's gorge rises, and, in his fancy, he rushes
through the creaking door and out into the fresh rain-washed night;

for he cannot tolerate the sermon's "mingled weft/ Of good and ill."
Truth, it appears, is so much a matter of individual interpretation
that in the search for certainty one grasps only frustration. Truth
can be made to look false "in the natural fog of the good man's mind,"
like the halos the fog casts around the roadside lamps. Is the nimbus
of light around a fog-girt lamp true or false? Who knows? "Truth
remains true, the fault's in the prover. . . ." Man's mind is imperfectly
capable of seizing upon truth with certainty. Indeed, what commonly
passes for truth is what proves agreeable to our preconceptions.
"Truth" is enormously convincing "to those convinced before." He
looks at the risen moon, which is partly hidden by the prison of
clouds in the west ("For what purpose the winds knows best,/ Who
changes his mind continually") and feels a pantheistic apperception
of the wisdom of nature that is rare in Browning. Man cannot fathom
the reasons of nature:

> —In youth I looked to these very skies,
> And probing their immensities,
> I found God there, his visible power;
> Yet felt in my heart, amid all its sense
> Of the power, an equal evidence
> That his love, there too, was the nobler dower.
> For the loving worm within its clod
> Were diviner than a loveless god
> Amid his worlds, I will dare to say.
> You know what I mean: God's all, man's nought:
> But also, God, whose pleasure brought
> Man into being, stands away
> As it were a handbreadth off, to give
> Room for the newly-made to live,
> And look at him from a place apart,
> And use his gifts of brain and heart,
> Given, indeed, but to keep forever.
> Who speaks of man, then, must not sever
> Man's very elements from man . . . .[17]

17. Ll. 279-297.

It is clear that to Browning love is "the nobler" dower, but it is equally clear that God created man to "use his gifts of brain and heart . . . ." Browning, indeed, is severe upon those blind critics of the cosmic plan who denigrate man and insist that because his gifts are incomplete he should not use them. These men, by severing "Man's very elements from man . . . ," abuse God's gifts and seek to thwart God's plan. Man's mind (power) is coeval with heart (love); but—and this is the first clear statement in Browning of the arresting idea—love is fundamentally unlike mind or power in that its sum cannot be increased. Weak man may learn through knowledge how to lift mountains when he marries the strength of his hand to an engine, Browning says,

> But love is the ever-springing fountain:
> Man may enlarge or narrow his bed
> For the water's play, but the water-head—
> How can he multiply or reduce it?
> As easy create it, as cause it to cease;
> He may profit by it, or abuse it,
> But 't is not a thing to bear increase
> As Power does: be love less or more
> In the heart of man, he keeps it shut
> Or opes it wide, as he pleases, but
> Love's sum remains what it was before.[18]

In his youth the heavens seemed to give man the promise that the Eternal First and Last would never bestow "less than man requires" to comprehend the word of him "who endlessly was teaching," although the path of knowledge extends through the whole life of man and into the infinite as well. Just to understand what "love can do in the leaf or stone" he "must go on learning endlessly." Here is the clearest kind of evidence that God's gifts to man are nicely gauged to our needs, neither too great nor too small, and the divine commission is to use them all together in "learning endlessly" the wonders of the creation. How disheartened Browning would have felt had he known

---

18. Ll. 318-328.

that he would be placed with the opponents of the mind! In reality
he states with absolute clarity that the sum of knowledge not only
may be but must be enlarged from birth to death. Love, a fixed quantity, affords a test of whether man elects to shut his heart or open it
wide, as man can make a stream run swift and clear by straightening
and clearing its bed, even though the ever-springing fountain cannot
be forced to yield more water. Love is given to us complete; knowledge
is given to us in the germ, to be nurtured without cease.

As he contemplates the heavens, the clouds part, revealing a perfect
moon-rainbow, which assumes mystical significance:

> 'T was a moon-rainbow, vast and perfect,
> From heaven to heaven extending, perfect
> As the mother-moon's self, full in face.
> It rose, distinctly at the base
> With its seven proper colors chorded,
> Which still, in the rising, were compressed,
> Until at last they coalesced,
> And supreme the spectral creature lorded
> In a triumph of whitest white,—
> Above which intervened the night.[19]

The rainbow, like Shelley's dome of many-colored glass, is a Platonic
symbol of Browning's philosophy of the imperfect and the function
of the struggle for perfection. Like David in "Saul," he hears God,
"the triumph of whitest white," call his name, and his brain, "Glutted
with the glory," bursts asunder to relieve itself of the "too-much glory,"
which falls to the ground in "mazy error." In his dream he fancies
that he asks God's permission to build "Service-tabernacles three,"

> "Where, forever in thy presence,
> In ecstatic acquiescence,
> Far alike from thriftless learning
> And ignorance's undiscerning,
> I may worship and remain!"[20]

---

19. Ll. 385-394.
20. Ll. 415-419.

In these lines is the substance of Browning's theory of knowledge. Man must renounce "thriftless learning" and ignorance equally. The proper study of man is what the mind of man can understand and what will not burst his brain with the white light. One must contemplate the prismatic colors of the moon-rainbow—the wondrous cosmos, dimly discerned—not the light of God. It is clear that Browning is not opposed to following any path of inquiry that might be included in the curriculum of a university, with one possible exception: extra-sensory perception and inquiry into the occult. It is by no means sure that he would oppose even these studies, for the light they shed seems sufficiently impure; but the recollection of Mr. Sludge inclines one to feel that Browning might class such pursuits as "thriftless learning."

Outside the little chapel, Browning sees the Master, arrayed in flowing robes, but with his face averted at the poet's departure from God's house, and he implores God's pardon:

> "I thought it best that thou, the spirit,
> Be worshipped in spirit and in truth,
> And in beauty, as even we require it—
> Not in the forms burlesque, uncouth,
> I left but now as scarcely fitted
> For thee . . . ." [21]

God turns the full light of his countenance upon him and he falls, "saturate with brightness" and dismayed. He is caught up in the whirl and drift of the flowing garments and whisked off to St. Peter's in Rome, the stronghold and symbol of ritualistic and unreasoning faith:

> Their faith's heart beats, though her head swims
> Too giddily to guide her limbs,
> Disabled by their palsy-stroke
> From propping mine. [22]

---

21. Ll. 467-472.
22. Ll. 611-614.

As it must be on earth, truth, as perceived by Roman Catholicism, is "obscured/ By errors and perversities . . . ," but not so fully that no smoulder or spark of flame appears through the smoke; but such anti-intellectualism, Browning feels, does violence to God's gift of mind, which is "the clue" granted to man to guide his footsteps:

> But I, a mere man, fear to quit
> The clue God gave me as most fit
> To guide my footsteps through life's maze.... [23]

He finds the love of the first Christians enormously appealing, but he is repelled by their unfortunate contempt for the mind: "the antique sovereign Intellect" was "hurled/ From the throne he reigned upon . . . ."And with the dethronement of intellect, disappeared the poetry and rhetoric of Greece and Rome, leaving hearts set free in "imbecility." "Filthy saints," feeling the lusts of the flesh, unreasoningly condemned a beautiful statue of Aphrodite and broke her nose to inhibit concupiscence in others; music became mere hog-grunts; and love became "the all-sufficient." [24] Love is not all sufficient for man, and Browning (in incantatory lines reminiscent of Smart's *A Song to David*) rejects the early Christian anti-intellectual zeal, along with contemporary Catholicism, because of its contempt for God's gift of mind:

> They take, as it were, a padlock, clap it tight
> On their southern eyes, restrained from feeding
> On the glories of their ancient reading,
> On the beauties of their modern singing,
> On the wonders of the builder's bringing,
> On the majesties of Art around them.... [25]

---

23. Ll. 623-625.

24. James Fotheringham, writing in his *Studies in the Poetry of Robert Browning* (London, 1887), pp. 207-208, assumes that Browning approved the dethronement of intellect by the early Christians: "Above all the error there was and is love—the greatest thing; the love that gave Christianity its first power, in the might of which it conquered 'the sovereign intellect,' and made a new world, and in time a new art—though always more or less 'blind.' " It was not only blind, affirms Browning, but imbecilic, hideous, and bigoted.

25. Ll. 718-723.

In a passage of perfect clarity, he sums up his "new resolves":

> So I summed up my new resolves:
> Too much love there can never be.
> And where the intellect devolves
> Its function on love exclusively,
> I, a man who possesses both,
> Will accept the provision, nothing loth,
> —Will feast my love, then depart elsewhere,
> *That my intellect may find its share.*[26]

This judgment Browning never abandoned. Love always remained for him life's supreme value, and there can never be too much love; but it does not follow that man is a measure that can be filled to the brim with love alone, to the exclusion of the mind, which God has given as "clue." Illimitable love in no wise precludes full development and use of the intellect, for man's capacity is not that of a bucket.

Browning next flies in the company of the berobed figure to Göttingen, where the high-cheekboned professor, bent with his cranium's over-freight, is breaking into his Christmas-Eve discourse. This scene may appear to the unwary as evidence of Browning's anti-rationalism and elevation of love as the sole guide needful to man. The burden of the professor's speech is that reason must be man's sole guide to prevent his swerving from the well-heads of knowledge. He represents the higher critics, perhaps specifically David Friedrich Strauss, author of *Das Leben Jesu,* which had shaken the foundations of orthodox faith. After Strauss had sifted the Biblical story to remove inconsistency and imposture, all that was left "for residuum" was a mere man. Browning, who detested the higher criticism for its attempt to supplant the heart by intellect and the supernatural by reasoned argument, finds the lecture hall an "exhausted air-bell." The struggles between Papist and Dissenter, he notes, may make truth's atmosphere "grow mephitic" by impregnating its clarity with "frankincense's fuming," on the one hand, or the vulgar odor of meat and garlic, on the other;

---

26. Ll. 731-738. The italics are mine.

but poisoned air is better than the vacuity left by the critic's pumping out all love, the life-giving oxygen.

> But the Critic leaves no air to poison;
> Pumps out with ruthless ingenuity
> Atom by atom, and leaves you—vacuity.
> Thus much of Christ does he reject?
> And what retain? His intellect?
> What is it I must reverence duly?
> Poor intellect for worship, truly. . . .[27]

One is well advised to be cautious in concluding that because the intellect is not to be worshipped it is not to be used.

It is as foolish to adore the mind as to worship "simple work of nomenclature" or to deify Harvey for discovering and naming the circulation of the blood.

> But if the common conscience must
> Be ultimately judge, adjust
> Its apt name to each quality
> Already known,—I would decree
> Worship for such mere demonstration
> And simple work of nomenclature,
> Only the day I praised, not nature,
> But Harvey, for the circulation.
> I would praise such a Christ, with pride
> And joy, that he, as none beside,
> Had taught us how to keep the mind
> God gave him. . . .[28]

The rational viewpoint in matters of the spirit is less satisfactory than either the individualistic nonconformist or the unquestioning ritualistic viewpoint; for they allow love. None of the three is entirely acceptable or perfect, for perfection, he again affirms, is fatal to growth. Clearly as Browning chooses the little chapel with all of its smells and snuffles, he would, if forced to make a choice, choose unreasoning love

---

27. Ll. 911-917.
28. Ll. 966-977.

over unloving reason; but man is never asked to make such a choice,
for it is entirely contrary to God's whole scheme of things. The re-
sounding denunciation of the arid professor should not blind one to
Browning's umbrage at Rome's dethronement of reason. He discovers
that God's truth lies traced upon man's breast to be discerned if man
will but exercise his gifts. There is an inward light, but man must
bring wholeness of effort to discover it. He elects the non-conformist
chapel by a choice involving both heart and head, not one alone:

> I then, in ignorance and weakness,
> Taking God's help, have attained to think
> My heart does best to receive in meekness
> That mode of worship, as most to his mind,
> Where earthly aids being cast behind,
> His All in All appears serene
> With the thinnest human veil between....[29]

Evidence from *Easter-Day* may seem to demonstrate Browning's
contempt for science. Such passages as those expressing distaste for
the collector of bugs and the equally absurd snuffboxes are well
known:

> "One friend of mine wears out his eyes,
> Slighting the stupid joys of sense,
> In patient hope that, ten years hence,
> 'Somewhat completer,' he may say,
> 'My list of *coleoptera!*'
> While just the other who most laughs
> At him, above all epitaphs
> Aspires to have his tomb describe
> Himself as sole among the tribe
> Of snuffbox-fanciers, who possessed
> A Grignon with the Regent's crest."[30]

The poem is an imaginary dialogue in Browning's mind between
two men of differing religious positions: one, a man of easily attained

29. Ll. 1301-1307.
30. Ll. 150-160.

faith; and the other, a moderate skeptic, who longs for intellectual certitude. Just prove to me, the skeptic says, that the smallest of God's commandments is indeed God's, and what injunction would a sane man need to pay obedience? To man's certainty of the shortness of life and of the inevitability of death, add certainty of survival and reward or punishment, and man can rationally compute, "Weigh loss and gain together . . ." and give his body to the axe or faggot for Christ's sake in confidence of full compensation for his martyrdom. The man of faith replies that indeed this is the point whereon all turns, but that if rational certitude were given him and he could in full confidence "joint" the "flexile finite life" into the "fixed and infinite," he would spurn mere life. The skeptic admits that some doubt must be mixed with faith, if faith is to be, but he still wants proof that God's reign is based upon exacter laws than man perceives. " 'In all God's acts— (as Plato cries/ He doth)—he should geometrize.' " The man of faith says that the doubt would keep up with the proof, for the world groans in such travail that more than intellectual certainty must support faith. Thus, a scientific faith is absurd, and "Frustrates the very end 't was meant/ To serve," answers the man of faith:

> "So, I would rest content
> With a mere probability,
> But, probable; the chance must lie
> Clear on one side,—lie all in rough,
> So long as there be just enough
> To pin my faith to, though it hap
> Only at points: from gap to gap
> One hangs up a huge curtain so,
> Grandly, nor seeks to have it go
> Foldless and flat along the wall."[31]

He cites the collectors of bugs and snuffboxes, together with those who devote their lives to blindfold chess, as evidence, not that these activities are in themselves bad, but that men in their diversity of inclinations

---

31. Ll. 126-135.

and interests pursue widely different lives, have different faiths, and require different support for belief.

In the concluding vision of Judgment Day, the speaker is condemned to glut his senses upon the things of the world, which in life he has worshipped. At first his doom seems light indeed, and he exults in the inexhaustible joys of the world. He picks up a leaf and recollects how many varieties of ferns exist for man's collection, study, and delight,

> Each as distinct and beautiful
> As this, the very first I cull.
> Think, from the first leaf to the last!
> Conceive, then, earth's resources! Vast
> Exhaustless beauty, endless change
> Of wonder! And this foot shall range
> Alps, Andes,—and this eye devour
> The bee-bird and the aloe-flower? [32]

A voice informs him of his folly. It is "well" to welcome so God's variegated earth and all its wonder, but the earth is only God's antechamber, and the business of the wise man is to study the things of earth to postulate the glories of the next life. All partial beauty is but a pledge of the coming plenitude of beauty. The uses of mind are not decried or depreciated, but study for itself alone is not enough, good as it is. Plenitude will belong to those who look through science to God, he is assured; but he still cannot be disabused of the belief that mind is an absolute value:

> I cried in anguish: "Mind, the mind,
> So miserably cast behind. . . .
> . . . .
>   Mind is best—
> I will seize mind, forego the rest,
> And try how far my tethered strength
> May crawl in this poor breadth and length.

---

32. Ll. 742-749.

> Let me, since I can fly no more,
> At least spin dervish-like about
> (Till giddy rapture almost doubt
> I fly) through circling sciences,
> Philosophies and histories!"[33]

As he utters these defiant words, he knows that "to know," like to feel is still of earth.

> "I have reached the goal—
> 'Whereto does knowledge serve!' will burn
> My eyes, too sure, at every turn!
> I cannot look back now, nor stake
> Bliss on the race, for running's sake.
> The goal's a ruin like the rest!"[34]

Nothing in life is a goal in itself—not art, not science, not knowledge, not even earthly love. All of these values are to help man prefigure infinity through "grasps of guess,"

> "Which pull the more into the less,
> Making the finite comprehend
> Infinity. . . ."[35]

The poet, like the scientist, must see through art to eternity, and work through partial knowledge to show truth by means of fable, the world of spirit, as of sense, being plain to him, " 'but not too plain,'" lest earth turn heaven. Science and the mind are no less proper for man than art, so long as they are means to an end—to sting man " 'with hunger for full light.'" The great vision of Judgment Day teaches him that love is the basis of God's plan; that the test of life is conducted through the agency of frustration, ignorance, and doubt; and that knowledge is a valid tool—but only a tool—for man's dim perception of infinity through the imperfection of the finite.

---

33. Ll. 864-882.
34. Ll. 896-901.
35. Ll. 906-908.

III

The clearest warning in Browning of the dangers of attaining while in the flesh the secret of the Absolute is best illustrated in the resurrection of Lazarus in "An Epistle Containing the Strange Medical Experience of Karshish, the Arab Physician." Karshish is both a medical doctor and natural scientist, "the not incurious in God's handiwork," who writes in ill-concealed shame of the assent his spirit longs to accord to the religion of Christ. To hide from his mentor, Abib, the excitement which grips him in facing the implications of the resurrection of Lazarus, he sprinkles throughout his letter bits of scientific observation gleaned from his travels; but his heart is not in such scientific findings but in an apparent suspension of natural law, which, if true, must alter all of man's values. Karshish, like Cleon, cannot quite take the step from science to faith, but he is closer to acquiescence in the great discovery than Cleon, who rejects Christianity summarily, without the travail of spirit that the physician experiences.

The burden of the poem is the disastrous effects upon Lazarus of his three days' exposure to the white light beyond the borders of life. He is like a child, witless with the overburden of his knowledge. None of life's values have meaning any longer, for life keeps no secrets from him. He has been robbed of ignorance and doubt, the essence of earthly existence. He sits in placid reflection, unmoved, undisturbed, uninterested; for his vision of total truth has deprived his renewed earthly sojourn of purpose. He can know neither the simple joys nor the sorrows of his fellows:

> ...we call the treasure knowledge, say,
> Increased beyond the fleshly faculty—
> Heaven opened to a soul while yet on earth,
> Earth forced on a soul's use while seeing heaven:
> The man is witless of the size, the sum,
> The value in proportion of all things,
> Or whether it be little or be much.[36]

---

36. Ll. 139-145.

Exposure to the infinite has destroyed him. Only his body remains on earth; his mind and heart are still fixed upon the wonders which alone have worth for him. Karshish, the scientist, "knows" that the truth of the supposed return from death is but "a case of mania—sub-induced/ By epilepsy, at the turning point/ Of trance prolonged unduly some three days. . . ." His mind tells him that the proper business of man is to reject all superstition and "fantastic" revelation alike; but his spirit, thwarted though it is by mind, apprehends the appalling significance of the resurrection. In the conclusion of the epistle, he bursts the fetters of intellect in an emotional outburst which must have disturbed Abib's trust in the balance of his protégé:

> The very God! think, Abib; dost thou think?
> So, the All-Great, were the All-Loving too—
> So, through the thunder comes a human voice
> Saying, "O heart I made, a heart beats here!
> Face, my hands fashioned, see it in myself!
> Thou hast no power nor mayst conceive of mine,
> But love I gave thee, with myself to love,
> And thou must love me who have died for thee!"
> The madman saith He said so: it is strange.[37]

For one moment he intuitively perceives a ray from the white light of the great mystery, but his rationalistic habits are too strong to allow his spirit free reign. The tragedy of Karshish is not that he is an intellectual, but that he has atrophy of the spirit so that the infinite moment of divine revelation passes him by.[38] But how close he comes to the Truth, to which he has dedicated his mind, but not his heart!

Cleon, unlike Karshish, knows that he has failed, although he has excelled in all the arts and has written three books on the soul "Proving absurd all written hitherto,/ And putting us to ignorance again." His frustration and sense of failure result from an uneasy conviction

---

37. Ll. 304-312.
38. See Richard D. Altick, "Browning's 'Karshish' and Saint Paul," *Modern Language Notes*, LXXII (November, 1957), 494-496, for an expression of the supposed anti-intellectual theme of the poem: "In terms of Browning's constant exaltation of the lessons of the soul over those of the mind, where Paul was strong, Karshish was weak." (p. 495)

that he is incomplete. Life, he feels, must be viewed as a whole, "not analyzed to parts,/ But each part having reference to all. . . ." Unlike Karshish, Cleon is both an intellectual and a creative artist; but even these together, without love and the vision of eternity, are incomplete. He has been a skillful botanist, wise in the cross-pollination of flowers; but knowledge alone is arid, and a fact is just one fact the more, unless it be placed with other facts to form a picture, however imperfect, of the divine plan:

> Suppose the artist made a perfect rhomb,
> And next a lozenge, then a trapezoid—
> He did not overlay them, superimpose
> The new upon the old and blot it out,
> But laid them on the level in his work,
> Making at last a picture; there it lies.[39]

But man lost his way when he emerged from the lower forms of life, because he sought to gain the heights by mind alone:

> We called it an advance, the rendering plain
> Man's spirit might grow conscious of man's life,
> And, by new lore so added to the old,
> Take each step higher over the brute's head.
> This grew the only life, the pleasure-house,
> Watch-tower and treasure-fortress of the soul,
> Which whole surrounding flats of natural life
> Seemed only fit to yield subsistence to;
> A tower that crowns a country. But alas,
> The soul now climbs it just to perish there![40]

The Tower of Babel leads to death of the soul, but neither Cleon nor Browning denounces the use of mind. Cleon, miserable as he is, still is sure that "to know is something," but "knowing naught, to enjoy is something too." The rower with the moulded muscles is nearer joy and wholeness than he, and the fair slave girl is a greater ode than

---

39. Ll. 83-88.
40. Ll. 227-236.

Cleon's love ode, for life is a wholeness greater than art, which is a part of the whole. In facing old age and death, he sees clearly the poverty of his vision. His subconscious urges belief in a future state, but he is fettered by the mind-forged manacles and cannot believe what his mind does not give assent to.

The pitiable woman in "James Lee's Wife," unlike Cleon, dimly descries life's law in her desolation. Life is limitation—limitation of bliss and beauty and joy and knowledge equally. The sad song of the wailing winds is of the "limit time assigns" to all things mortal:

> Nothing endures: the wind moans, saying so;
> We moan in acquiescence: there's life's pact,
> Perhaps probation—do *I* know?
> God does: endure his act![41]

Her resignation appears on the surface to illustrate the value of calculated ignorance; but she is in reality urging on man the recognition of the limitation of mind set by God, not further limitation set by man.

St. John in "A Death in the Desert" utters on his deathbed an anachronistic reading of life, proper to the age of Darwinian skepticism. In his treatment of the doctrine of wholeness, the function of ignorance, and the role of the mind, the words of the divine are of first importance in understanding Browning's attitude toward the intellect. Man, he says, has three souls which make up one soul, the wholeness which is man: one soul, a soul of "each and all the bodily parts"; a second soul

> ...which, seated in the brain,
> Useth the first with its collected use,
> And feeleth, thinketh, willeth,—is what Knows. ...

and a third soul

> ...that uses both the first,
> Subsisting whether they assist or no,

---

41. VI. "Reading a Book, under the Cliff," ll. 72-75.

> And, constituting man's self, is what Is—
> And leans upon the former, makes it play,
> As that played off the first. . . .[42]

These three souls of man—"What Does, what Knows, what Is; three souls, one man"—are absolutely interdependent. St. John is not anti-intellectual. He finds the soul not fettered by either mind or flesh, but dependent on both equally for its wholeness and health. He preaches no romantic doctrine of intuitionism, but rather, "reasoning from my knowledge," he teaches men to believe for love's sake. Predictably, he holds the belief that the test of life is conducted through ignorance and doubt, a lesson which he has but recently learned, in his extreme old age. Indeed, before coming to the cave, where he is attended by his four faithful comrades and the small boy, he comforted himself with belief in the illusion that in the age of anti-Christ he could die secure in the knowledge that "We had the truth, might leave the rest to God." But the nearness of death has taught him sorely that facts snap and truth is a shifting path through dark and rugged terrain, where man gropes "for foothold through a blank profound." As death approaches nearer and the test of life concludes, the veil of youth and strength which blinds man's eyes from truth wears thin and lets man see "to the universal prick of light," a common theme in Browning. His dying words, spoken in the radiance of his earthly glimpse of the Absolute, concern directly the nature of truth and the uses of the mind:

> "—this gift of truth
> Once grasped, were this our soul's gain safe, and sure
> To prosper as the body's gain is wont,—
> Why, man's probation would conclude, his earth
> Crumble; for he both reasons and decides,
> Weighs first, then chooses: will he give up fire
> For gold or purple once he knows its worth?
> Could he give Christ up were His worth as plain?"[43]

---

42. Ll. 90-99.
43. Ll. 287-294.

It is not given to man to know without the travail of exercising thought and choice that Christ is the ultimate and eternal value, as man had to discover by his own wits the worth of fire.

Herein lies for St. John the reason that God did not permit his saints to establish with indubitable proof the "truth safe forever." Immediately doubt and skepticism began their silent work of subverting truth, which must ever be rediscovered to keep it truth. The doubters, while admitting that the old ones who reported at first hand of Christ were right in the main, also held that youth can reach where "age gropes dimly." New shrewd tongues of the higher critics began their distressing clamor; and in the anguish of doubt Christians implore him to give them certainty, "tell the whole mind out," and so destroy all doubt at a stroke. John replies that man's vision of truth is evolutionary, growing with his growth and needs. In earlier times man needed the myth that the sun was drawn across the heavens by yoked steeds—and this "truth" proved sufficient for a time; we know now that " ' "what made and drives/ The sun is force, is law, is named, not known. . . ." ' " Our progress toward truth is half error and half truth; in fact, we have exchanged one myth for the myth of nomenclature. Apollo has become "force" or "law," but are we much closer to the truth? In the dawn of man's childhood, it was believed that the sun arose or set at improbable times, or even stood still upon occasion, to threaten or reward or terrify man into obedience; but as man has progressed and put away childish things, miracles have ceased and natural law is not abrogated for the instruction of grown men:

> "That help, he needed once, and needs no more,
> Having grown but an inch by, is withdrawn:
> For he hath new needs, and new helps to these."[44]

As mythology and superstition served their purpose and are gone, so man's proud scientific triumphs will be superseded by later truths, which will in turn erode away:

---

44. Ll. 425-427.

"This imports solely, man should mount on each
New height in view; the help whereby he mounts,
The ladder-rung his foot has left, may fall,
Since all things suffer change save God the Truth.
Man apprehends Him newly at each stage
Whereat earth's ladder drops, its service done;
And nothing shall prove twice what once was proved.
You stick a garden-plot with ordered twigs
To show inside lie germs of herbs unborn,
And check the careless step would spoil their birth;
But when herbs wave, the guardian twigs may go,
Since should ye doubt of virtues, question kinds,
It is no longer for old twigs ye look,
Which proved once underneath lay store of seed,
But to the herb's self, by what light ye boast,
For what fruit's signs are. This book's fruit is plain,
Nor miracles need prove it any more.
. . . .
What? Was man made a wheelwork to wind up,
And be discharged, and straight wound up anew?
No!—grown, his growth lasts; taught, he ne'er forgets:
May learn a thousand things, not twice the same."[45]

Those who believe that Browning execrated the mind might with
profit study this passage. Man must employ all of his faculties in his
never-ending search for truth, but he must progress by mind from
"truth" to "truth"—as it is given to man to see truth. It is fatal to dog-
matize and stagnate. We see so much of the world as " 'God wills for
his purpose.' "

Richard D. Altick, in "The Private Life of Robert Browning," expresses the traditional interpretation of the poem as a thundering
denunciation of intellect:

Instead [of meeting the higher critics on their own ground], he re-
treated to his own citadel and, loftily disdaining arguments of his
adversaries, insisted upon his one cherished principle of faith— the faith
that men hold, intuitively, even mystically, the knowledge of God and

---

45. Ll. 428-451.

His love which is impossible to anyone who relies on the deceptive charms of reason. The more he became aware, as the years passed, of the swelling tide of rationalism and agnosticism, the more passionately he insisted that divinely granted intuition was the only means to truth.[46]

This judgment is not supported by the poem.

It would be difficult to find a nobler passage in praise of man's intellect than the following:

> "I say, the acknowledgement of God in Christ
> Accepted by thy reason, solves for thee
> All questions in the earth and out of it,
> And has so far advanced thee to be wise.
> Wouldst thou unprove this to re-prove the proved?
> In life's mere minute, with power to use that proof,
> Leave knowledge and revert to how it sprung?
> Thou hast it; use it and forthwith, or die!" [47]

It is clear, I trust, that reversion to the "how" of phenomena means the attempt to seize absolute truth. It is " 'Death and the sole death' " when a man seeks such forbidden truth and gains darkness for light, ignorance from knowledge. As a stomach surcharged with indigestible fare starves for want of food it can assimilate and as a lamp may be extinguished by repletion of oil, he says, so man finds death if he seeks God's knowledge. In words reminiscent of the Great Chain of Being, St. John finds man midway between God and the beasts, with one distinctive mark alone: " 'God is, they are,/ Man partly is and wholly hopes to be.' "

> "Such progress could no more attend his soul
> Were all it struggles after found at first
> And guesses changed to knowledge absolute,
> Than motion wait his body, were all else
> Than it the solid earth on every side,
> Where now through space he moves from rest to rest.
> Man, therefore, thus conditioned, must expect

---

46. *Yale Review*, XLI (1951), 259.
47. Ll. 474-481.

> He could not, what he knows now, know at first;
> What he considers that he knows to-day,
> Come but to-morrow, he will find misknown;
> Getting increase of knowledge, since he learns
> Because he lives, which is to be a man,
> Set to instruct himself by his past self:
> First, like the brute, obliged by facts to learn,
> Next, as a man may, obliged by his own mind. ...'"[48]

God's gift to man, St. John says, is that he conceives of truth and yearns to attain it, " 'catching at mistake,/ As midway help till he reach fact indeed.' " Far from being a pronouncement hostile to mind, this is an admirable statement of the scientific method which has served man well in his progress toward knowledge. Nothing could be more liberal and humane than the insistence that knowledge never be permitted to become entrenched in dogma, immune from examination and repudiation if found false. St. John, speaking the thoughts of Browning, urges perpetual inquiry with the open and searching mind.

One may object that in Browning there is an inconsistency in his view of the consequences of striving to know the Absolute: sometimes man is warned that "sole death" is the infallible result of such hubris; at other times he is merely cautioned that a foray beyond the veil leads to sure frustration, the veil in reality being of adamantine impregnability. If one cannot cross the boundary, wherein is the harm in trying, since he is protected by his fleshly limitations from attaining the knowledge which would mean death? The presumption is that the sin is of the same species though perhaps of a different order if man seeks to breach the walls by impotence or strength; in the end it is not well, whatever be the consequences.

IV

The Ring and the Book includes the most closely reasoned examination of the nature of truth and the limitations of man's mind in Browning's middle period. The Pope's magnificent soliloquy, which is

---

48. Ll. 589-603.

usually judged to be the most eloquent statement of Browning's philosophy, may justly be considered as of special significance. Indeed, from first to last Browning's masterpiece is a drama of human error, weakness, and limitation, with particular emphasis on the nature of truth. E. D. H. Johnson, in *The Alien Vision of Victorian Poetry,* sees the work as an indictment both of social and religious institutions and of the intellect. He makes much of the conclusion, which he takes to be the theme of the work, that truth is many things and commonly reflects the bias, distortion, and self-interest of each individual:

> . . . our human speech is naught,
> Our human testimony false, our fame
> And human estimation words and wind.[49]

Robert Langbaum, however, in his judicious study *"The Ring and the Book:* a Relativist Poem," wisely notes that Browning, far from counseling man to suspend the offices of mind, urges man to seek the truth through the "machinery of understanding":

> In other words, in trying to adapt the machinery of understanding to the truth, which remains always in advance of the machinery, man advances his moral understanding.[50]

The sordid story of the "Old Yellow Book" became an admirable means of showing that truth is on earth always relative and subjective, never in pure form, but always fused with its matrix of infinite complexity. No one person has truth: not Caponsacchi, not Pompilia, not even the Pope; for it is the care of "the angel of this life" to shield men from full truth, "lest men see too much at once." Man's task is to search within the ring of testimony, surmise, and lies for the truth as

---

49. XII, 834-836. Hoxie N. Fairchild ("Browning the Simple-Hearted Casuist," *University of Toronto Quarterly,* XVIII, No. 3 [April, 1949], 234-240) sees "in *The Ring and the Book* that the struggle between subtle brain and simple heart grows most acute." In this well-balanced study, however, Fairchild does not find Browning at enmity with mind, even though the poet "seldom fails," he says, "to make the speaker expose the 'real' truth which underlies the surface play of intellectual sophistication"—an entirely valid observation.

50. *PMLA,* LXXI (March, 1956), 143.

he sees it through the use of all his faculties. "The God-glimpse must suffice," for pure truth blinds. The murder trial is a microcosm wherein life's principle of test, testimony, and judgment is seen. "Fancy with fact is just one fact the more," and the amalgam of truth and fancy making *The Ring and the Book* is hardly different from that making the "Old Yellow Book."

> Are means to the end, themselves in part the end?
> Is fiction which makes fact alive, fact too?
> The somehow may be thishow.[51]

Browning gives us in his great work exactly what life gives us:

> —No dose of purer truth than man digests,
> But truth with falsehood, milk that feeds him now,
> Not strong meat he may get to bear some day. . . .[52]

The quest for truth, which is but the good and the beautiful by a different name, is man's prime duty: ". . . there's nothing in nor out o' the world/ Good except truth. . . ." But man is fated to search forever in the deceptive depths of a pool, which leads his arm waveringly, "lets fall wide/ O' the mark its finger. . . ." The statements of Half-Rome, the Other Half-Rome, and Tertium Quid are merely aspects of "the world's guess, as it crowds the bank o' the pool. . . ," each seeing truth through the filter of his own inclination.

Half-Rome looks into the depths of the pool at truth and finds it to square with his own bias of the moment. Because his wife is all too familiar with a gallant, Guido appears patently guiltless, the type of manliness in defense of home. The Other Half-Rome, feeling for truth "with a like swerve, like unsuccess,—/ Or if success, by no skill but more luck," finds the pool perplexing. A man wearing pink, Browning says, will pick a runner who wears a pink scarf over one who wears drab; and such are the powers of self-deception, he will be certain that his choice was rationally made. Tertium Quid, a nobleman

---

51. I, 698-700.
52. I, 822-824.

of cultivated speech and critical mind, assesses the case in "selectest phrase" and with less bias, but with a grasp of truth not conspicuously firmer than that of his fellows. His sophisticated conclusion ("The long and the short is, truth seems what I show") is that of other men. His judicious weighing of evidence and reluctance to betray vulgar bias by hasty judgment reveal more sensitivity and refinement than the other two mouthpieces of the Roman populace can show, but truth and superficial cultivation of objectivity should not be confused.

E. D. H. Johnson, in *The Alien Vision of Victorian Poetry,* cites Guido's intellectuality as the *fons et origo* of his repellent villainy. I should judge that his villainy is repellent, not because he is an intellectual, but because he is a scoundrel without spirit or the capacity for love. Here is a precise illustration of Browning's concept of wholeness. Guido is found reprobate, not because he is the thinking man, but because one of his triumvirate of souls—the heart, or spirit—is dead, leaving only mind and body alive, and these are therefore warped. Iago is a villain because he is a heartless blackguard, not because he is an intellectual, although his twisted and brilliant mind helped perfect his villainy. There is no such thing in Browning as an "excess" of mind so long as the other two souls are functioning. A man of minimum intellect and little learning—a Caliban, for example— can be overintellectual if he has allowed his small gift of mind to destroy his other powers. It is as erroneous to find Browning deprecating the intellect as it is to suggest that he extolled the virtues of poverty because he deplored the corrosive effects of greed. The greatest intellectual in all of Browning is the Pope, the most rational and clearheaded spokesman the poet created to utter his most carefully reasoned beliefs. At no time is the Pope carried away with emotion, visited with intuitive certitude, or otherwise aided to form his decision by the intervention of means that transcend the mind. Like all men, he gropes through uncertainty, using all of his powers in the knowledge that God would not give man capacities he is forbidden to use. That he speaks Browning's most thoughtful words of doubt of man's capacity to seize truth in all its purity is certainly not valid grounds for considering him to be anti-intellectual. He knows that though he

is a Pope he is yet a man, with all of man's capacity for seizing error
for truth and for abusing the powers of intellect to the detriment
of spirit, a knowledge which reflects an anachronistic awareness of
the nineteenth-century spirit of intellectual skepticism.

Guido's defense, which may appear on the surface to be an indictment of the reason as much as of Guido, is the most brilliant casuistic
employment of reason in a bad cause to be seen among Browning's
villains, but the intellect is not on trial. Guido essays every rational
appeal which may influence the decision of the court, it is true; but
far more effective are his emotional appeals. His first speech begins
and ends, not on a syllogistic note, but on apologetic grimaces of pain
and allusions to the rack. He suggests that he has suffered more than
enough already for any fancied wrongdoing he might be charged
with, his shoulder blade and wrist being dislocated and his hand torn
with the pincers. The emotional appeal on which his defense rests
may, of course, be partially attributed to calculation, but the skill
with which he makes his appeal suggests that he is not pure intellect
alone.

> Then will I set my son at my right-hand
> And tell his father's story to this point,
> Adding "The task seemed superhuman, still
> I dared and did it, trusting God and law:
> And they approved of me: give praise to both!"
> And if, for answer, he shall stoop to kiss
> My hand, and peradventure start thereat,—
> I engage to smile "That was an accident
> I' the necessary process,—just a trip
> O' the torture-irons in their search for truth,—
> Hardly misfortune, and no fault at all."[53]

Guido urges in his defense *honoris causa,* the sanctity of marriage,
the supremacy of the husband, and his right and duty to exact obedience and wreak vengeance to protect the home. The weakness in
his case, as he well knows, is his failure to act in hot blood when he

---

53. V, 2037-2047.

caught up with the fugitives in Castelnuovo outside Rome and his commission of cold-blooded murder eight months later. He carefully builds up a picture of himself as a man of hot blood, quick to love and anger, tempered by mildness and almost superhuman forbearance; but in his sanctimonious protestations of reverence for marriage, he reveals himself to be a liar. To convince the court that he is not the dry stick of a man which he is, he postulates his ardent conduct in an imagined adulterous affair:

> Had it been some friend's wife, now, threw her fan
> At my foot, with just this pretty scrap attached,
> "Shame, death, damnation—fall these as they may,
> So I find you, for a minute! Come this eve!"
> —Why, at such sweet self-sacrifice,—who knows?
> I might have fired up, found me at my post,
> Ardent from head to heel, nor feared catch cough.
> Nay, had some other friend's . . . say, daughter, tripped
> Upstairs and tumbled flat and frank on me,
> Bareheaded and barefooted, with loose hair
> And garments all at large,—cried "Take me thus!
> Duke So-and-So, the greatest man in Rome—
> To escape his hand and heart have I broke bounds,
> Traversed the town and reached you!"—then, indeed,
> The lady had not reached a man of ice!
> I would have rummaged, ransacked at the word
> Those old odd corners of an empty heart
> For remnants of dim love the long disused,
> And dusty crumblings of romance![54]

A true hot-blooded gallant proves himself a man of ice if he spurns an adulterous union, on the premise, widely held, that only one's own marriage is sacred:

> Pompilia's duty was—submit herself,
> Afford me pleasure, perhaps cure my bile.
> Am I to teach my lords what marriage means,

---

54. V, 676-694.

> What God ordains thereby and man fulfils
> Who, docile to the dictate, treads the house?[55]

He similarly traps himself in a web of falsehood which a more intelligent man would have avoided. He denounces Pompilia as a cold temptress who shunned his embraces and who destroyed him through her calculating hatred:

> Such was the pact: Pompilia from the first
> Broke it, refused from the beginning day
> Either in body or soul to cleave to mine,
> And published it forthwith to all the world.
> No rupture,—you must join ere you can break. . . .[56]

Later, in describing his Christian fortitude in the face of provocation, he recalls how Pompilia lay in his bosom; and he tells of "a whisper" in his ear to test Pompilia in the home of the Comparini by the words: "Open to Caponsacchi!"

> And then,—why, even then, I think,
> I' the minute that confirmed my worst of fears,
> Surely,—I pray God that I think aright!—
> Had but Pompilia's self, the tender thing
> Who once was good and pure, was once my lamb
> And lay in my bosom, had the well-known shape
> Fronted me in the door-way,—stood there faint
> With the recent pang perhaps of giving birth
> To what might, though by miracle, seem my child,—
>
> .   .   .   .
>
> I had paused.[57]

Guido, then, is sentenced to the block because he is a murderer, a loveless and twisted liar, a man dead in soul. Had his mind been more potent by thrice, he would not have been a scoundrel if he had been a whole man. As he is, his intellect, divorced from heart, makes him Browning's matchless villain.

---

55. V, 716-720.
56. V, 605-609.
57. V, 1627-1640.

The Pope, in sentencing Guido to death, examines with such anxious care the bases of man's knowledge and the limitations of mind that the whole book may falsely be taken as an indictment of man's reason and a frank substitution of instinct for intellect. The course of his argument may properly be considered to be basic to an understanding of Browning's attitude toward the mind.

At the beginning of his discourse, the Pope is sitting down to read, as is his daily habit, a history of the popes, so that he may "take instruction" from the precedent their conduct affords; but history, even of the men of God, is a fabric of deception and half-truth reflecting man's infinite capacity for error and evil. The shameful schism in the church, during the course of which Pope Stephen denounced the late Pope Formosus as an imposter and commanded that his corpse be exhumed and set before him in a ghastly trial, he finds to be an example of man's regard for propriety and truth when they are set against self-interest. Upon the death of Stephen, Pope Romanus reversed the judgment of the tribunal and pronounced Formosus the true representative of God and Stephen as accursed. Next, Pope Theodore reversed this reversal; and so the grim comedy of self-interest and falsity continued through the lives of several popes.

> Which of the judgments was infallible?
> Which of my predecessors spoke for God?
> And what availed Formosus that this cursed,
> That blessed, and then this other cursed again? [58]

He, the latest Pope in turn, is called upon to pass judgment upon Guido, and if the testimony of history is a tissue of lies, what can he believe of the testimony of the trial, where bias is all in all? His argument for a time seems to tend toward the view that since the mind cannot determine truth, it were best to throw mind overboard and consult intuition or revelation; but this is precisely what the Pope does not mean. Like St. John, he recognizes that life tests man through ignorance, and the issue of Guido's life or death differs only

---

58. X, 150-153.

in degree, but not in kind, from all other decisions life exacts of a man, wherein he is tested. Throughout a sombre winter's day, the old Pope has pored over the dismal records of the trial, "With winter in my soul, beyond the world's. . . ." He knows well that most of what he reads is false:

> Truth, nowhere, lies yet everywhere in these—
> Not absolutely in a portion, yet
> Evolvible from the whole: evolved at last
> Painfully, held tenaciously by me.
> Therefore there is not any doubt to clear. . . .[59]

It is important to remember that, with full knowledge of the elusive nature of truth and the incidence of falsehood in the testimony, he yet studies the court records with care "through the sombre wintry day" and at the end of his perusal, "there is not any doubt to clear." Does this mean that he has certitude of seeing absolute and total truth? By no means, but he is confident that he has truth in so far as it is given to him to perceive it, and he accepts this "truth" as an adequate basis for action just as he accepts all of life's limitations. Every man every day judges Guido and renders his verdict from imperfectly perceived truth, for Guido's trial is life in little, and the records of the trial are the records of all history. If while on a walk through the countryside, he says, he should come across a man bitten by an adder and in his ignorance he should bleed the victim for supposed epilepsy, with fatal consequences,

> What other should I say than "God so willed:
> Mankind is ignorant, a man am I:
> Call ignorance my sorrow, not my sin!"[60]

---

59. X, 228-232. Robert Langbaum, in *"The Ring and the Book: a Relativist Poem,"* p. 141, finds that the Pope "relies not upon logic to make his judgments, but upon talent, intuition, insight, the advantages of his own character gained through a long experience of life and people." True, the Pope, being whole, relies not upon one faculty alone, but upon them all, working in harmony. It is equally true that the Pope does not scorn logical processes.

60. X, 256-258.

This pragmatic view of truth is quite the opposite of the paralysis of will that results from a defeatist belief in nescience. Ignorance is a limitation, not a blessing, certainly not a condition to be cultivated for the furtherance of intuitionism and entry of the white light.

Much has been made over such statements as the following:

> . . . who trusts
> To human testimony for a fact
> Gets this sole fact—himself is proved a fool. . . .[61]

A. K. Cook cites these words, which Browning himself delivers *in propria persona,* as proof that he "constantly declares that human testimony is worthless."[62] Neither the Pope nor Browning ever says this, of course. What he does say is that human testimony, like all other things in this world, is part truth and part falsehood; and so man is faced with a constant challenge of discerning as best he can what he can find of truth, not giving up the offices of the mind without reflection. To do so is indeed to be a fool.

> "God who set me to judge thee, meted out
> So much of judging faculty, no more:
> Ask Him if I was slack in use thereof!"[63]

In these three lines may be seen in simple clarity Browning's trust in the intellect. Man will be ultimately judged on how well he used God's gifts; a man may be a fool to trust human testimony without examination, but a greater fool by far is the man who is slack in the uses of mind.

> Man must tell his mate
> Of you, me and himself, knowing he lies,
> Knowing his fellow knows the same,—will think
> "He lies, it is the method of a man!"
> And yet will speak for answer "It is truth"

---

61. XII, 598-600.
62. *A Commentary on Browning's "The Ring and the Book"* (London, 1920), p. 207.
63. X, 264-266.

> To him who shall rejoin "Again a lie!"
> Therefore these filthy rags of speech, this coil
> Of statement, comment, query and response,
> Tatters all too contaminate for use,
> Have no renewing: He, the Truth, is, too,
> The Word. We men, in our degree, may know
> There, simply, instantaneously, as here
> After long time and amid many lies,
> Whatever we dare think we know indeed
> —That I am I, as He is He,—what else?
> But be man's method for man's life at least![64]

Fortified by his assurance that God commissions man to use man's methods, he scorns the doubts and paralysis of decision which would be the natural fruit of nescience: "I shall face Guido's ghost nor blench a jot." He is old and exhausted from his application to the evidence, but he is confident that he has used the instrumentalities as a man must. Hard study is good; its perversion is bad. The fox-faced Abate, the horrible priest, is worse than Guido, the Pope declares, for he is all guile and hypocrisy:

> Armed with religion, fortified by law,
> A man of peace, who trims the midnight lamp
> And turns the classic page—and all for craft,
> All to work harm with, yet incur no scratch![65]

He pronounces man's intellect the "sword, the energy his subtle spear,/ The knowledge which defends him like a shield. . . ."; but the mind can be twisted into the paths of evil.

The Pope, like Browning, believes that life's crown is not the intellect but a beautiful soul. Speaking of Pompilia, he finds her white as snow in her innocence and purity. Man's mind and knowledge

> . . . make not up, I think,
> The marvel of a soul like thine, earth's flower
> She holds up to the softened gaze of God!

64. X, 366-381.
65. X, 884-887.

> It was not given Pompilia to know much,
> Speak much, to write a book, to move mankind,
> Be memorialized by who records my time.[66]

Pompilia is not shrouded in the white radiance of spirit because she is unread and illiterate. It was given to Browning to know much, to speak more, to write a very great deal, and to move mankind far more than he could have predicted; and yet we know that he never felt his irregular erudition to menace the health of his soul. Man's mind is for life. It is a convex glass to "gather all the scattered points" in the immensity of sky—to give wholeness to man's triple soul. "The little mind of man" is reduced to a "littleness that suits his faculty," but the Pope never suggests that since it is small man should make it smaller. The Bible says that we see as in a glass darkly, but it does not command us to seek blindness. All things from the insect to the angel are given their "just length and breadth,/ Due facet of reflection. . . ." Man's intelligence, like the insect's and the angel's, is "ample." In reference to a scriptural tale, he says that he does not hesitate to apply to it the test of mind as well as heart. Blind, emotional faith is not demanded:

> There is, beside the works, a tale of Thee
> In the world's mouth, which I find credible:
> I love it with my heart: unsatisfied,
> I try it with my reason, nor discept
> From any point I probe and pronounce sound.
> Mind is not matter nor from matter, but
> Above,—leave matter then, proceed with mind!
> Man's be the mind recognized at the height,—
> Leave the inferior minds and look at man!
> Is he the strong, intelligent and good
> Up to his own conceivable height? Nowise.
> Enough of the low,—soar the conceivable height. . . .[67]

Here is the reverse of anti-intellectualism. Even God's works and

---

66. X, 1012-1017.
67. X, 1343-1354.

plan may be examined by man's mind as well as heart. Where mind proves unable to comprehend, "I reach into the dark,/ Feel what I cannot see, and still faith stands. . . ." This is as clear as any other statement in Browning of his faith in intellect. A child fancies that the sea roars in anger, the Pope notes by way of analogy, and such an explanation is sufficient to his needs; but "Man makes acoustics deal with the sea's wrath," for he uses his mind to gain greater knowledge. For all of man's science, of course, the sound remains the same; and man is very far from full truth. The Pope says that a child may believe that the lightning is a real arrow shot to pierce his eyes; a man of science may smile at such naïveté, "but shuts his lids the same." "Lightning's cause comprehends nor man nor child." The context makes it clear that the Pope does not intend to challenge the accuracy of our knowledge of the physical world, which may afford a valid explanation of the "cause" of lightning. The Pope refers, not to the physical cause, but to the First Cause, the cause behind the cause, which man, for all his science, must seek as does the child. "So much, no more two thousand years have done!"

Such statements as this prompted Henry Jones to write near the conclusion of his *Browning as a Philosophical and Religious Teacher:*

> I have tried to show that Browning's theory of life, in so far as it is expressed in his philosophical poems, rests on agnosticism; and that such a theory is inconsistent with the moral and religious interests of man. The idea that truth is unattainable was represented by Browning as a bulwark of the faith, but it proved on examination to be treacherous. His optimism was found to have no better foundation than personal conviction, which any one was free to deny, and which the poet could in no wise prove. The evidence of the heart, to which he appealed, was the evidence of an emotion severed from intelligence, and, therefore, without any content whatsoever. 'The faith,' which he professed, was not the faith that anticipates and invites proof. . . . In casting doubt upon the validity of knowledge, he degraded the whole spiritual nature of man; for a love that is ignorant of its object is a blind impulse, and a moral consciousness that does not know the law is an impossible phantom—a self-contradiction.[68]

68. Glasgow, 1902, pp. 321-322.

This statement is a classical example of purity of error rarely attained through human faculties. Browning held no "agnostic"—Jones consistently misuses the term—belief in the futility of mind; he did not say that man cannot attain truth, in the usual sense of the word; he did not sever the head hygienically from the heart; he did not say that faith should be spared examination by the mind. The charge that Browning's religion should have rested not upon personal conviction but upon axiom and corollary which can be tested and proved seems to make all religious belief whatever impossible. Love and faith alike ultimately rest on the evidences of things not seen. I have yet to meet the man who has attained absolute knowledge either of God or of his beloved. It is strikingly perverse to charge that Browning "degraded the whole spiritual nature of man" throughout a lifetime devoted with singleness of purpose to the elevation of man's spiritual nature. Jones insists that as there are "not two kinds of righteousness and mercy; there are not two kinds of truth," and for the poet to deny that man can attain on earth truth whole and absolute is to be "disloyal to the fundamental principle of the Christian faith which he professes."

> Human nature is not "cut in two with a hatchet," as the poet implies that it is. There is in man a lower and a higher element, ever at war with each other; still he is not a mixture, or an agglomerate, of the finite and the infinite. A love perfect in nature cannot be linked to an intelligence imperfect in nature; if it were, the love would be either a blind impulse or an erring one.[69]

Far from believing that human nature is a duality of head and heart, sundered by an illimitable gulf, Browning insisted on the unity of the triple soul of man. The statement that a love perfect in nature is impossible if the intelligence is not in the same happy state, begs the question; for Browning believed that mortality implied imperfection in all things, love included. Even little Pippa knows that God's love transcends in nature all forms of earthly love, good as they are.

---

69. Pp. 328-329.

In fact, earthly love and knowledge and faith all rest in varying degrees upon trust. It is difficult to share Jones's conviction that these beliefs make Browning a traitor to Christianity, for the Bible includes them also: "for we walk by faith, not by sight,"[70] said Paul; and even more pointedly, "Now faith is assurance of things hoped for, a conviction of things not seen. For therein the elders had witness borne to them. By faith we understand that the worlds have been framed by the word of God, so that what is seen hath not been made out of things which appear."[71] Additional examples may readily be supplied by anyone familiar with the scriptures.

Perhaps the single utterance of the Pope which on the surface appears most strongly to betray distrust of learning, particularly of scientific learning, is the following:

> Thus, bold
> Yet self-mistrusting, should man bear himself,
> Most assured on what now concerns him most—
> The law of his own life, the path he prints,—
> Which law is virtue and not vice, I say,—
> And least inquisitive where search least skills,
> I' the nature we best give the clouds to keep.
> What could I paint beyond a scheme like this
> Out of the fragmentary truths where light
> Lay fitful in a tenebrific time?[72]

Does Browning literally mean that man should busy himself with the law of his own life and with virtue and should not investigate the arcana of meteoritics? Does he deprecate the natural sciences? To conclude so does violence to all of Browning; but, then, this has happened with moderate regularity. The clouds here are not literal clouds, but are the veil separating life and death; and once again Browning is cautioning man against the folly of seeking the Absolute.

---

70. II Cor. V.7.
71. Hebrews XI. 1-3.
72. X, 1747-1756.

When the Pope says that "We have got too familiar with the light," does he reveal a sentimental affection for horny-handed illiteracy as an earnest of spiritual excellence? Not at all. He is yearning for a return of the thrill of the early Christian days, "When the whole truth-touched man burned up, one fire," before the world had its way.

It is not the light but man's intellectual pride in the light that is culpable. The Pope hears the new tribunal, "now/ Higher than God's —the educated man's!" urging that he pardon Guido:

> Remonstrants on each side commence
> Instructing, there's a new tribunal now
> Higher than God's—the educated man's!
> Nice sense of honor in the human breast
> Supersedes here the old coarse oracle—
> Conforming none the less a point or so
> Wherein blind predecessors worked aright
> By rule of thumb.... [73]

"The spirit of culture speaks," and culture is what the world in its blindness calls the twisted and partial development of one faculty, mind, at the expense of soul. The Pope says nothing against culture in the proper sense; but he fears that perversity masquerading as culture will bring back "Civilization and the Emperor" to supplant "Christianity and Pope."

Evidence that the weary and disheartened Pope fears not the mind alone but also the heart as distorted in the "new order of things" is seen in his picture of the experimentalist of the new order:

> Here comes the first experimentalist
> In the new order of things,—he plays a priest;
> Does he take inspiration from the Church,
> Directly make her rule his law of life?
> Not he: his own mere impulse guides the man—
> Happily sometimes, since ourselves allow
> He has danced, in gayety of heart, i' the main

---

73. X, 1969-1976.

> The right step through the maze we bade him foot.
> But if his heart had prompted him break loose
> And mar the measure? Why, we must submit,
> And thank the chance that brought him safe so far.[74]

As dangerous as pride of intellect is "the instinct of the world/ Ruling its household without tutelage." And tutelage surely implies learning, the acquisition of knowledge, and the use of intellect. With these reflections, the Pope sends his verdict to the Governor.

---

74. X, 1904-1914.

CHAPTER II

THE DIVINE AGENCY OF IGNORANCE:
THE PERIOD OF GRAY ARGUMENT

> I say, o'erstep no least one of the rows
> That lead man from the bottom where he plants
> Foot first of all, to life's last ladder-top. . . .
> · · · · · · · · · · · · · ·
> Live and learn,
> Not first learn and then live, is our concern.
> —"Parleyings with Christopher Smart"

I

It should prove useful to examine separately the period to which Browning himself supplied the name—the period of "my mere gray argument." True, in using the phrase in the parleyings with Christopher Smart, he did not intend to label the last half of his literary life, but the name, perhaps unfortunately, has stuck. The poems after 1870 are increasingly argumentative and philosophical, occasionally knotty and crabbed; but they are never without interest and rarely without a glow of his earlier lyricism. William Clyde DeVane, following Jones, discovers in the later period a marked growth in the poet's anti-intellectualism,[1] a final surrender of faith in the mind as an instrument in the pursuit of understanding. It behooves us to study well the poems beginning with *Fifine at the Fair* (1872).

---

1. Cf. Robert W. Hartle's article ("Gide's Interpretation of Browning," *Studies in English*, XXVIII [1949], 244-256), in which he appears to assume that Browning's "renunciation of reason" is so well established as to need no further proof. Hartle discovers Gide's admiration for Browning to rest in their similar renunciation of rational culture: "Gide has renounced rational culture in favor of life. To try to understand his ideas, then, as being the expression of a rational culture will be futile; and unless we reject him—as Santayana does Browning—because of his renunciation of reason, we must, I believe, try to understand him on his own terms."

It is strange to find substantial agreement on the role of the mind between the Pope and the unspiritual rake, Don Juan, whose defense of infidelity in *Fifine at the Fair* has puzzled the public and critics alike. Don Juan carefully develops the central beliefs of the Pope on the function of ignorance as a test in life, the futility and even the dangers of overintellectualism gained at the expense of wholeness.[2] We grope through life, he says, to "reach knowledge by ignorance. . . ." He finds, in line with his theme of the therapeutic values of adultery and the virtues of kept women, that "the proper goal for wisdom was the ground/ And not the sky." One should be lowly wise and not fret "on altitudes of self-sufficiency," not investigate the region beyond man's proper boundaries, but "welcome what is." All life, he says, is flux, and change is the only changeless thing. Each generation feels that earlier times lived in darkness and error and that truth shines forth in all its whiteness only *now;* but all of man's temples suffer decay, and the temples of the mind suffer most of all:

> But are they only temples that subdivide, collapse,
> And tower again, transformed? Academies, perhaps!
> Domes where dwells Learning, seats of Science, bower and hall
> Which house Philosophy—do these, too, rise and fall,
> Based though foundations be on steadfast mother-earth,
> With no chimeric claim to supermundane birth,
> No boast that, dropped from cloud, they did not grow from ground?
> Why, these fare worst of all! these vanish and are found
> Nowhere, by who tasks eye some twice within his term
> Of threescore years and ten, for tidings what each germ
> Has burgeoned out into, whereof the promise stunned
> His ear with such acclaim,—praise-payment to refund
> The praisers, never doubt, some twice before they die
> Whose days are long i' the land.[3]

Similarly religion itself suffers the ravages of time and is patched up and plastered over; but natural philosophy, supposedly an exact science, proves least exact. For thirty years, Don Juan laments, he

---

2. The principal discussion of *Fifine at the Fair* appears in the chapter "Browning's Casuists."
3. Ll. 1913-1926.

has been agape "to learn how tadpole turns to frog," and thrice at least some "fire-new fabric" of truth has sent its sparks upward for men to hail as the living truth:

> Alack, Philosophy!
> Despite the chop and change, diminished or increased,
> Patched-up and plastered-o'er, Religion stands at least
> I' the temple-type. But thou? Here gape I, all agog
> These thirty years, to learn how tadpole turns to frog;
> And thrice at least have gazed with mild astonishment,
> As, skyward up and up, some fire-new fabric sent
> Its challenge to mankind that, clustered underneath
> To hear the word, they straight believe, ay, in the teeth
> O' the Past, clap hands and hail triumphant Truth's outbreak—
> Tadpole-frog-theory propounded past mistake!
> In vain! A something ails the edifice, it bends,
> It bows, it buries . . . Haste! cry "Heads below" to friends—
> But have no fear they find, when smother shall subside,
> Some substitution perk with unabated pride
> I' the predecessor's place![4]

Truth, he discovers, is always built upon the sands, "Though stationed on a rock," and so suffers decay. It matters not how massive appears the rock on which truth is stationed, for the rock in its turn rests on shifting sands. The truth that lasts man his lifetime "does well," he says; but in spite of this lesson each generation seizes upon the latest discovery, hypothesis, or theory—Browning surely had in mind Darwinism, the higher criticism, and neo-rationalism—as imperishable: "yesterday's doctrine dead, this only shall endure!"

Don Juan, even though arguing in a bad cause, does not mean that man can know nothing and thus should shelve his mind as a means only of error. The sands upon which the rock of truth rests are the equivalent of the veil between life and death. Let man probe knowledge ever so far, he will arrive at a point beyond which he cannot probe. If this theory of knowledge be considered anti-intellectual, then the greatest living atomic scientists are anti-intellectual. Every

---

4. Ll. 1926-1941.

working hypothesis of the structure of the atom and the nature of the chemical bond is founded ultimately upon ignorance. Because certain laws of cause and effect may be derived and demonstrated upon demand, theories that appear consonant with what is known are derived; and these theories properly constitute the laws of science until they are unseated by others.

That Don Juan does not single out science to demonstrate the darkness whence all our light derives is seen in his picture of vain man, glorying in his art, and looking backward in contempt from the vantage point of his proud eminence to the low hills of the past. Indeed, the peak on which man stands looks to his eyes like the roof of the world, with no superior peaks on either side.

The mystery of Stonehenge is used as a symbol of the riddle of existence beyond man's capacity to explore. In one of the apparently anti-intellectual passages in Browning, Don Juan says that "Learning" expends great labor over the mystery of the monoliths, "While Ignorance reads right":

> How does it strike you, this construction gaunt and gray—
> Sole object, these piled stones, that gleam unground-away
> By twilight's hungry jaw, which champs fine all beside
> I' the solitary waste we grope through? Oh, no guide,
> Need we to grope our way and reach the monstrous door
> Of granite! Take my word, the deeper you explore
> That caverned passage, filled with fancies to the brim,
> The less will you approve the adventure! such a grim
> Bar-sinister soon blocks abrupt your path, and ends
> All with a cold dread shape,—shape whereon Learning spends
> Labor, and leaves the text obscurer for the gloss,
> While Ignorance reads right—recoiling from that Cross!
> Whence came the mass and mass, strange quality of stone
> Unquarried anywhere i' the region round? Unknown!
> Just as unknown, how such enormity could be
> Conveyed by land, or else transported over sea,
> And laid in order, so, precisely each on each,
> As you and I would build a grotto, where the beach

> Sheds shell—to last an hour: this building lasts from age
> To age the same. But why? [5]

If this passage means that ignorance, not learning, is the proper tool for archaeological exploration (taken as a type for all science), there could be no defense against the charge of the grossest anti-intellectualism. The words do not, however, say that ignorance is a dependable guide, to be preferred to learning, but that since the druid mystery, which is a symbol for all inscrutable mystery of life, can never be understood by man, ignorance, through a sort of instinctual sapience, recoils from examination of the cross. Browning does not say that ignorance, in reading right, solves the mystery; to read "right" is to forswear the attempt to delve into ultimate secrets. An uninformed guess, it is suggested, without either examination or evidence, may by mere chance come as close to the truth as science can in matters which science is unqualified to examine. Science can tell whether the stone is granite or sandstone and perhaps can disclose many facts about the druid cult, but the land behind the veil is as inscrutable to learning as to ignorance. Learning, applied to matters beyond man's ken, will give us a "prosy wherefore," of as little value as "Ignorance Surmising" in the mouth of an illiterate peasant lad or lass. Whence came the druids? Whither did they go? These are the eternal questions of mankind, the prime movers of his mind and spirit, and great care is exercised in the scheme of things to shield man's eyes from such truth, lest the mind and the spirit die. The individual soul, working through "the shows of sense/ Which, ever proving false, still promise to be true," is kept at stretch in life's moral gymnasium.

Don Juan, speaking for Browning, denies that all of mankind's efforts to discover truth arrive at nescience. Falsity contaminates man's truth in all conceivable degrees, according to the divine plan, and man's duty is to move from imperfect truth to a better truth throughout life, from birth to death:

---

5. Ll. 2048-2067.

> . . . truth successively takes shape, one grade above
> Its last presentment, tempts as it were truth indeed
> Revealed this time; so tempts, till we attain to read
> The signs aright, and learn, by failure, truth is forced
> To manifest itself through falsehood. . . .[6]

The lines that follow are a noble tribute to truth as man's goal in
life, in seeking which he sees the "value of a lie"—to show forth the
beauty of the light of truth in contrast to the darkness of the false:

> His problem posed aright
> Was—"From the given point evolve the infinite!"
> Not—"Spend thyself in space, endeavoring to joint
> Together, and so make infinite, point and point:
> Fix into one Elvire a Fair-ful of Fifines!"[7]

II

Monsieur Léonce Miranda, in *Red Cotton Night-Cap Country; or
Turf and Towers,* is the central figure in an allegory of man's struggle
for truth. He builds a tower, or belvedere, as a symbol of his spiritual
aspiration and yearning to see the white light which man must leave
this dull world to perceive. Turf, symbolic of the world, the flesh,
and human error, lies before him, strewn with "the ravage of opinion,"
for each man's conjecture is partially or largely false. In his search
for truth, he stumbles from lie to lie, to madness and suicide. This is
the price man pays for erecting on earth a tower to elevate himself
above the issues of life in his desire to see into heaven:

> If we have souls, know how to see and use,
> One place performs, like any other place,
> The proper service every place on earth
> Was framed to furnish man with: serves alike
> To give him note that, through the place he sees,

6. Ll. 2192-2196.
7. Ll. 2294-2298.

> A place is signified he never saw,
> But, if he lack not soul, may learn to know.
> Earth's ugliest walled and ceiled imprisonment
> May suffer, through its single rent in roof,
> Admittance of a cataract of light
> Beyond attainment through earth's palace-panes
> Pinholed athwart their windowed filagree
> By twinklings sobered from the sun outside.[8]

In these thirteen lines, which are spoken by Browning himself, is the heart of his philosophy of the imperfect and also the refutation unmistakable of those who charge him with hostility toward the mind. Man "may learn to know" from the evidences of this earth, and if his soul be not dead, he may even project his knowledge into a prevision of eternity. But death is the result of spurning life's instrumentalities and limitations.

It is the "check that gives the leap its lift," but how can one reconcile Browning's belief in the use of mind with the following charge that cultivated souls often or always are a nullity?

> The nullity of cultivated souls,
> Even advantaged by their news from Vire,
> Only conduces to enforce the truth
> That, thirty paces off, this natural blue
> Broods o'er a bag of secrets, all unbroached,
> Beneath the bosom of the placid deep,
> Since first the Post Director sealed them safe. . . .[9]

In the passage which follows Browning makes it clear that not he but a "possible objector" charges cultivated souls with nullity:

> . . . nullity
> And ugliness, the taunt be his, not mine
> Nor yours. . . .[10]

---

8. I, 58-70.
9. I, 87-93.
10. I, 101-103.

And a few lines below he says that "The learned eye is still the loving one!"

The moral of *Red Cotton Night-Cap Country* Browning states directly:

> Take its moral first.
> Do you advise a climber? Have respect
> To the poor head, with more or less of brains
> To spill, should breakage follow your advice!
> Head-break to him will be heart-break to you
> For having preached "Disturb no ruins here!
> Are not they crumbling of their own accord?
> Meantime, let poets, painters keep a prize!
> Beside, a sage pedestrian picks his way."
> A sage pedestrian—such as you and I!
> What if there trip, in merry carelessness,
> And come to grief, a weak and foolish child?
> Be cautious how you counsel climbing, then![11]

One should distrust towers, which often are a mash of rottenness inside, "Symbolic partial-ravage,—keep in mind!" Man were well advised to plant the foot warily, even straggle into the rubbish that life plants in man's path, rather than "To foot it fast and easy" up the tower of pride.

Poor Miranda, one of Browning's certifiable psychotics, was born the pawn of his father's passionate Castilian blood and his mother's cold French reason. "Such mixture makes a battle in the brain/ Ending as faith or doubt gets uppermost. . . ." He thus becomes symbolic of man's struggle for a settled faith and the fate that awaits him the moment all doubts are gone.

Miranda falls in love with Clara de Millefleurs at first sight by a notable instance of the operation of elective affinities, "Such potency in word and look hath truth." They live together in an irregular liaison for many years, their love being as "true" as earth permits:

---

11. II, 94-106.

> Truth I say, truth I mean: this love was true,
> And the rest happened by due consequence.
> By which we are to learn that there exists
> A falsish false, for truth's inside the same,
> And truth that's only half true, falsish truth.
> The better for both parties! folk may taunt
> That half your rock-built wall is rubble-heap:
> Answer them, half their flowery turf is stones![12]

In spite of the truth of their love, Miranda is torn by guilt and in-decision. His heart tells him that his love, because true, is holy; but his received social and religious convictions war against his heart; and he is not strong enough to find in human love the evidence of divine sanction which he seeks or to renounce the liaison and find peace within the grace of the church. In short, he cannot choose between turf, the symbol of earth, the flesh, and mortal love; and tower, the complex symbol of man's spiritual aspirations, the Virgin, and the yearning for the Absolute. Predictably, Browning's heart sides with turf:

> Chance
> Or purpose,—who can read the mystery?—
> Combined, I say, to bid "Entrench yourself,
> Monsieur Léonce Miranda, on this turf,
> About this flower, so firmly that, as tent
> Rises on every side around you both,
> The question shall become,—Which arrogates
> Stability, this tent or those far towers?
> May not the temporary structure suit
> The stable circuit, co-exist in peace?"[13]

The tent is a shadowy symbol of the structure of expediency, essen-tial to man who cannot live wholly on turf or tower, and symbol-izes both the liaison, unsanctified except by the heart, and the day-

---

12. II, 457-464.
13. II, 934-942.

to-day compromise man makes between the demands of flesh and
the aspiration of spirit. Since nothing in life is in pure form, the
flimsy tent is man's symbol of pragmatic living, the way of the world:

> Outside the turf, the towers: but, round the turf,
> A tent may rise, a temporary shroud,
> Mock-faith to suit a mimic dwelling-place:
> Tent which, while screening jollity inside
> From the external circuit—evermore
> A menace to who lags when he should march—
> Yet stands a-tremble, ready to collapse
> At touch of foot: turf is acknowledged grass,
> And grass, though pillowy, held contemptible
> Compared with solid rock, the rampired ridge.
> To truth a pretty homage thus we pay
> By testifying—what we dally with,
> Falsehood, (which, never fear we take for truth!)
> We may enjoy, but then—how we despise![14]

Miranda, torn between the demands of hot passion and cold reason,
finds his wavering faith shattered by the higher criticism. He longs
for a miracle that will exorcise all doubts of mind and give him
peace; but none comes. In the meanwhile, he is further torn between
fear of examining the origins of faith and hope that in doing so he
may find the proof he seeks:

> Now, into the originals of faith,
> Yours, mine, Miranda's, no inquiry here!
> Of faith, as apprehended by mankind,
> The causes, were they caught and catalogued,
> Would too distract, too desperately foil
> Inquirer.[15]

Analysis is powerless to prove the origins of faith, the roots of human
belief which lie hidden in obscurity, for these are matters proper to
infinity and God. It cannot detect or trace the wire thread of truth

---

14. II, 341-354.
15. III, 786-791.

within the fluffy silk twist of faith, which "Men call their rope, their real compulsive power." How can man reduce quantities to their opposites—"value to zero"—and then bring zero back "To value of supreme preponderance?" Lazarus, as we have seen, did so, but at what a price! In a passage that is central in understanding Browning's attitude toward inquiry into things forbidden, he says that man should be practical and spare his pains in parading useless proofs of what needs no proof on earth. It is just as well, for proof is not within man's power:

> Therefore the course to take is—spare your pains,
> And trouble uselessly with discontent
> Nor soul nor body, by parading proof
> That neither haply had known ailment, placed
> Precisely where the circumstance forbade
> Their lot should fall to either of the pair.
> But try and, what you find wrong, remedy,
> Accepting the conditions: never ask
> "How came you to be born here with those lungs,
> That liver?" But bid asthma smoke a pipe,
> Stramonium, just as if no Tropics were,
> And ply with calomel the sluggish duct,
> Nor taunt "The born Norwegian breeds no bile!"
> And as with body, so proceed with soul:
> Nor less discerningly, where faith you found,
> However foolish and fantastic, grudge
> To play the doctor and amend mistake,
> Because a wisdom were conceivable
> Whence faith had sprung robust above disease.
> Far beyond human help, that source of things![16]

The business of man is to be pragmatic: smoke a healing weed for asthma and purge the sluggish duct with calomel; and inquire only into the curative effects of the remedy, not into the metaphysics of physic. The soul, likewise, does not bear scrutiny with profit to man. Whether the sickness be of the body or the soul, "Never mind the

---

16. III, 822-841.

cause,/ *Fons et origo* of the malady:/ Apply the drug with courage!"
There are two stages in man's inquiry into mystery: the first stage is
"the stare/ Of apprehension at the invisible. . . ." Straightway enters
divergency of mind from mind: "leave this first! /Little you change
there!" The second stage, man's proper use of mind, is the pragmatic
stage which man learns from the abrasions and contusions gained
from the first stage:

> What comes afterward—
> From apprehended thing, each inference
> With practicality concerning life,
> This you may test and try, confirm the right
> Or contravene the wrong which reasons there.
> The offspring of the sickly faith must prove
> Sickly act also: stop a monster-birth!
> When water's in the cup and not the cloud,
> Then is the proper time for chemic test:
> Belief permits your skill to operate
> When, drop by drop condensed from misty heaven,
> 'T is wrung out, lies a bowlful in the fleece.
> How dew by spoonfuls came, let Gideon say:
> What purpose water serves, your word or two
> May teach him, should he fancy it lights fire.[17]

The apparent sense of this passage, which may betray the reader
into the belief that Browning sturdily opposed theoretical science, is
that man may examine the water in his cup for bacteria and even
boil it suitably, but meteorology should form no part of his studies.
Browning means no such thing. When water is in the cup and not
the cloud, he says, is the time for a *chemic test,* for the simple reason
that man cannot test water that he cannot get to. How can a chemist
test water for its properties and potability when it is still in the clouds?
Browning does not say that the study of weather, trade winds, and
cloud formations is not proper for man. Nor does he deny that the
scientific explanation for the precipitation of dew is a proper subject
of investigation. He says that the significance of Gideon's story of

---

17. III, 846-860.

how "dew by spoonfuls came" is a sterile point of inquiry. Indeed, both the dew and the clouds serve Browning here and elsewhere as symbols of heaven and the divine mystery; and this is exactly what the context makes it clear that he intends. He is opposed to abstruse metaphysics, not to physics. The dew is not the literal droplet of water which is economically important to horticulture and therefore to be studied, but rather it is the symbol for God's infinite secret.

Miranda, maddened by his religiosity, doubts, and sin, symbolically spurns his mistress by plunging her love letters into the fire, "Letters and coffer and both hands to boot. . . ." until all is consumed and the bones of his hands are carbonized—an unhappy consequence of imperfect wholeness, which today might be called schizophrenia. His hideous atonement brings no cure and no peace, for his mania to seize absolute truth through divine revelation continues. He prays that God will for once manifest His presence by suspending the law of gravity as he jumps in safety from his belvedere. This prayer for suspension of the physical law is symbolic of his desire to float at will between the flesh and the spirit by suspension of the moral law for him alone. In his leap from the tower, he finds the death which awaits all men who seek to transcend the limitations of life in the search for forbidden powers.

The world pronounces his act suicide, but not Browning. Miranda's madness lay in his hubris, in his war against self, in his yearning to attain the tower while enjoying the fleshly delights of turf. "Mad!" says the world,

> No! sane, I say.
> Such being the conditions of his life,
> Such end of life was not irrational.
> Hold a belief, you only half-believe,
> With all-momentous issues either way,—
> And I advise you imitate this leap,
> Put faith to proof, be cured or killed at once!
> Call you men, killed through cutting cancer out,
> The worse for such an act of bravery?
> That's more than I know. In my estimate,

> Better lie prostrate on his turf at peace,
> Than, wistful, eye, from out the tent, the tower,
> Racked with a doubt. . . .[18]

If one shatters the wholeness that alone brings life meaning, if man elects to build both tent and tower in order to have in life both earth and heaven, if man seeks to probe the veil for certitude which, if gained, would nullify life's meaning, then it is better to put all upon one test, though death be the result. It is interesting that Browning finds that Miranda made too little use of mind, not too much. His "heart was wise according to its lights/ And limits; but the head refused more sun,/ And shrank into its mew, and craved less space." His intellect should have been occupied with the issues of life:

> He might have opened eye, exerted brain,
> Attained conception as to right and law
> In certain points respecting intercourse
> Of man with woman. . . .[19]

He was culpable because

> . . . the sense of him should have sufficed
> For building up some better theory
> Of how God operates in heaven and earth. . . .[20]

III

The wealthy nameless young man in *The Inn Album,* like Léonce Miranda, has a yearning for towers, but his is the ivory tower of scientific investigation. The older man, also unnamed, shows him the folly of expending his days pursuing natural science, "Or, very like, astronomy . . ." just on the chance that he might give to science "one more asteroid." Almost consistently when Browning shows the

---

18. IV, 351-362.
19. IV, 745-748.
20. IV, 752-754.

aridity to which science leads, if pursued without regard for wholeness, he employs astronomy, the stars, clouds, rainfall, asteroids, or
dew to illustrate man's unwise aspirations to forbidden learning. At
other times he uses natural beauty as a symbol of the divine plan of
creation into which one must not peer too recklessly:

> Beauty's the prize-flower which dispenses eye
> From peering into what has nourished root—
> Dew or manure: the plant best knows its place.
> Enough, from teaching youth and tending age
> And hearing sermons,—haply writing tracts,—
> From such strange love-besprinkled compost, lo,
> Out blows his triumph! Therefore love's the soil
> Plants find or fail of.[21]

It is clear, I trust, that this passage is no more a dark warning against
the study of the workings of moisture and barnyard fertilizer upon
the growth of flowers than the earlier passage is an admonition
against the use of telescopes. It is, rather, a clear warning against
hubris.

Among the strikingly anti-primitivist passages in Browning is the
story told by the young cousin, also nameless, of her marriage to a
poor parish priest and her life in a simple rustic village. The priest
is the embodiment of dogmatic irrationality. Walled around with his
narrow faith, he is like a man at the bottom of a well who sees above
only one round of blue: " 'Faith: he had faith in dogma, small or
great,' " but in nothing else, for he entertains the liveliest suspicion
of mind. Like Carlyle, his one rule of life, from childhood, is Obey!
Labor! Any scholarship he might have had shriveled away; but if he
is pictured as a mindless lout, the village is even worse. Not since
Crabbe's village has such a repellent picture of primitive life been
put into verse:

> "These four years I have died away
> In village-life. The village? Ugliness

---

21. III, 231-238.

> At best and filthiness at worst, inside.
> Outside, sterility—earth sown with salt
> Or what keeps even grass from growing fresh.
> The life? I teach the poor and learn, myself,
> That commonplace to such stupidity
> Is all-recondite. Being brutalized
> Their true need is brute-language, cheery grunts
> And kindly cluckings, no articulate
> Nonsense that's elsewhere knowledge. Tend the sick,
> Sickened myself at pig-perversity,
> Cat-craft, dog-snarling,—maybe, snapping. . . ."[22]

Faith without mind and love of life is death, the cousin discovers. Her narrow, self-righteous husband perversely holds that man's best faculty is " 'idiocy/ Man's only guide while act was yet to choose. . . .' " He is the anti-intellectual that Browning is often pictured as being. His wife, speaking for Browning, condemns such a perverse view as opposed to God's general ordinance:

> "This doctrine, which one healthy view of things,
> One sane sight of the general ordinance—
> Nature,—and its particular object,—man,—
> Which one mere eye-cast at the character
> Of Who made these and gave man sense to boot,
> Had dissipated once and evermore. . . ."[23]

Like Browning, she recognizes that the romanticizing of primitive ignorance is vicious folly: " 'Ignorance is not innocence but sin—/ . . . Ignorance/ Being, I hold, sin ever, small or great.' "

Such a theme is not at all inconsistent with the dying words of the man in "Pisgah-Sights. I. ," as approaching death teaches him the function of life's evil. Good wants evil, and joy demands sorrow, as in life angel weds devil, he discovers—but even in the hour of death the ultimate "why" eludes him. Man should submit and not inquire into such things:

---

22. IV, 298-310.
23. IV, 402-407.

> "Which things must—*why* be?"
> Vain our endeavor!
> So shall things aye be
> As they were ever.
> "Such things should *so* be!"
> Sage our desistence!
> Rough-smooth let globe be,
> Mixed—man's existence![24]

No obscurantist, he has exercised his mind, "Peering and prying" into life, as man should; the sage man desists only from prying into infinity.

"Pisgah-Sights. II." includes some most disturbing evidence of apparent distrust not only of man's mind, but of man's whole capacity to cope with life. Browning asks whether if granted a second life he would elect to strive against life's greed and ambition or bypass life and so pass to fruition. Predictably, of course, he replies that he would strive for the same objects, taking life on its own terms, not on those of the infinite. The blind mole shall mine for deniers throughout its three score and ten years, and the dazed hawk shall soar in the sun—each obeying the law of his own nature. The law of man's life is that

> "Turf 't is thy walk's o'er,
> Foliage thy flight's to."[25]

Stanza III is the perplexing stanza:

> Only a learner,
> Quick one or slow one,
> Just a discerner,
> I would teach no one.
> I am earth's native:
> No rearranging it!
> *I* be creative,
> Chopping and changing it?

---

24. Ll. 17-24.
25. Ll. 15-16.

This seems to say that life as it is, is perfect; whatever is, is right; this is the best of all possible worlds; and, of course, this is precisely what it does say, provided we understand that Browning is talking of the divine plan, not of the day-to-day frustrations of life, which are indubitable evils, working toward undeniable good. This being so, man should acquiesce in the plan, though not in the evil, which must be combated to further the plan. As God allowed Moses near the end of his life to view from the top of Mt. Pisgah the land which he was not allowed to enter, so God permits man, as death approaches, a glimpse into the infinite. With such knowledge, he chooses to love God down in the darkness of this world, lest through misapplication of mind, he prove, in the manner of Strauss and Renan, God to be not a star but a mere glowworm.

In "Fears and Scruples," a companion poem in the *Pacchiarotto* volume, Browning attacks more directly the agnosticism of the higher criticism. Of old he loved an unseen friend, whose letters of love he has accepted on faith; but now the critics say the letters are "forgeries from A. to Z." He wishes that it were possible to muzzle the foolish mouths that give him pain, or that the absent friend would refute them with a word or wink; but the friend remains silent. Some critics, he notes, contest his belief that ignorance is part of life's test, asserting that his friend perhaps is testing the acuity of his vision and will punish him for failing to see through solid bricks; but Browning silences their carping voices:

> Hush, I pray you!
> What if this friend happen to be—God? [26]

Man is not asked to see through solid bricks into eternity. Life measures man's faith against his doubts and ignorance, not against absolute certitude.

Similarly, in "Natural Magic" when the lady brings love into the bare room and all darkness and cold vanish, the change does not admit of rational examination. "All I can sing is—I feel it!" Love, like

---

26. Ll. 47-48.

God, is properly to be felt by love, not to be examined in a centrifuge. When reason and love are in conflict in an affair of the heart, choose love. In "Bifurcation" the disappointed lover asks that his faithless mistress have inscribed on her tombstone:

> "I loved him; but my reason bade prefer
> Duty to love, reject the tempter's bribe
> Of rose and lily when each path diverged,
> And either I must pace to life's far end
> As love should lead me, or, as duty urged,
> Plod the worn causeway arm-in-arm with friend.
> So, truth turned falsehood: *'How I loathe a flower,*
> *How prize the pavement!'* . . . ."[27]

When the reason counsels duty at the expense of love, truth turns falsehood, for the heart is always the highest power of man, though by no means always opposed to mind.

In "Numpholeptos," Browning's most obscure and metaphysical short poem, the theme is again the tragic frustration of finite man in pursuit of the infinite. The letter that Browning wrote to Furnivall to silence the fantastic speculations of the Browning Society may be useful, not so much to throw light upon the meaning of the verse, as to make the poem itself seem clear in contrast to the prose. Browning cites the title, meaning "caught or entranced by a nymph," to refute the interpretation that the poem concerns "a woman-lover."

> An allegory, that is, of an impossible ideal object of love, accepted conventionally as such by a man who, all the while, cannot quite blind himself to the demonstrable fact that the possessor of knowledge and purity obtained without the natural consequences of obtaining them by achievement—not inheritance—such a being is imaginary, not real, a nymph and no woman; and only such an one would be ignorant and surprised at the results of a lover's endeavour to emulate the qualities which the beloved is entitled to consider as pre-existent to earthly experience, and independent of its inevitable results.
>
> I had no particular woman in my mind; certainly never intended to

---

27. Ll. 3-10.

personify wisdom, philosophy, or any other abstraction; and the orb, raying colour out of whiteness, was altogether a fancy of my own. The "seven spirits" are in the Apocalypse, also in Coleridge and Byron: a common image.[28]

The important thing to remember is that the man of earthly limitations is on an endless and impossible quest for "an impossible ideal object of love . . . a nymph and no woman"—in short, the theme once again of the finite in hopeless search for the infinite. She is "gold above my clay," too bright for human eyes to see:

> As my lips now kiss
> Your feet, my arms convulse your shrouding robe,
> My eyes, acquainted with the dust, dare probe
> Your eyes above for—what, if born, would blind
> Mine with redundant bliss, as flash may find
> The inert nerve, sting awake the palsied limb,
> Bid with life's ecstasy sense overbrim
> And suck back death in the resurging joy—
> Love, the love whole and sole without alloy![29]

The familiar imagery of the folly of man's quest for the Absolute, "the love whole and sole without alloy!" immediately places this poem among the poems warning against hubris. His eyes are acquainted with the dust—life—and yet he dares probe the infinite at his great peril. He sets out repeatedly on the fruitless quest, journeying down the prismatic colors successively, hoping to return unstained by the colors of the world as evidence of his purity to match her whiteness—in Browning always the symbol of infinity. She is both the source and tomb of the prismatic colors, which symbolize mortality; and between the white radiance and the rainbow colors there is "divorce/ Absolute, all-conclusive!" At last the man rejects the unfair conditions of the quest. It is impossible for a mortal to attain the white light; and it is unfair for the nymph to be granted this purity without experiencing the trial and failure which the quest exacts of mortals:

---

28. *Browning Society Papers*, II, 338. Quoted in DeVane, *A Browning Handbook*, pp. 360-361.

29. Ll. 26-34.

> No more seeking love
> At end of toil, and finding, calm above
> My passion, the old statuesque regard,
> The sad petrific smile!
>
> O you—less hard
> And hateful than mistaken and obtuse
> Unreason of a she-intelligence!
> You very woman with the pert pretense
> To match the male achievement! Like enough!
> Ay, you were easy victors, did the rough
> Straightway efface itself to smooth, the gruff
> Grind down and grow a whisper,—did man's truth
> Subdue, for sake of chivalry and ruth,
> Its rapier-edge to suit the bulrush-spear
> Womanly falsehood fights with![30]

But this insurgency is just "The true slave's querulous outbreak!" And again he fares forth on the hopeless quest—the symbol of the fate of man in search for an unattainable goal beyond the world.

IV

La Saisiaz, one of the first long poems of "gray argument," includes Browning's most direct and personal examination of the riddle of existence; the problems of human suffering, doubt, and ignorance; and the role of human limitation in all of the poetry of his middle and later periods, not excluding *Christmas-Eve and Easter-Day.* As such, it is of central importance in any study of Browning's view of the mind. It was composed in the deep sorrow and travail of spirit occasioned by the death of his friend Anne Egerton Smith, who died on September 14, 1877. She and Browning were to climb Mt. Salève, a few miles from Geneva, symbolically to " 'take a foretaste, match by stealth/ Sight and sound, some unconsidered fragment of the hoarded

---

30. Ll. 130-143. See Hoxie N. Fairchild's revealing essay challenging the belief that Browning bound himself to certain rules supposedly set up by *The Nineteenth Century* for contributions to "A Modern Symposium": "La Saisiaz and the *Nineteenth Century,*" *Modern Philology,* XLVIII, No. 1 (August, 1950), 104-111.

wealth.' " On the morning of their proposed climb, as described in the poem, the poet awaits the arrival of his friend, but she does not come; for she has gone to discover directly the heart of the mystery in death, not waiting for a symbolic foretaste.

More honest doubt and despair appear in *La Saisiaz* than in any other of the poems. Perhaps it is less a sermon of "gray argument" than a personal heart-searching and lament for the trials of life, as if he felt that he must measure the validity of his optimistic philosophy against the challenge of his loss:

> Call this—God, then, call that—soul, and both—
>   the only facts for me.
> Prove them facts? that they o'erpass my power of
>   proving, proves them such:
> Fact it is I know I know not something which is
>   fact as much.
> What before caused all the causes, what effect of
>   all effects
> Haply follows,—these are fancy. Ask the rush if it
>   suspects
> Whence and how the stream which floats it had a rise,
>   and where and how
> Falls or flows on still! What answer makes the rush
>   except that now
> Certainly it floats and is, and, no less certain
>   than itself,
> *Is* the everyway external stream that now through
>   shoal and shelf
> Floats it onward, leaves it—may be—wrecked at last,
>   or lands on shore
> There to root again and grow and flourish stable evermore.[31]

This sounds certain enough, but the line following reveals vitiating doubt: "—May be! mere surmise not knowledge: much conjecture styled belief. . . ." Rare in Browning is the tired admission that only

---

31. Ll. 222-232.

hope of another and better existence makes this one tolerable: ". . . take the hope therein away,/ All we have to do is surely not endure another day."

In the depths of gloom, he utters what seems to be an appallingly narrow view of the capacity of man's mind. Man, he seems to say, is limited only to the cerebration implied in *Sum*; *non cogito*. Man's knowledge apparently is limited to the testimony of his imperfect senses and reflections concerning his own experience; everything else is mere surmise:

> Cause before, effect behind me—blanks! The midway
> point I am,
> Caused, itself—itself efficient: in that narrow
> space must cram
> All experience—out of which there crowds conjecture
> manifold,
> But, as knowledge, this comes only—things may be as
> I behold,
> Or may not be, but, without me and above me, things
> there are;
> I myself am what I know not—ignorance which proves
> no bar
> To the knowledge that I am, and, since I am, can
> recognize
> What to me is pain and pleasure: this is sure, the
> rest—surmise.
> If my fellows are or are not, what may please them
> and what pain,—
> Mere surmise: my own experience—that is knowledge,
> once again![32]

Does this represent a narrower view of the intellect than he expressed before? Clearly not. The terminology is somewhat different, but the idea is familiar. All knowledge outside the fact of one's existence is a fusion of the false and the true, involving inevitably faith and surmise.

---

32. Ll. 255-264.

All of man's conclusions, from the most naïve guesses to the most
sapient findings of the physicist, partake alike of error in their several
degrees, and likewise some shred of truth lightens the lump of every
lie. Certainly Browning is not counseling aggressive distrust of the
intellect or trust in the intuitions, as Henry Jones supposes. Jones finds
that Browning, especially from the time of *La Saisiaz* on, "condemned
all knowledge" in his incredible theory of nescience:

> Now, Browning held, not only that no certain knowledge is attain-
> able by man, but also that such certainty is incompatible with moral life.
> Absolute knowledge would, he contends, lift man above the need and
> the possibility of making the moral choice, which is our supreme
> business on earth. Man can be good or evil, only on condition of being
> in absolute uncertainty regarding the true meaning of the facts of nature
> and the phenomena of life.
>   This somewhat strange doctrine finds the most explicit and full ex-
> pression in *La Saisiaz*.[33]

This is such a basic misunderstanding of Browning that it should
be examined closely. Browning did say, of course, that absolute certainty is denied man, but he never said that man should weary of
progressing by means of mind and spirit through the partial truths
that are stepping stones upward to absolute truth that lies beyond the
border of life. Browning does not say that absolute knowledge—and
by this Browning does not mean certainty of any of the phenomena
of life, but rather total understanding of absolute truth, with the veil
rolled completely away—would make a moral choice impossible for
man. He says that it would make any other choice impossible. Man
could make the choice, but it would be a directed verdict, for a total
vision of the Absolute would make unwisdom and sin unthinkable.
The assumption that if man is denied total knowledge he is totally
impotent in his progress toward truth would have shocked Browning,
as it would shock any one wise enough to know that man's most
certain knowledge is based upon surmise, assumption, and reasoned

---

33. *Browning as a Philosophical and Religious Teacher, op. cit.*, pp. 228-229.

guesses, which support very well indeed the practical fruits of man's mind. Jones's last statement that man must be in "absolute uncertainty regarding the true meaning of the facts of nature and the phenomena of life" is quite false. There is a slippery play on the word *absolute* here. "Absolute uncertainty" is a far different thing from "uncertainty about the Absolute." The first would cripple every undertaking of man and reduce him to impotent paralysis; but the other spurs man onward toward the final truth, which cannot be attained. Man is granted sufficient certainty of the facts relevant to life to invite progress. Man "believes" according to bias or evidence, which is rarely conclusive. A balance has two pans, and the descent of one is not proof that nothing is in the other. Browning believed that man would indeed be paralyzed without the need to exercise judgment and make nice distinctions. He constantly counseled man to make do with what imperfect knowledge he has until better knowledge comes along. Jones concludes that he condemned the mind as quite useless, since it is powerless to secure perfect knowledge. He fails to see that Browning's position was precisely that of the eminent scientist Sir James Jeans, who likened the world to a vast hall with infinitely varied bell-pulls depended through holes which pierce the ceiling, into which man is denied entrance. Man pulls the ropes and rings the invisible bells in every sequence and combination. He labors and learns and records the results of his findings; theory, assumption, and surmise he then bases upon what facts are known; but he never penetrates the adamantine ceiling, wherein is concealed the mystery of which he can only postulate and conjecture the purpose and meaning.

Browning agrees that truth is relative, varying from person to person: "Knowledge stands on my experience: all outside its narrow hem,/ Free surmise may sport and welcome!" My neighbor, he says, being color-blind, fancies the grass to be red. If we were the only two persons on earth, with no third to act as referee, it would be impossible to distinguish between the false and the true testimony of our senses. We assume that the grass is "green," because this is the sound the man of normal vision utters to describe the color. In the simplest things, reflection reveals the most creaking structure of assumption piled on assumption underlying "truth." Belief in the existence of Timbuktu rests upon a complex of faith and assumption that unsettles belief if thought upon too closely. We assume that Timbuktu exists because testimony uniformly supports the belief, and because it is unreasonable to suppose that a fiction of such antiquity and so little motive would be everywhere attested by men of grave comportment. And we believe in spite of the knowledge that the earth is the grave of myth and legend of the past and will equally hold the dust of our most revered fallacies, superstitions, and solemn error. This is life, and according to Browning it is the height of wisdom to acquiesce in life's plan by fighting defeatism and conquering the dark:

> —learn life's lesson, hate of evil, love of good,
> As 't is set me, understand so much as may be understood—
> Solve the problem: "From thine apprehended scheme of
>   things, deduce
> Praise or blame of its contriver. . . ."[34]

I fail to understand De Vane's discovery that in *La Saisiaz* Browning shows "the characteristics of his later thinking, that our human knowledge is of no use whatever in solving the riddle of our doubtful doom. In short, we cannot prove anything about God by our human intellects, and must resort to the intuitive knowledge of our hearts."[35] Browning never said that the mind is useless either in solving the practical problems of life or in attaining some insight into the heavenly plan. Between the intuitive knowledge of our hearts and our intellects there is neither antagonism nor gulf. The dejected tone of personal loss in *La Saisiaz* has betrayed many readers into the belief that beginning with the poem Browning entered into a period of militant anti-intellectualism in which he deprecated the use of the mind or held that the mind has no power whatever that man may trust to.

---

34. Ll. 285-288.
35. *A Browning Handbook* (New York, 1935), p. 377.

> Wisdom—that becoming wise meant making slow and
>   sure advance
> From a knowledge proved in error to acknowledged
>   ignorance? [36]

Such a question does not imply that the life of man is a sure progress from knowledge to nescience, from light to dark; it means that as man progresses from dark to light, he discards the partial truths that ignorance embraces as imperishable. It is valid progress to proceed from falsehood tinctured with truth to truth tinctured with falsehood—the heart of Browning's theory of knowledge. The wisest of men have come to the end of their lives with the certitude that they are sure of only one thing: that they know nothing. No one fancies that they mean to say they are vacuous; everyone knows that they are wise enough to perceive the vast mysteries of life and death on to which their lifetime of study and reflection has opened a few doors. Surely this is what Browning meant when he said:

> —Wherefore? whereto? ask the whirlwind what the
>   dread voice thence explains!
> I shall "vindicate no way of God's to man," nor
>   stand apart,
> "Laugh, be candid!" while I watch it traversing
>   the human heart.
> Traversed heart must tell its story uncommented
>   on: no less
> Mine results in "Only grant a second life, I acquiesce
> In this present life as failure, count misfortune's
>   worst assaults
> Triumph, not defeat, assured that loss so much the
>   more exalts
> Gain about to be. For at what moment did I so advance
> Near to knowledge as when frustrate of escape from
>   ignorance?" [37]

---

36. Ll. 339-340. Cf. F. E. L. Priestley ("A Reading of *La Saisiaz*," *University of Toronto Quarterly*, XXV, No. 1 [October, 1955], p. 53): ". . . Reason and Fancy in actuality cooperate in the search for truth, as the dialogue [in *La Saisiaz*] suggests."
37. Ll. 354-362.

In *Two Poets of Croisic* he expressed it in another way: "Who knows most, doubts most. . . ." It takes knowledge to recognize the immensity of one's ignorance.

Browning's famous outburst of human weariness, deplored as inconsistent with his robust optimism, is in my opinion one of the treasures that humanize the man:

> I must say—or choke in silence—"Howsoever came
>   my fate,
> Sorrow did and joy did nowise,—life well weighed,—
>   preponderate." [38]

This warmly human judgment no more means that he found life an intolerable burden than that he found the human mind, God's gift, a futile and treacherous adjunct for man's increased misery.

In the debate, umpired by the soul, Reason tells Fancy that "Living here means nescience simply: 't is next life that helps to learn," and adds that man should "Shut those eyes, next life will open,—stop those ears, next life will teach. . . ." Reason is not in despair counseling man to go through life with eyes and ears shut because they are instruments only of error. Man is to shut his eyes to the riddle which only the next life can solve. Such a passage must be matched with Reason's further statement of confidence in mind to gain upon truth:

> In this first
> Life, I see the good of evil, why our world began
>   at worst:
> Since time means amelioration, tardily enough displayed,
> Yet a mainly onward moving, never wholly retrograde.
> We know more though we know little, we grow stronger
>   though still weak,
> Partly see though all too purblind, stammer though
>   we cannot speak. [39]

This is the true theme of the poem—man grows through knowledge

---

38. Ll. 333-334.
39. Ll. 413-418.

upward; man is no more doomed to absolute ignorance than to absolute knowledge, both of which would make life a mockery. *Nescience* as used by Browning never means "total ignorance," but rather limited truth or truth tinged by untruth, "the right and the wrong, now tangled," as he phrased it in the poem. In the next life the knot will be untied, not cut by a sword.

The Two Poets of Croisic illuminates the discussion of man's limitation of mind. René Gentilhomme, like Lazarus, is given through a blinding flash of lightning a direct revelation of God and truth—or so he fancies. To many, the consequences of a vision of the Absolute to a minor poet would be of no moment whatever, but Browning "intimately" cares to know how a fellow creature comported himself after God dealt directly with him. Did his reason melt in the white flash of truth? Did he, reduced to smiling idiocy, live out an ordinary life? How many problems the answers to these questions would solve! Can a man, so visited by truth, go back to life "nor find things out of joint?"

> I think no such direct plain truth consists
> With actual sense and thought and what they take
> To be the solid walls of life: mere mists—
> How such would, at that truth's first piercing, break
> Into the nullity they are![40]

Since we no longer live in the age of miracles and direct revelation of God, we must play the pageant out with due regard for the tourney regulations: no thunder-clap revelations of truth will guide us, but simulated thunder-claps which "tell us counterfeited truths. . . ." These simulated thunder-claps are not direct acquisition of knowledge, but rather the earnest of heaven which music may bring to the soul or which beauty may promise:

> So do we gain enough—yet not too much—
> Acquaintance with that outer element
> Wherein there's operation (call it such!)

---

40. Ll. 489-493.

> Quite of another kind than we the pent
> On earth are proper to receive. Our hutch
> Lights up at the least chink: let roof be rent—
> How inmates huddle, blinded at first spasm,
> Cognizant of the sun's self through the chasm![41]

The nescience to which he refers in this Platonistic passage is un-mistakably ignorance, not of temporal phenomena, but of "that outer element"—the truth behind the grave which is providentially screened from man's eyes. Our senses recoil from "aught beyond the dim and dense" of this earth, for what man, grown familiar with eternity, will be content to grope thereafter "among groundlings"? Although knowledge of the stars (*i.e.,* the Absolute) is shut from man, "what flowers make glad the ground!" Gentilhomme, Browning is sure, scorned human praises after his ears, "all atingle," had heard the "tones few hear and live, but none forget." Thus, he stopped writing verse, the proper employment of earth, for after his divine experience the trick of riming seemed poor employment.

Near the end of the poem appears a tribute to truth and to its su-preme importance in the lives of men. These words hardly sound as if Browning wrote them in a dark obscurantist mood:

> But truth, truth, that's the gold! and all the good
> I find in fancy is, it serves to set
> Gold's inmost glint free, gold which comes up rude
> And rayless from the mine. All fume and fret
> Of artistry beyond this point pursued
> Brings out another sort of burnish: yet
> Always the ingot has its very own
> Value, a sparkle struck from truth alone.[42]

In the prefatory poem to *Dramatic Idyls, Second Series* (1880), man's fatuous pride of intellect is satirized with directness uncommon in Browning. Doctors A and B, specialists in the care and cure of the

---

41. Ll. 513-520.
42. Ll. 1209-1216.

body, are in complete disagreement in the sickroom; and yet men pretend to omniscience in matters of the soul:

> "You are sick, that's sure,"—they say:
> "Sick of what?"—they disagree.
> " 'T is the brain"—thinks Doctor A;
> " 'T is the heart"—holds Doctor B;
> "The liver—my life I'd lay!"
> "The lungs!" "The lights!"
> > Ah me!
> So ignorant of man's whole
> Of bodily organs plain to see—
> So sage and certain, frank and free,
> About what's under lock and key—
> Man's soul!

In "Ixion" he says that modern man, living in an atmosphere of rational skepticism, should recall that "Ixion the cherished/ Minion of Zeus grew vain, vied with the godships and fell" through arrogance.

Jochanan, in "Jochanan Hakkodosh," Israel's wisest, perfectly expresses Browning's theory of man's limited mind. As he lies on his deathbed, his admiring followers gather around to hear the truth that is said to sit on the lips of dying men. The learned rabbi groans, for he has learned only that he knows nothing. He has, indeed, been almost inspired in his folly: he married unwisely, imagining that a rose lip signifies meekness and discretion in a bride; he abused his mind by filling it with rubbish when he might have loaded it with "lore"; and as a warrior he shivered his sword upon a stone. " 'In dwarf's-play spent/ Was giant's prowess. . . .' " His followers propose to implement the resource of the Targums—to buy more life for the master by donations of an equal length of life from the days of lesser lives. Jochanan, tired and unhopeful of attaining wisdom through a gift of days, accepts only one year, three months each from the lover, the poet, the warrior, and the statesman. At the end of each quarter, he bitterly recognizes the futility of the experiment. As the quarter-year of lustihood, the lover's gift, ends, his admirers come to him for the pearls of wisdom that must surely fall from his lips after the miraculous extension of life:

> "Make appear
>
> "Thy profit from experience! Plainly state
> How men should Love!" Thus he: and to him thus
> The Rabbi: "Love, ye call it?—rather, Hate!
>
> "What wouldst thou? Is it needful I discuss
> Wherefore new sweet wine, poured in bottles caked
> With old strong wine's deposit, offers us
>
> "Spoilt liquor we recoil from, thirst-unslaked?" [43]

Disillusionment, complete and total, has been the fruit of his unnatural experiment. Age's hard cold knowledge has unhappily succeeded to the ignorance of youth, and the youthful, happy dreams, "Fresh as from Paradise," fare as does the pigeon returning to the fancied security of its nest and finding the coils of a snake awaiting to embrace it.

> "See, Eve stands supreme
>
> "In youth and beauty! Take her for thy bride!
> What Youth deemed crystal, Age finds out was dew
> Morn set a-sparkle, but which noon quick dried
>
> "While Youth bent gazing at its red and blue
> Supposed perennial,—never dreamed the sun
> Which kindled the display would quench it too." [44]

Not only does age find the crystal of youth turn to impermanent dew; in his impotence, he still is attracted physically to women, and like the simple steer, he is the miserable slave to impulses that cannot be understood or satisfied.

---

43. Ll. 276-283.
44. Ll. 300-306.

At the end of the summer quarter, he is in despair, indeed. Youth is the period of arrogant discontent with indirect half-measures, when war appears to be the " 'straight way through lands yet unexplored/ To absolute Right and Good. . . .' " But age, with rheumy eye and sickened heart, sees the folly of attempting to attain to absolute truth:

> "Ay, thus we prattle—young: but old—why, first,
> Where's that same Right and Good—(the wise inquire)—
>
> "So absolute, it warrants the outburst
> Of blood, tears, all war's woful consequence,
> That comes of the fine flaring?"[45]

Our enemies pay tribute to the same Right and Good which we claim to be our own exclusively.

Autumn brings the end of the third quarter of protracted life, the gift of the poet. Tsaddik, the spokesman for the faithful, visits his master in joy and hope, for after three months' extension of life spent in contemplation of poetry, Jochanan surely will have found truth. The lute has the power to reveal the secret that shall lift man above the brutes "As only knowledge can." But the old man is without hope:

> "A fount unsealed"
> (Sighed Jochanan) "should seek the heaven in leaps
> To die in dew-gems—not find death, congealed
>
> "By contact with the cavern's nether deeps,
> Earth's secretest foundation where, enswathed
> In dark and fear, primæval mystery sleeps—
>
> "Petrific fount wherein my fancies bathed
> And straight turned ice. My dreams of good and fair
> In soaring upwards had dissolved, unscathed
>
> "By any influence of the kindly air,
> Singing, as each took flight, The Future—that's
> Our destination, mists turn rainbows there,

---

45. Ll. 398-402.

> "Which sink to fog, confounded in the flats
> O' the present!" [46]

At the end of the year, as time revokes the gift of the statesman, Tsaddik returns again. Jochanan, who has hoped to attain absolute knowledge, attains what appears to be absolute pessimism. The "science of Man's life," which he has wanted to bequeath to man, can be written very briefly: " 'one blank's the whole!' "

Alarms and rumors of a new persecution of the Jews drive Tsaddik and his companions from the city for a period of three months. Upon their return, they find the sage still alive, but his despair has given way to serenity and happiness, the fruits of man's prime lesson in life: " *'Ignorance confirmed/ By knowledge ....'* " He has attained "utter acquiescence" in God's plan, which is not to permit man to view absolute knowledge but, paradoxically, to permit him to gain absolute acquiescence in his inability to attain it.

> "The power to work this miracle at last,—
> Exceeds my guess. Though—*ignorance confirmed*
> *By knowledge* sounds like paradox, I cast
>
> "Vainly about to tell you—fitlier termed—
> Of calm struck by encountering opposites,
> Each nullifying either!" [47]

Perhaps no better phrase to describe Browning's theory of knowledge could be found than "ignorance confirmed by knowledge," which is not at all the same as "knowledge confirmed by ignorance." The truly ignorant man is unaware of the depths of his imperception, but the man of learning finds that each new ray of light reveals a vast darkness unsuspected before. In the wisdom that death brings to man, Jochanan learns that opposites bring opposites: hate brings love, sorrow brings delight, pain brings joy, and ignorance brings knowledge, "each nullifying either"—which argues well that knowledge, far from

---

46. Ll. 508-521.
47. Ll. 682-687.

being totally useless, is an essential to life, without which man could never progress toward truth.

V

Ferishtah's Fancies (1884) includes the fullest and most varied treatment of God's plan of bringing man to light through the darkness of imposed ignorance to be found in Browning's later period. It ranks philosophically with *Christmas-Eve and Easter-Day, The Ring and the Book,* and *La Saisiaz;* and more apparent anti-intellectualism, pernicious nescience, and despair of the role of the mind appear in it than in any other of Browning's works. Jones finds in it, as everywhere else as well, that "the absolute dualism of the old ascetics between flesh and spirit, sense and reason, find their accurate parallel in Browning's teachings. . . . No professed agnostic can condemn the human intellect more utterly than he does."[48]

In the first fancy, "The Eagle," Ferishtah, before he has become dervish, makes two interesting points. As Ferishtah walks through the woods one evening, he sees a nest of starving ravens, their mother lying dead at the foot of the tree. As he reflects on the cruelty of fate, an eagle swoops down, feeds the younglings, and flies away. Astonished, Ferishtah concludes that one should have faith in providence and take no thought for the morrow; surely it is an apparent object lesson that man demonstrates imperfect faith if he toils unremittingly for a livelihood when " 'Providence cares for every hungry mouth!' " Full of these relaxing notions, he muses for days, refusing food and drink in his admiration of the symbolism; but in his idleness he sleeps and dreams that God chides him for perverse misuse of his faculties. Should man play the helpless birdlings and await succor, or should he be the eagle? Once seen, the import of the adventure is clear to Ferishtah; and, chagrined at man's capacity for seizing an error for truth, he resolves to go to Ispahan, where he may be the eagle to the soul-starved masses.

---

48. Pp. 220-221. Jones's consistent misuse of the word *agnostic* should be noted. A true agnostic is marked by thoughtful questioning, not distrust of mind.

A similar theme, illustrating the pitfalls of judgment, informs "The Melon Seller," number two in the series. Ferishtah, midway on the course to dervishhood, meets on the road a poor melon-seller, who for peculation was reduced from his position as prime minister to the Shah. Ferishtah, only partially wise, commiserates with him, asking whether his fall from twelve years of high station does not make him curse God. The beggar, with luminous brow, replies:

> "Fool, does thy folly think my foolishness
> Dwells rather on the fact that God appoints
> A day of woe to the unworthy one,
> Than that the unworthy one, by God's award,
> Tasted joy twelve years long? Or buy a slice,
> Or go to school!"
>   To school Ferishtah went. . . .[49]

After his schooling, Ferishtah keeps school himself to preach the wisdom of the degraded beggar: if we receive good at God's hand, shall we not also receive evil? This truth should be transparent to all, he feels, "But great wits jump"—*i.e.,* jump to conclusions, electing as most valid the belief that is most congenial to their uses or bent.

"Shah Abbas," number three of the fancies, continues the examination of man's perception of truth and the nature of belief. Ferishtah is now a full dervish and speaks with ripe wisdom. Yakub, his pupil, asks him whether one may believe on hearsay evidence such a story as that of Shah Abbas, who, by report, caught a stag with one hand and slew a lion with one blow of the other and yet who died upon finding a spider in his wine cup. Ferishtah admits the validity of such evidence, for the story stands "clear-chronicled," and the facts in the matter, as reported by the cup-bearer who witnessed the lion slaying, are recounted with perfect fidelity by all. The pupil objects that it is folly to credit a cup-bearer's tale above the testimony of man's experience which the tale does violence to. His master replies, in this Socratic dialogue, that the confusion arises from faulty nomenclature. The word *belief* should not mean " 'easy acquiescence of mankind/ In

---

49. Ll. 27-32.

matters nowise worth dispute. . . .' " Our self-interest is not affected by the account of prodigious valor, and since chronicles assure us that Abbas did live and reign and die somehow, we easily believe. But self-interest and private bias operate powerfully upon any belief that affects them. Yakub can accept the story, for he is indifferent to it; but if the present shah should levy a double tax on Yakub because, by chance, the pupil should be found to be a direct descendant of the same cup-bearer who, it is reported, killed Shah Abbas by serving a spider in a wine cup, then this indeed would be matter for "belief." The victim of double taxation would demand incontrovertible proof and would reject all hearsay as inadmissible evidence, and, in short, would not believe.

A second parable illustrates another facet of faith. Yakub recounts the fiction of Tahmasp, who saw his beloved devoured by a nine-headed snake. Yakub's heart is much affected by the pathos of the story, but his intellect is outraged by the palpable myth of a snake with nine heads, when everyone knows, " 'No snake boasts more than three!' " The tears which the pathos of the story elicits are forgotten as he laughs at the childish beliefs that earlier times gave assent to. Belief is a complex thing. It is undeniably an advance to reject a myth of a snake more generously endowed with heads than the well-authen-ticated tri-headed serpents of which only the perverse doubt the exist-ence. Lies rarely yield to total truth at one stroke.

Ferishtah narrates the parable of the reported return to his home of Ishah, whom twenty people saw die in the late war. His two sons, upon hearing the report, react in accordance with their natures and self-interest. One son rejoices and believes, for he loves his father and instinctively elects belief over unbelief. Another son, following his inclination in turn, scorns the rumor and holds to the testimony of the twenty eyewitnesses. Upon the arrival of the father, the believer is praised; the doubter, scorned. Yakub, who is impressed by the cogency of the parable, perceives the truth that Ishah would be a fool if he did not prize " 'Mere head's work less than heart's work.' " Knowing that he is ready to make his point, Ferishtah asks, " 'Is God less wise?' "

Browning's belief that in life the heart and love are the supreme values and the final arbiter for man is clear enough; but less clear is his theme of the interdependence of mind and heart, so often seen in earlier works. Ferishtah, a model of sapience, is not counseling anti-rational dependence on emotion as a sole guide. He is urging the point that reason is easily deceived and must work with the heart. One cannot reason in a vacuum, nor is faith to be attained solely by intellect, but by head and heart working together in wholeness, with the heart being the higher court if differences between the two must be resolved. One should not, like Yakub, seek belief only through the agency of the mind and weigh only statistics in the balance of life. In matters of "faith," which is based on the evidence of things not seen as well as seen, the heart is supreme; but Browning no more rejects the reason than he does the digestive or lymphatic system. Browning recognized the semantic confusion that had arisen between *belief* and *faith*. Both terms, in effect, mean much the same thing, and Browning deplored the fission of man's faculties, which together fulfill their indivisible functions.

Fancy four, "The Family," illustrates another problem of faith: the rationale of prayer to a God who, being omniscient and omnipotent, presumably does not need instruction in his duty from man. That the matter was a lively issue is everywhere attested, but nowhere better than in Tyndal's absurd proposal that the value of prayer be tested by praying vigorously for the patients on one side of a hospital ward and leaving the patients on the other side to the uninstructed conscience of the deity. This travesty of the statistical method of arriving at truth illustrates perfectly the stupidity committed under the banner of reason. Against such a background as this, Browning, through Ferishtah, relates the tale of Shiraz's wife, whose leg a world-renowned leech says must be amputated forthwith to save her life from the bite of a serpent. The husband, acquiescent, sadly replies, " ' "Thou knowest: be it so!" ' " The eldest son, being differently constituted, remonstrates with the physician and prays for a gentler way, perhaps soon to be discovered by science. The second son denounces the prescription as needless and cruel: " ' "save the limb thou must and

shalt!" ' " The youngest son, pert and aping sapience, seeks favor in
the eyes of the doctor by groveling acquiescence: " ' "the Leech knows
all things, we are ignorant;/ What he proposes, gratefully accept!" ' "
With his pharisaical arrogance, he adds that even if science should
supply him with an unguent bound to heal the limb, he would not
dare to try it in defiance of the leech's verdict. All the points of view
except the last one are understandable and acceptable in frail man;
the "chit," while pretending to understanding, is imitating omniscience in his heartless inhumanity:

    "Ah, the young devil!"

                    "Why, his reason chimed
Right with the Hakim's."

                    "Hakim's, ay—but chit's?
How? what the skilled eye saw and judged of weight
To overbear a heavy consequence,
That—shall a sciolist affect to see?
All he saw—that is, all such oaf should see,
Was just the mother's suffering."

                    "In my tale,
Be God the Hakim: in the husband's case,
Call ready acquiescence—aptitude
Angelic, understanding swift and sure:
Call the first son—a wise humanity,
Slow to conceive but duteous to adopt:
See in the second son—humanity,
Wrong-headed yet right-hearted, rash but kind.
Last comes the cackler of the brood, our chit
Who, aping wisdom all beyond his years,
Thinks to discard humanity itself:
Fares like the beast which should affect to fly
Because a bird with wings may spurn the ground,
So, missing heaven and losing earth—drops how
But hell-ward? No, be man and nothing more—
Man who, as man conceiving, hopes and fears,
And craves and deprecates, and loves, and loathes,

And bids God help him, till death touch his eyes
And show God granted most, denying all."[50]

Browning's theme is that man's prime duty is to be a man, living as man must according to the dictates of both heart and head, rejecting neither. The head alone can make a very good case indeed for the folly of lessoning God in the performance of his Godhead, but man, not being all head, finds that the heart in grief overrules the head, and man prays. God is angered neither by man's prayers for the recovery of his loved ones nor by his fullest uses of mind in seeking a cure. Man must be man and nothing more, and it is in his nature to do both of these things. The use of medicines and vaccines, the fruits of mind, is perfectly proper; perhaps the bite of the serpent is a test of man's use of his talents, and, indeed, God may elect to answer prayer, not through direct intervention, but through the agency of a cure discovered happily in time.

The lyric accompanying "The Family" illustrates the theme that man should not aspire to Godhead, but should be content to be man, uncomplaining of his limited mental powers:

Man I am and man would be, Love—merest man and nothing more.
Bid me seem no other! Eagles boast of pinions—let them soar!
I may put forth angel's plumage, once unmanned, but not before.

. . . .

Good you are and wise, full circle: what to me were more outside?
Wiser wisdom, better goodness? Ah, such want the angel's wide
Sense to take and hold and keep them! Mine at least has never tried.

"The Sun," fancy number five, develops the familiar idea of life's limitations and the duty of man to make fullest use of his faculties in spite of their imperfection. Man must use man's tools even though they may never be honed to perfection. Ferishtah sees a man cuff and kick another for saying that "God once assumed on earth a human shape." The sage defends man's belief in partial truth until a better truth comes along. If man is to be man, he must not reject knowledge

---

50. Ll. 50-74.

because it is imperfect, any more than he should reject life because it is not heaven. The quest for perfection is the thing. The Persians, he says, evolved sun worship in their early times out of simple human need to believe something:

> "During our ignorance"—
> Began Ferishtah—"folk esteemed as God
> Yon orb: for argument, suppose him so,—
> Be it the symbol, not the symbolized,
> I and thou safelier take upon our lips.
> Accordingly, yon orb that we adore
> —What is he? Author of all light and life:
> Such one must needs be somewhere: this is he.
> Like what? If I may trust my human eyes,
> A ball composed of spirit-fire, whence springs
> —What, from this ball, my arms could circle round?
> All I enjoy on earth. By consequence,
> Inspiring me with—what? Why, love and praise."[51]

It was but natural then to ascribe supernatural powers to the object that gave light and warmth and crops. Fire symbolized power, until, through learning, fire became only fire; and then sun worship gave way to another belief, for it had served its function. As primitive man might worship a gardener for the gift of a succulent fig, a man who has advanced in mind " 'by just progression slow and sure/ To some prime giver . . . ' " leaves behind such a limited vision. Man needs some belief, false or no, and it will grow with man's growth and needs. If man can believe that the sun once was flesh, although the belief is absurd, the man of no belief at all should " ' "stand appalled before/ Conception unattainable by me/ Who need it most." ' " Man's supreme function is to progress to the highest conception of the prime giver and to return love for love according to his capacity.

> "My part
> Is plain—to meet and match the gift and gift
> With love and love, with praise and praise, till both

---

51. Ll. 18-30.

Cry 'All of us is thine, we can no more!'
So shall I do man's utmost—man to man. . . ."[52]

Man is bound by " 'man's conditions neither less nor more' " and so he is " 'plainly bound/ To take man's truth for truth and only truth. . . .' " Nothing could afford clearer evidence of Browning's pragmatic acceptance of man's limitations and his equally firm belief that man must not reject the uses of mind because he knows they are imperfect. He must never embrace a belief in the futility of human knowledge.

The theme of "Mihrab Shah" is Browning's usual justification of evil and ignorance in a world created by an all-wise and all-powerful God. These trials, which serve as a test, have their obverse sides, pain bringing joy when pain ceases. In words reminiscent of both Marcus Aurelius and Carlyle, he says that instead of complaining against misfortune, one should marvel at the miracle that keeps one's head from tumbling from the neck and that restrains one's cane, if dropped, from taking off for the stratosphere, as might very well happen under a different set of natural laws. As things stand, man does not feel compelled to carry a weight upon his shoulders to avoid the dangers of going into orbit unexpectedly, "upwards to perdition"; and man may doff his hat without fear of decapitation. An inquirer who has cured a painful scorpion sting by timely application of a "virtuous root" ruefully asks why God created scorpions for man's annoyance. The wise dervish replies that all evil is essential as a test of man's powers and as bond between men. Man exercises his mind in finding the "medicinable" root, he gains in love and pity, and he grows in understanding of earth as a means of descrying God's plan and the rewards of eternity. There is no direct answer to the question why scorpions were created; an appeal is made to the pragmatic virtues inherent in the workings of all evil whatever. Ferishtah demonstrates proof of his argument by cleverly inducing the sceptic to admit that all of the Shah's virtues have not won his love; but the dreadful ulcer, eating

---

52. Ll. 78-82.

away the stomach of the beneficent ruler, wins his pity. Pain welds
bonds of brotherhood beyond the power of beneficence.

Unfortunately Ferishtah makes his own thinly stretched theme absurd by ending:

> "Thanks to God
> And love to man,—from man take these away,
> And what is man worth? Therefore, Mihrab Shah,
> Tax me my bread and salt twice over, claim
> Laila my daughter for thy sport,—go on!
> Slay my son's self, maintain thy poetry
> Beats mine,—thou meritest a dozen deaths!
> But—ulcer in the stomach,—ah, poor soul,
> Try a fig-plaster: may it ease thy pangs!"[53]

One wonders by what casuistry Browning would reconcile his doctrine
that man must live as mere man, following the dictates of his nature,
with such sublime pity for an ailing monarch whose rectitude has
been marred by his debauching of the man's daughter, murdering his
son, levying unjust taxes, and, to crown the list of irregularities, boast-
ing of supremacy in verse. One sadly muses on the more human, if
unholy, joy that might suffuse the heart of the outraged subject, as he
prays that the cure be long deferred and of exceeding pain.

Hoxie N. Fairchild finds in Browning's theory of the function of
evil an almost perfect parallel with Pope's belief in the *Essay on Man*
that

> The bliss of man, could pride that blessing find,
> Is not to think or act beyond mankind.

He cites "Mihrab Shah" to prove that "If there were no pain, there
would be no human pity. Why then presume to revise God's work by
attempting to abolish evil?"[54] In the answer to the question lies the
gulf separating Pope and Browning. The couplet is indeed a perfect
expression of Browning's belief, if it means that one should accept the

---

53. Ll. 128-136.
54. "Browning's 'Whatever Is, Is Right,'" *College English,* XII (April, 1951), p. 381.

limitations God has set upon man and upon life. Both poets would have agreed fully in the wisdom of man's acceptance of life's rules and conditions. Pope, arguing from the Great Chain of Being, saw the inevitability of an ordered creation, the necessity of each link in the scale of creation, and the function of man's link in holding together the grand plan. He also saw the fundamental sin of aspiring to ascend beyond one's preordained link, to usurp another's place in the scale. Man's greatest wisdom, therefore, is to submit, but in this submission there is far more passivity and stagnation than one finds in Browning. The Great Chain of Being supplied the negative comfort of inevitability: this is the best of all possible worlds, and the wise man accepts the evils of the world with whatever cheer the knowledge can give him that somehow in the dim Master Plan they all have to be. Browning held the opposite belief. Accept the laws of life even though this is far from being the best of all possible worlds. The plan of the world is perfect, precisely because it challenges man to make life better. It is a world teeming with evils which are put here, not to see whether man can tolerate them blindly in the belief that they subserve a far-off good but to see whether he will meet the challenge of their day-to-day presence and fight them until he blows the slug horn before the squat dark tower of death.

"A Camel Driver," seventh of the series, repudiates the concept of damnation and illustrates the folly of applying the laws of human reason and necessity to God. It is proper to punish and even execute malefactors as a deterrent to others, but it does not follow that damnation would have a similar function or justification. Man, with his human intellect, sees parallels where none exist. It is a misuse of the mind to ascribe to God the motives and methods proper to man, just as it is intellectual arrogance to scale the wall and attempt to pry into the secrets of infinity:

> "Reason aims to raise
> Some makeshift scaffold-vantage midway, whence
> Man dares, for life's brief moment, peer below:
> But ape omniscience? Nay! The ladder lent
> To climb by, step and step, until we reach

> The little foothold-rise allowed mankind
> To mount on and thence guess the sun's survey—
> Shall this avail to show us world-wide truth
> Stretched for the sun's descrying? Reason bids
> 'Teach, Man, thy beast his duty first of all
> Or last of all, with blows if blows must be,—
> How else accomplish teaching?' Reason adds
> 'Before man's First, and after man's poor Last,
> God operated and will operate.'
> —Process of which man merely knows this much,—
> That nowise it resembles man's at all,
> Teaching or punishing."[55]

One thing to Browning was sure: God would never limit man's understanding and then damn him for having an understanding that is limited. Man does well to comport himself as a man must. Browning pushes the doctrine so far that one must be on guard against the conclusion that he espouses the untenable belief that ignorance can do no wrong and knowledge somehow carries the seed of sin:

> "Ask thy lone soul what laws are plain to thee,—
> Thee and no other,—stand or fall by them!
> That is the part for thee: regard all else
> For what it may be—Time's illusion. This
> Be sure of—ignorance that sins, is safe.
> No punishment like knowledge! Instance, now!
> My father's choicest treasure was a book
> Wherein he, day by day and year by year,
> Recorded gains of wisdom for my sake
> When I should grow to manhood. While a child
> Coming upon the casket where it lay
> Unguarded,—what did I but toss the thing
> Into a fire to make more flame therewith,
> Meaning no harm? So acts man three-years old!
> I grieve now at my loss by witlessness,
> But guilt was none to punish."[56]

---

55. Ll. 61-77.
56. Ll. 87-102.

Whether one holds that hell indubitably is hell, with certifiable brim-
stone, he should not be blind to the praise of mind in these lines, or
the lament for man's ignorance. Here is no reckless invitation to sin
under the protection of the triple-brass shield of ignorance; man pays
well for his sins, and no punishment is more real than the knowledge
of one's wrongdoing and loss. Ferishtah grieves for his deprivation of
his father's words of wisdom and learning, which he lost through
immaturity of mind.

"Two Camels" is Ferishtah's parable of two camels which journey,
laden with costly bales, from Nishapur to Sebzevar, for their beloved
master, symbol of God. One camel, his judgment clouded with asceticism, declines the wholesome feed provided for him against the rigors
of the journey, preferring to munch mouldy bran by way of mortify-
ing the flesh to please his master. The other camel rejoices in the
luscious provender and crams himself without stint in preparation for
the task ahead. The first camel, predictably, breaks down, his pack
rejoices the robbers, and his carcass nourishes the vultures; while the
second camel, sustained by ample nourishment, triumphantly enters
Sebzevar with his burden intact. Browning detested asceticism, which
holds that man can best please God by self-denial, mortification of the
flesh, and starvation of the mind.

> "What imports
> Fasting or feasting? Do thy day's work, dare
> Refuse no help thereto, since help refused
> Is hindrance sought and found. Win but the race—
> Who shall object 'He tossed three winecups off,
> And, just at starting, Lilith kissed his lips' ? "[57]

The proper study of man is life, and all faculties are his to use in his
study. To scorn nourishment for the body, the mind, or the spirit is
to strew the wasteland with bones. Ferishtah says that a doctor upon
being called to help the sick does not cry, " ' "Let me, first of all, discard my health!" ' "

---

57. Ll. 59-64.

> "No, Son: the richness hearted in such joy
> Is in the knowing what are gifts we give,
> Not in a vain endeavor not to know!"[58]

Ignorance, like sickness of the body, is a form of disease, and to cultivate either is evil and madness.

The brief lyric following "Two Camels" interestingly explains how
the pursuit of science, far from being an abuse of man's intellect, can
give useful knowledge and at the same time help man prefigure the
infinite by analogy. A chemist by mixing two chemicals causes an
explosion. From apparently inert "nothings" comes a very real "something," which lets the spectators learn "what was" and imagine "what
might be." The lessons of life are to school a man through exercise of
mind and imagination to "conceive/ What a heaven there may be."

In "Cherries," number nine in the fancies of the wise dervish, the
theme is that in God's sight there is no first or last. Ferishtah tells the
parable of the slave who wanders into the Shah's palace in Ispahan:

> "As duty bade,
> He enters in the courts, will, if he may,
> See so much glory as befits a slave
> Who only comes, of mind to testify
> How great and good is shown our lord the Shah.
> In he walks, round he casts his eye about,
> Looks up and down, admires to heart's content,
> Ascends the gallery, tries door and door,
> None says his reverence nay: peeps in at each,
> Wonders at all the unimagined use. . . ."[59]

Gold and jewels lie about, but above are wonderful lamps which
attract the eye upward. Their unimagined use is beyond the limited
capacity of the slave, but he is granted full right to explore to his
heart's content: " 'None says his reverence nay. . . .' " He discovers
a small nook with his own name above the door, a cosy abode just
suited to his limited desires and capacities. Within this little world, he

---

58. Ll. 84-86.
59. Ll. 24-33.

can speculate without stint upon the light cast by the sun within the minaret, which he scarce guesses the "good of."

> "Never too much, by parity, of faith
> In impuissance, man's—which turns to strength
> When once acknowledged weakness every way." [60]

Man has just the optimum capacity of understanding: enough to permit wonder and adoration in the presence of God's surpassingly beautiful plan, but not enough knowledge to stale the wonder by familiarity.

The conclusion is a direct warning against the sin of intellectual pride and presumptuous prying into the infinite:

> "Nor waste thy power of love in wonderment
> At what thou wiselier lettest shine unsoiled
> By breath of word. That this last cherry soothes
> A roughness of my palate, that I know:
> His Maker knows why Mushtari was made." [61]

Mushtari, the symbol of the hereafter, is best left to the mind of God; the cherry, the symbol of all matter on this side of the infinite, is man's to enjoy and study.

A parallel idea is even more forcefully emphasized in "Plot-Culture," number ten of Ferishtah's lessons to his followers. The wise man urges that human conduct be judged by its fruits, regardless of the pronouncements of society. Right and wrong are highly personal matters between man and God. An irreverent disciple baits Ferishtah by asking what would happen if he should make love to Ferishtah's daughter under cover of the night and the palms.

> "Thou wouldst not stand
> Distinctly Man,"—Ferishtah made reply,
> "Not the mere creature,—did no limit-line
> Round thee about, apportion thee thy place

---

60. Ll. 54-56.
61. Ll. 97-101.

> Clean-cut from out and off the illimitable,—
> Minuteness severed from immensity.
> All of thee for the Maker,—for thyself,
> Workings inside the circle that evolve
> Thine all,—the product of thy cultured plot.
> So much of grain the ground's lord bids thee yield
> Bring sacks to granary in Autumn! spare
> Daily intelligence of this manure,
> That compost, how they tend to feed the soil:
> There thou art master sole and absolute
> —Only, remember doomsday!" [62]

God gives man a large measure of freedom in the exercise of conduct and moral choice. There are certainly no prohibitions on man's use of mind; man need only bring his grain in autumn to the granary and there render up his account.

The most significant of all the fancies is "A Pillar at Sebzevar," which may betray one into belief that it inveighs against reliance on mind. The key to the poem may be found in the first lines as "the foolishest of all the company" groans that knowledge is nescience:

> "Knowledge deposed, then!"—groaned whom that most grieved
> As foolishest of all the company.
> "What, knowledge, man's distinctive attribute,
> He doffs that crown to emulate an ass
> Because the unknowing long-ears loves at least
> Husked lupines, and belike the feeder's self
> —Whose purpose in the dole what ass divines?" [63]

Ferishtah, paradoxically, seems to agree with him, for all his learning proved false, or largely so, and in his old age he is left with only one certainty, that he can love without limit:

> "Friend," quoth Ferishtah, "all I seem to know
> Is—I know nothing save that love I can
> Boundlessly, endlessly. My curls were crowned

---

62. Ll. 31-45.
63. Ll. 1-7.

> In youth with knowledge,—off, alas, crown slipped
> Next moment, pushed by better knowledge still
> Which nowise proved more constant: gain, to-day,
> Was toppling loss to-morrow, lay at last
> —Knowledge, the golden?—lacquered ignorance!
> As gain—mistrust it! Not as means to gain:
> Lacquer we learn by. . . ."[64]

It is unfortunate that these lines may erroneously be interpreted to mean that since we know in advance, from the evidence of the past, that whatever we hold as truth will prove in time to be falsehood, the wise man should realize the futility of all mental employments whatever and should begin to love boundlessly, endlessly, as a remedy to frustration. Ferishtah's apparent condemnation of knowledge as lacquered ignorance may strike the unwary as proof of Browning's genuine anti-intellectualism. It should be noted that immediately thereafter Ferishtah says that man should not mistrust knowledge and study as a means to gain, for they are what man learns by. Indeed, the counsel to mistrust knowledge "as gain" means that man should not consider any information as final or complete or immune from re-examination and inquiry. Dogma means death to the mind and to progress.

> "We learn,—when what seemed ore assayed proves dross,—
> Surelier true gold's worth, guess how purity
> I' the lode were precious could one light on ore
> Clarified up to test of crucible.
> The prize is in the process: knowledge means
> Ever-renewed assurance by defeat
> That victory is somehow still to reach. . . ."[65]

The figure of speech is enlightening: earthly knowledge, like ore in the lode, is impure with dross, but man is not advised to scorn the mine because he must purify the gold and discard impurity. The real worth of searching for the gold of knowledge lies in the "guess" how

---

64. Ll. 8-17.
65. Ll. 18-24.

precious the pure ore will be in the next life, to urge man on to aspire to truth.

In love, Ferishtah says, success is sure, and attainment is no delusion whatever:

> "Love—trust to! Be rewarded for the trust
> In trust's mere act. In love success is sure,
> Attainment—no delusion, whatsoe'er
> The prize be: apprehended as a prize,
> A prize it is."[66]

Does Browning intend to delude us into believing that all love is wise and right and fruitful of bliss however misdirected, that the state of marriage guarantees happiness, or that the man in love is immune to pain? To suppose so is to be impervious to the whole of Browning. The long list of desperately unhappy romances and rejected suitors immediately makes such a notion absurd. The ideal called love is pure and perfect, according to Browning, differing fundamentally from knowledge in that it is a fixed and completed quantity, not to be increased as knowledge may be enlarged; but, although love itself is pure, it surely can be misdirected, misapplied, and abused even though the ideal itself remains unsmirched. It is important not to fall into the mistaken belief that Browning discovered a polarity between love and knowledge: the one being totally good, the other being absolutely illusory. A child who desires the sun is spared the consequences of his attempt to grasp it, but he can seize an orange, Ferishtah explains. The orange he secures may or may not have juice, but, like love, the impulse to desire the orange is good. We can attain love; we can only pursue truth. Both activities together make up the whole of life, not love alone.

Ferishtah knows that man by nature is inclined to dogma and unreasoning acceptance of half-truths. This is the curse that threatens him:

---

66. Ll. 26-30.

> "This constitutes the curse that spoils our life
> And sets man maundering of his misery,
> That there's no meanest atom he obtains
> Of what he counts for knowledge but he cries
> 'Hold here,—I have the whole thing,—know, this time,
> Nor need search farther!' "[67]

Man is indeed unwise to scorn the imperfect pleasure and learning of the world in visionary pursuit of impossible attainments:

> "Fool not thus
> In practising with life and its delights!
> Enjoy the present gift, nor wait to know
> The unknowable. Enough to say 'I feel
> Love's sure effect, and, being loved, must love
> The love its cause behind,—I can and do!'
> Nor turn to try thy brain-power on the fact,
> (Apart from as it strikes thee, here and now—
> Its how and why, i' the future and elsewhere)
> Except to—yet once more, and ever again,
> Confirm thee in thy utter ignorance. . . ."[68]

The sense of this, it is hoped, is clear. Man's brain-power should be applied to earth, not to the inscrutable "how" and "why" which lie secure from man's eyes among the secrets of the infinite. These are the things of which man is doomed to "utter ignorance" and which defy his "longing looks." The distressing lines that follow must be considered in their context if one is to be spared an unwise conclusion:

> "Wholly distrust thy knowledge, then, and trust
> As wholly love allied to ignorance!
> There lies thy truth and safety."[69]

Nothing could be more natural than to assume that an indictment of open hostility to mind might safely rest on these three lines alone,

---

67. Ll. 39-44.
68. Ll. 48-58.
69. Ll. 64-66.

but it should by now be clear that Browning's advice to distrust knowledge means nothing more than to keep the spirit of inquiry as insurance against petrifaction of mind and to bend one's energies to the things of earth rather than of the Absolute. The belief that he recommended an unfurnished mind as the proper soil for love is an error which does violence to Browning's noble concept of love and also to man, made in the image of God to strive toward perfection with all his power. The ignorance to which love is to be allied is, naturally, ignorance of what death alone can inform man about.

> "By Sebzevar a certain pillar stands
> So aptly that its gnomon tells the hour;
> What if the townsmen said 'Before we thank
> Who placed it, for his serviceable craft,
> And go to dinner since its shade tells noon,
> Needs must we have the craftsman's purpose clear
> On half a hundred more recondite points
> Than a mere summons to a vulgar meal!'
> Better they say 'How opportune the help!
> Be loved and praised, thou kindly-hearted sage
> Whom Hudhud taught,—the gracious spirit-bird,—
> How to construct the pillar, teach the time!'
> So let us say—not 'Since we know, we love,'
> But rather 'Since we love, we know enough.' "[70]

The uses of the pillar, which was given to man by the master craftsman, should not be scorned until the hour when all secrets behind the veil are revealed to man. We know enough to love the beneficent creator. How foolish to suspend thanks and joy and use at once until knowledge is absolute!

Ferishtah advises his disciples to doubt knowledge " 'Even wherein it seems demonstrable.' " But the essence of scholarship is to check and recheck evidence, lest error creep into the canon for all time. Love and pleasure surely "are," but knowledge only "may be." He does not say that knowledge cannot be. Knowledge and nescience are

---

70. Ll. 76-89.

not interchangeable terms, even though much knowledge proves spurious.

Ferishtah concludes his harangue with an inspiriting invitation to rational inquiry:

> "Consider well!
> Were knowledge all thy faculty, then God
> Must be ignored: love gains him by first leap.
> Frankly accept the creatureship: ask good
> To love for: press bold to the tether's end
> Allotted to this life's intelligence!"[71]

The dervish is far too wise and humane to counsel intellectual activity if he believes that knowledge is wholly useless or perhaps pernicious to man.

In "A Bean-Stripe: Also Apple-Eating"—which I fancy is the gauchest title in Victorian poetry—Ferishtah continues his philosophical rationale of man's limited vision. Black beans and white beans when mixed look gray at a distance, but they remain black and white. Life is made up of black moments and white moments. The clear-eyed man sees life as white, tinged with black, not black, lightened with white. A life all white would stifle hope:

> ("Black, not White,
> Never the whole consummate quietude
> Life should be, troubled by no fear!—nor hope—
> I'll say, since lamplight dies in noontide, hope
> Loses itself in certainty. Such lot
> Man's might have been: I leave the consequence
> To bolder critics of the Primal Cause;
> Such am not I: but, man—as man I speak:
> Black is the bean-throw: evil is the Life!")[72]

Full knowledge, absolute certainty, means death to man, and existence grows impossible, says the dervish.

---

71. Ll. 133-138.
72. Ll. 32-40.

> "Here and there a touch
> Taught me, betimes, the artifice of things—
> That all about, external to myself,
> Was meant to be suspected,—not revealed
> Demonstrably a cheat,—but half seen through,
> Lest white should rule unchecked along the line:
> Therefore white may not triumph."[73]

Ferishtah's humanity is nicely demonstrated in his protestation that life has never shown him total black—"black's soul of black"—beyond the power of white to disintensify, but

> "... such may wreck
> My life and ruin my philosophy
> To-morrow, doubtless: hence the constant shade
> Cast on life's shine,—the tremor that intrudes
> When firmest seems my faith in white."[74]

He has no answer for the question why some men are singled out for special sorrow, for the answer to this ancient riddle lies beyond man's powers of inquiry: "'Man's impotency, God's omnipotence/ These stop my answer.'" Again he advises his followers to mind the issues of life, not of infinity:

> "How I bear the sun,
> Beat though he may unduly, that I know:
> How blood once curdled ever creeps again,
> Baffles conjecture. . . ."[75]

Man is granted in life none of these absolutes, which belong solely to the Primal Cause. Like the aphis on his leaf, man's vision is sorely limited; but then what need has an aphis for understanding of relativity or the quantum theory?

> "To know of, think about—
> Is all man's sum of faculty effects

---

73. Ll. 193-199.
74. Ll. 203-207.
75. Ll. 229-232.

> When exercised on earth's least atom, Son!
> What was, what is, what may such atom be?
> No answer! Still, what seems it to man's sense?
> An atom with some certain properties
> Known about, thought of as occasion needs,
> —Man's—but occasion of the universe?
> Unthinkable, unknowable to man." [76]

If a knowledge of relativity, the quantum theory, or curved space is pertinent to man's comfort, happiness, or progress in knowledge of his world, then it is wholly good even though man will never attain whole truth; but if such knowledge in no wise can further man and is knowledge lying beyond man's world, to seek it out is folly.

The lovely "Epilogue" to *Ferishtah's Fancies* concludes with one of the most heart-warming and human notes to be found among Browning's later works. After hailing the "wonder crowning wonder" of life for the brave fighter against evil, Browning suddenly experiences the chill of doubt which gives the ring of sincerity to the series of Fancies:

> Only, at heart's utmost joy and triumph, terror
> Sudden turns the blood to ice: a chill wind disencharms
> All the last enchantment! What if all be error—
> If the halo irised round my head were, Love, thine arms?

How good it is to know that Browning too experienced, once at least, the chill wind of disenchantment!

VI

Apollo's speech to the Fates in the Prologue to the *Parleyings with Certain People of Importance in Their Day* is a summary of Browning's theory of knowledge and limitation of mind. Although man is circumscribed in his search for truth,

---

76. Ll. 366-374.

> 'T is Man's to explore
> Up and down, inch by inch, with the taper his reason:
> No torch, it suffices—held deftly and straight.
> Eyes, purblind at first, feel their way in due season,
> Accept good with bad, till unseemly debate
> Turns concord—despair, acquiescence in fate.[77]

In the "Parleyings with Bernard de Mandeville" Browning reveals a unique misunderstanding of the cynical philosophy of the Dutch physician, as has been demonstrated by DeVane, which might be taken as the most telling evidence Browning supplied unconsciously in support of his belief that man has a conspicuous talent for being deceived. It is one of the ironies of literary history that Browning hailed Mandeville as a fellow idealist who saw the planned harmony between evil and good and, most ironic of all, who "hailed truth's triumph." In any event, the supposed kinship between the two encouraged Browning to speak in his own person with candor on his theory of knowledge:

> Here we alive must needs deal fairly, turn
> To what account Man may Man's portion, learn
> Man's proper play with truth in part, before
> Entrusted with the whole. I ask no more
> Than smiling witness that I do my best
> With doubtful doctrine: afterward the rest!
> So, silent face me while I think and speak!
> A full disclosure? Such would outrage law.
> Law deals the same with soul and body: seek
> Full truth my soul may, when some babe, I saw
> A new-born weakling, starts up strong—not weak—
> Man every whit, absolved from earning awe,
> Pride, rapture, if the soul attains to wreak
> Its will on flesh, at last can thrust, lift, draw,
> As mind bids muscle—mind which long has striven,
> Painfully urging body's impotence

---

77. Ll. 180-185.

> To effort whereby—once law's barrier riven,
> Life's rule abolished. . . .[78]

Mandeville, who agrees with Browning's theory of the mind, discovers man's intellectual arrogance to stem from an overweening fancy, which prompts him to attempt to " 'cram inside/ His finite God's infiinitude,' " a task that is as futile as assaying to crowd the universe into the earth's vault. Man's duty is to " 'Abjure each fond attempt to represent/ The formless, the illimitable!' " And mankind has long recognized the futility of addressing mind to the "nature of the essence":

> "Drag what lurks
> Behind the operation—that which works
> Latently everywhere by outward proof—
> Drag that mind forth to face mine? No!"[79]

Man realizes that his proper sphere of study is what may prompt his steps or thaw his blood—these are "truer to the mark" than a half-surmise about the nature of the First Cause. "Mysteries/ At source why probe into?" he asks; and Browning, in the conclusion, agrees with man's judgment:

> Shall mind's eye strive
> Achingly to companion as it may
> The supersubtle effluence, and contrive
> To follow beam and beam upon their way
> Hand-breadth by hand-breadth, till sense faint—confessed
> Frustrate, eluded by unknown unguessed
> Infinitude of action? Idle quest!
> Rather ask aid from optics. Sense, descry

---

78. Ll. 13-30. Joseph E. Baker ("Religious Implications in Browning's Poetry," *op. cit.*, p. 145) assumes that Browning recognized Mandeville as the cynic that he was and yet found his own beliefs to be of a similar nature: "Browning recognizes his kinship with one eighteenth-century cynic, when he invokes Barnard Mandeville to refute Carlyle." If one accepts Baker's thesis that Browning was callously indifferent to sin and suffering, this interpretation follows nicely.

79. Ll. 273-276.

> The spectrum—mind, infer immensity!
> Little? In little, light, warmth, life are blessed—
> Which, in the large, who sees to bless? Not I
> More than yourself: so, good my friend, keep still
> Trustful with—me? with thee, sage Mandeville![80]

It should be clear that the folly of tracing the beams in the spectrum from their point of convergence, back through the lens, and up to the primal source refers not to any supposed futility of skill at the optical bench, but figuratively to the error of following light back to God in order to steal the secret of light. It would be incredible to applaud the scientific knowledge and acumen that gave man a lens for his use and in the same breath to deplore the very understanding of the principles of light which made the lens possible. Any research into the nature of light which might enlarge man's knowledge of his world or increase his well-being is man's proper employment, but the "white light" of absolute truth is off-limits to man.

The dialogue with Christopher Smart has one section in which anti-intellectualism may be suspected. Browning is following his argument that man is given sufficient insight into the strength and beauty of the world for comprehension of life's lesson. He laments in some bitterness that modern man wants the secrets of heaven before mastering the lessons of earth:

> Oh, yes—
> The other method's favored in our day!
> The end ere the beginning: as you may,
> Master the heavens before you study earth,
> Make you familiar with the meteor's birth
> Ere you descend to scrutinize the rose!
> I say, o'erstep no least one of the rows
> That lead man from the bottom where he plants
> Foot first of all, to life's last ladder-top:
> Arrived there, vain enough will seem the vaunts
> Of those who say—"We scale the skies, then drop

---

80. Ll. 309-321.

> To earth—to find, how all things there are loth
> To answer heavenly law: we understand
> The meteor's course, and lo, the rose's growth—
> How other than should be by law's command!"
> Would not you tell such—"Friends, beware lest fume
> Offuscate sense: learn earth first ere presume
> To teach heaven legislation.
>
> . . . .
>
>   Live and learn,
>   Not first learn and then live, is our concern.[81]

Life is greater than any of its parts, including both the arts and the
sciences. Nature, Browning says, was given to man for two reasons:
first, "to be by Man enjoyed"; and, second, to supply the means of
instruction, which is "enjoyment's fruit." It is true that man is clearly
warned to study earth before the heavens, but there can surely remain
no doubt that Browning is speaking figuratively.

The "Parleyings with Francis Furini," which includes Browning's
well-known attack on the methods of the evolutionists, may seem to
supply evidence of his opposition to science, especially to the theory
of evolution. The irony here is that Browning's lifelong message was
wholly evolutionary. In lines reminiscent of Goethe, he affirms that
man grows in mind and spirit by steps upward toward perfection,
which can never be attained. Growth is all to Browning: the progress
toward perfection rather than perfection itself informs all of Browning's thinking. What he objected to was the one-sidedness of the
evolutionists: they looked backward to see whence man had come,
not ahead to see whither he was going. Man seeks in vain to disperse
the clouds of ignorance by looking down, for light comes only from
above. Furini says:

>   "Evolutionists!
>   At truth I glimpse from depths, you glance from heights,
>   Our stations for discovery opposites,—
>   How should ensue agreement? I explain:

---

81. Ll. 239-265.

'T is the tip-top of things to which you strain
Your vision, until atoms, protoplasm,
And what and whence and how may be the spasm
Which sets all going, stop you: down perforce
Needs must your observation take its course,
Since there's no moving upwards: link by link
You drop to where the atoms somehow think,
Feel, know themselves to be: the world's begun,
Such as we recognize it. Have you done
Descending?" [82]

William Clyde DeVane, in his discussion of the "Parleyings with Francis Furini," finds that Browning "discounts the intellect altogether":

It is easy to see that this theory of the worthlessness of human intelligence ends inevitably in absolute scepticism. All ends in a blank darkness, which nothing can illumine. Browning's reason for degrading the intellect is of course that it impeaches what he wishes to believe. His purpose is to elevate in dignity the testimony that his feelings bring, that God is love and all is well with the world. And so the poet denies knowledge again: [83]

The quotation that follows the colon is the familiar statement that man is rounded by ignorance on all sides:

"Thus much at least is clearly understood—
Of power does Man possess no particle:
Of knowledge—just so much as shows that still
It ends in ignorance on every side. . . ." [84]

That this astonishing quotation does not reveal a new dark period in Browning's view of the mind or a convulsion in his faith in man's mind to attain knowledge is seen below, where he says that his knowledge is sufficient for his needs:

---

82. Ll. 265-278.
83. *Browning's Parleyings, the Autobiography of a Mind* (New Haven, 1927), pp. 188-189.
84. Ll. 281-284.

> "No, I have no doubt at all!
> There's my amount of knowledge—great or small,
> Sufficient for my needs: for see! advance
> Its light now on that depth of ignorance
> I shrank before from—yonder where the world
> Lies wreck-strewn,—evil towering, prone good—hurled
> From pride of place, on every side." [85]

This enlightening statement gives the lie to three sturdy fictions: one, that Browning believed literally that man can be certain of nothing; two, that knowledge is unattainable on earth; and three, that man should acquiesce in his nescience and rely upon the heart alone as a guide. He is " ' 'Twixt ignorance and ignorance enisled,' " but this is not the same thing as saying that he is ignorance surrounded by seas of ignorance. The ignorance on one side is " 'my Cause—that's styled/ God. . . .' " On the other is the next world, and " 'Light needs must touch on either darkness. . . .' " How far, he asks, can knowledge project a ray into the great dark of the beyond? Certainly not to the heart of the mystery, but for all that, man should " 'attempt to make the cloud disperse' " by climbing upward, " 'not from above but underneath.' "

> "Though Master keep aloof,
> Signs of His presence multiply from roof
> To basement of the building. Look around,
> Learn thoroughly,—no fear that you confound
> Master with messuage! He's away, no doubt,
> But what if, all at once, you came upon
> A startling proof—not that the Master gone
> Was present lately—but that something—whence
> Light comes—has pushed Him into residence?
> Was such the symbol's meaning,—old, uncouth—
> That circle of the serpent, tail in mouth?
> Only by looking low, ere looking high,
> Comes penetration of the mystery." [86]

---

85. Ll. 448-454.
86. Ll. 535-547.

Man should look around and learn thoroughly, looking from low to high, as a means of penetrating the mystery. As if fearful that this advocacy of mind might escape the hasty reader, Browning adds words that cannot be mistaken:

> In time let age advance
> And teach that knowledge helps—not ignorance—
> The healing of the nations. Let my spark
> Quicken your tinder![87]

These lines alone should resolve any doubts about Browning's respect for knowledge.

The "Parleyings with Gerard de Lairesse" hails man's progress from the early Greek times to the present. A sign of man's maturity is the death of Greek myth as a living force in his life, for his prime duty is to outgrow childhood, and the brain is to put aside the fancies of youth. At one time a rose was considered worthy of man's notice only as it was disentwined from Venus's wreath as she bent to kiss her deathly love. There was a time when man needed to haunt the air and gnome the mine, put color on what "were else a deadly ground," until the whole world became populous with nymph and satyr and all the rest of the supernatural machinery of man's youth. But now, Browning says, man is awake, has a mind and soul, nor wants "the wings of dreams" in his walk upward on the common surface of the earth. He need not repudiate the myths. No one of his "acquists" must man lose resignedly; but he must move beyond the need of fable to add meaning or color to his life. Man can and should use fancy and imagination

> . . . but somehow fact
> Has got to—say, not so much push aside
> Fancy, as to declare its place supplied
> By fact unseen but no less fact the same,
> Which mind bids sense accept.[88]

---

87. Ll. 565-568.
88. Ll. 149-153.

The function of the poet is not to return to ancient fable, but to proceed ever onward. It is always within his power to anchor his soul and brain to the past, sinking assuredly from great to small, but the world will not survive the moment man elects to repudiate progress:

> 'T is we see deeper. Progress for the bold!
> You saw the body, 't is the soul we see.
> Try now! Bear witness while you walk with me.
> I see as you: if we loose arms, stop pace,
> 'T is that you stand still, I conclude the race
> Without your company. Come, walk once more
> The "Walk": if I to-day as you of yore
> See just like you the blind—then sight shall cry
> —The whole long day quite gone through—victory![89]

Browning counsels Gerard to "stop further fooling" and, in accordance with the law of life, to progress beyond the painting of dead myths:

> Soul,
> Nothing has been which shall not bettered be
> Hereafter,—leave the root, by law's decree
> Whence springs the ultimate and perfect tree!
> Busy thee with unearthing root? Nay, climb—
> Quit trunk, branch, leaf and flower—reach, rest sublime
> Where fruitage ripens in the blaze of day![90]

All things, including intellect and knowledge, improve, for the only way is up. The sublime fatuity of this statement of faith, which makes one feel like weeping, should not blind one to what Browning implies about the mind. His concluding advice to the painter of Greek myths is to "do, and nowise dream," for the young significance of earth "is all to learn." The lore of the Greeks lies sleeping in the urn, but man now has much knowledge and more to learn:

---

89. Ll. 172-180.
90. Ll. 370-376.

> With so much knowledge is it hard to bear
> Brief interposing ignorance? [91]

The last of the parleyings, with Charles Avison, is the fullest statement among the group of Browning's theory of knowledge, and, ironically, a work in which much evidence may be misinterpreted in support of the belief that Browning had no respect whatever for mind. Perhaps the most electrifying of these exhibits is the following:

> Of all the lamentable debts incurred
> By man through buying knowledge, this were worst:
> That he should find his last gain prove his first
> Was futile—merely nescience absolute,
> Not knowledge in the bud which holds a fruit
> Haply undreamed of in the soul's Spring-tide,
> Pursed in the petals Summer opens wide,
> And Autumn, withering, rounds to perfect ripe,—
> Not this,—but ignorance, a blur to wipe
> From human records, late it graced so much.[92]

One pit to trap the unwary should immediately be recognized: the subjunctive *were* in the second line. This passage does not at all mean that in buying knowledge man is doomed to incur lamentable debts for spurious goods; Browning says that it would be a dreadful thing if this were man's fate. A second and better-hidden pitfall appears in the lines which follow:

> "Truth—this attainment? Ah, but such and such
> Beliefs of yore seemed inexpugnable
> When we attained them! E'en as they, so will
> This their successor have the due morn, noon,
> Evening and night—just as an old-world tune
> Wears out and drops away, until who hears

---

91. Ll. 417-418. See William L. Thompson's defense of Browning as a devoted classicist until his death ("Greek Wisdom and Browning," *Classical Journal*, XLV, No. 1 [May, 1950], 246-248) and Kenneth L. Knickerbocker's telling reply to the argument ("Greek Wisdom and Browning: a Reply," *Classical Journal*, XLV, No. 1 [May, 1950], 393-394).

92. Ll. 339-348.

> Smilingly questions—'This it was brought tears
> Once to all eyes,—this roused heart's rapture once?'
> So will it be with truth that, for the nonce,
> Styles itself truth perennial: 'ware its wile!
> Knowledge turns nescience,—foremost on the file,
> Simply proves first of our delusions." [93]

In the second from last line, the reference of the pronoun in " 'ware
its wile" is not to truth but to the false claim made for truth that it
is perennial—this is what man should beware of. If man expects
truth on earth to be everlasting and will settle for nothing less, then
he is the dupe of fate; but if he is wise enough to know that all things
mortal have their cycle of birth, life, and death, and that relative
truth is to be built on partial truth throughout the whole of man's
aspiration to absolute truth, then he comports himself in harmony
with God's plan.

Lest one doubt the meaning of the passage, Browning's extended
figure of building an arch over a gulf should disabuse him of error.
As a worker shapes his arch, laying stone upon stone across the gulf to
form a solid causeway,

> So works Mind—by stress
> Of faculty, with loose facts, more or less,
> Builds up our solid knowledge: all the same,
> Underneath rolls what Mind may hide not tame,
> An element which works beyond our guess,
> Soul, the unsounded sea—whose lift of surge,
> Spite of all superstructure, lets emerge,
> In flower and foam, Feeling from out the deeps
> Mind arrogates no mastery upon. . . . [94]

Is the causeway of no value—is it nescience—because the skilled
engineer cannot tame an "element which works beyond our guess"?
To conclude so is to disregard much of the vast artistic legacy left
by Browning. The bridge, man's structure of knowledge leading

---

93. Ll. 349-360.
94. Ll. 156-164.

to more nearly perfect truth and wholeness, should not be abandoned because of the builder's preoccupation with the mystery of the sea rolling beneath him. It is sufficient that he study the sea, its tides, and its forces to gain knowledge to the end that a better bridge may result. There will be time after the erection of the final span for the builder to plumb the riddle of the oceans.

The Epilogue to the *Parleyings,* "Fust and His Friends," is a fittingly clear refutation of all critics who have leveled the charge of anti-intellectualism against the poet. Browning identifies Dr. Faustus with Johann Fust, the banker at Mainz who lent money to Gutenberg to further the invention of printing, a confusion to which Defoe gave currency in his *Political and Modern History of the Devil.* Fust, who is credited inaccurately with the invention of printing, is visited by his friends who come to urge repentance upon him for supposedly selling his soul to the devil. They find the learned man buried in gloom, his head sunk on his desk; and they fancy that he is remorseful because of his compact with Satan and because of the fleshly excesses that marked his youth. But they misunderstand the cause. He has long since given over indulgence and craves pardon of God for his sins. He was equipped when young with the triumvirate of endowments, the triple soul that makes for wholeness: "culture of mind,/ Sound flesh and sane soul in coherence," and he abused his birthright—but not for this is he melancholy. He fears that his invention of printing may equally spread lies and truth. One of his visitors, judging Fust's sin to be the sin of pride, prescribes exorcism. First, however, they want to sing a psalm befitting the rites of exorcism, but their memories of the Latin are in disagreement. Hand-copied manuscripts are so rare and costly that none of the visitors has been granted more than glimpses of the treasured pages. Fust, sensing his triumph, retires to his printing shop, while his guests quarrel among themselves, and in five minutes he returns with perfect copies of the hymn for all. In joy, he sees the worth of his invention, which has the power to bring truth, which in turn has the power to smite falsehood.

> "Oh Word! Traverse world
> In sun-flash and sphere-song! Each beat of thy pinion
> Bursts night, beckons day: once Truth's banner unfurled,
> Where's Falsehood? Sun-smitten, to nothingness hurled!"[95]

Fust hails truth as God, and lies as God's foe. Truths inevitably change by the year, month, day, and hour; but how much truth is turned to error through slips of the pens held in the hands of weary scribes, their eyes "horny with poring" over manuscripts? The text is soon corrupted and corrupted yet again, with successive recopying adding error to error, till the snow of truth is soiled in the mire. God, Fust recalls, commanded man "to Know" and to yearn for the unreachable wholeness of God—the "Sole and single omniscience!"

> "Oh, Man's ignorance!" hear the fool whine!
> How were it, for better or worse, didst thou grunt
> Contented with sapience—the lot of the swine
> Who knows he was born for just truffles to hunt?—
> Monks' Paradise—"*Semper sint res uti sunt!*"
>
> No, Man's the prerogative—knowledge once gained—
> To ignore,—find new knowledge to press for, to swerve
> In pursuit of, no, not for a moment: attained—
> Why, onward through ignorance! Dare and deserve!
> As still to its asymptote speedeth the curve,
>
> So approximates Man—Thee, who, reachable not,
> Hast formed him to yearningly follow Thy whole
> Sole and single omniscience![96]

The phrase "onward through ignorance" means that man should progress not by means of ignorance, but by going through—passing beyond—it. The concept of man formed by God to yearn with all his being after knowledge is a fair statement of Browning's epistemology. It would be difficult, indeed, to find a more ecstatic hymn to God's

---

95. Ll. 292-295.
96. Ll. 416-428.

gift of eternal restlessness of mind to prick man onward toward the truth.

That Browning held to his lifelong faith in the intellect as an instrument, though purposely limited to further God's plan, may be discovered throughout his last volume, *Asolando*. In "Reverie" he has a vision of the coming day when "a veil is rent between/ Me and the truth. . . ." By affording man samples of infinity, life stimulates him to seek perfection:

> How but from near to far
> Should knowledge proceed, increase?
> Try the clod ere test the star![97]

Once again Browning hails the triple soul of man: body, mind, and spirit, which work together for wholeness:

> So, my annals thus begin:
> With body, to life awoke
> Soul, the immortal twin
> Of body which bore soul's yoke
> Since mortal and not akin.
>
> By means of the flesh, grown fit,
> Mind, in surview of things,
> Now soared, anon alit
> To treasure its gatherings
> From the ranged expanse. . . .[98]

Mind, working with body and spirit, can know what of life God makes clear to mortal sight; but Browning is as clear in his final work as he was in his youth that if man inquires into the activities of the First Cause, frustration awaits him:

> Thou earth that embosomest
> Offspring of land and sea—

---

97. Ll. 36-38.
98. Ll. 41-50.

How thy hills first sank to rest,
How thy vales bred herb and tree
Which dizen thy mother-breast—

Do I ask? "Be ignorant
Ever!" the answer clangs:
Whereas if I plead world's want,
Soul's sorrows and body's pangs,
Play the human applicant,—

Is a remedy far to seek?
I question and find response. . . .[99]

Man, he says, can no more withstand acknowledging and pursuing "resistless fact" than the clay can resist the potter's act. Man progresses thus from knowledge of the known to insight into the unknown, for "life is—to wake, not sleep. . . ."

Browning's poetry from *Pippa Passes* to *Asolando* gives a coherent and steady vision of the need for order and wholeness in man's life, for with these man is enabled to meet the test to which this world subjects him from birth to death. Evil and ignorance are all about him to see what he will do to combat them. By his actions he shall be judged. As life must finally be surrendered so that he may progress into the next life, so he is in a sense doomed, if his fate is looked upon narrowly. "He who findeth his life shall lose it," but only to gain the greater life. He who finds his life is the man who in wholeness uses all of God's gifts—mind, body, and spirit—in choosing his path to the Dark Tower, before which he shall neither be daunted nor afraid.

---

99. Ll. 101-112.

CHAPTER III

PROLOGUE TO A THEORY OF KNOWLEDGE:
PAULINE, PARACELSUS, AND SORDELLO

"Build on the human heart!"—Sordello

We have followed the path that Browning took in his quest for a satisfactory theory of knowledge, which led to the discovery of the triple soul and the concept of wholeness. There remain for examination the three early works, *Pauline, Paracelsus,* and *Sordello,* which are markedly autobiographical and unified in theme. Because of their unity, personal character, and difficulty (*Sordello* especially is renowned for its obscurity), I have elected to discuss these interesting works at the end rather than at the beginning of the examination of Browning's long quest, for their significance will be more readily seen in the light of the later works.

I

Pauline is a key poem in understanding Browning's preoccupation with epistemology: the role of mind, the pursuit of learning, and the limits placed upon human knowledge. It is difficult not to conclude that the young man of twenty (Browning's age at the time the poem was written) is the author disburdening himself of serious, if juvenile, reflections upon faith and doubt; the meaning of life; and the role of imagination, love, and the mind. In the poem the young man is beginning his search for a set of values. The fragment was to have been part of a whole comprising "the other novel, such an opera, such a speech, etc.," as Browning inscribed with expansive ambiguity on the fourth page of the copy which John Stuart Mill annotated and which

Browning gave to Forster; and "had for its object the enabling me to assume & realize I know not how many different characters. . . ."[1] Such a clear acknowledgment allays some of the critic's fears of being found guilty of ascribing too freely to the poet the views of the creatures of his invention. The danger of the biographical fallacy always remains, however, for no creation is ever completely identifiable with the creator.[2]

Pauline was written under the spell of Shelley and Voltaire. Browning first read Shelley in *Miscellaneous Poems,* a volume pirated by William Benbow in 1826. When he first read *Queen Mab* is uncertain, but its influence was major. For two years, until his eyesight suffered, Browning was a vegetarian, and, perhaps for an equal period, an atheist. At the time of the composition of *Pauline* he was neither.

The poem, in spite of the "yeasty incoherencies" which Douglas Bush finds it it, is to be numbered among the loveliest poems of youth in search of the answer to the riddle of existence. To dismiss the poem as absurd (as Bush does not) is to confess to imperfect sympathy with those yet young enough to demand that life yield both joy and meaning. Browning was a joyous amateur of the human heart in a happier day before the heart and head became the property of the professional psychologist and psychiatrist. It is difficult to regret Browning's amateur standing or to lament his ignorance of the *id* and the *superego.* The Browning who is read in the anthologies was that rarest of all human beings: a man both vitally alive and happy. For such indiscretions, many of his contemporaries and many people today cannot forgive him.

It is strange that so few people today like *Pauline,* for it is among the least bumptiously self-assured poems, written when Browning was deeply troubled and insecure and thus should appeal to our unhappy times.[3] The embarrassment *Pauline* brought its author, his attempts

---

1. Quoted in DeVane, *A Browning Handbook,* p. 37.

2. Parallels between the young poet and Browning may be seen in Richard D. Altick's "The Private Life of Robert Browning," *op. cit.*

3. Samuel C. Chew ("The Nineteenth Century and After" in *A Literary History of England,* ed. Albert C. Baugh [New York, 1948], p. 1393) admits that a few lines and passages give some evidence of greatness, which however, *Pauline,* "in its entirety, does not display."

to forget the unlucky poem, Rossetti's discovery of a copy in the British Museum fourteen years later and his astute guess that Browning was the author are part of literary history. There has been much speculation about the reasons for Browning's extreme reluctance to discuss the poem or even acknowledge its existence. The letters to Elizabeth Barrett early in 1846 show evidence that he was almost morbidly reluctant to let her see the book, which she wanted to read. He protested that the poem was foolish, but what he meant was that it revealed a side of him which he wished to conceal from the world:

> Will you, and must you have 'Pauline'? If I could pray you to revoke that decision! For it is altogether foolish and *not* boylike—and I shall, I confess, hate the notion of running over it—yet commented it must be; more than mere correction! I was unluckily *precocious*—but I had rather you *saw* real infantine efforts (verses at six years old, and drawings still earlier) than this ambiguous, feverish—Why not wait?[4]

It seems clear that he was reluctant to forward the poem for her perusal not because it was childish or ineptly written—he was willing to show worse things—but because he did not want her to look into a sickness of the psyche which by 1846 he was hopeful of curing. Pauline's young suitor is a man with a split personality, yearning for all things and fearful that he may attain false goals. The struggle in his soul between mysticism and realism, romantic subjectivity and rational objectivity, and escapism and activism informs the poem throughout.

Pauline, like the two poems which followed it, is a nineteenth-century treatment of hubris and its effect on the wholeness of personality. In the poem a nameless young man pours out his story of error, sin, and pride to Pauline, who, rivaling Griselda, must surely be the second most patient young woman in the history of literary confession, as she certainly is the most silent. She apparently accepts unquestioningly his imperious statement:

---

4. *The Letters of Robert Browning and Elizabeth Barrett Barrett, 1845-1846* (2 vols.; New York, 1898), I, 400.

> Thou lovest me;
> And thou art to receive not love but faith,
> For which thou wilt be mine, and smile and take
> All shapes and shames, and veil without a fear
> That form which music follows like a slave. . . .[5]

This unilateral position would be intolerable if Pauline were to be considered a real woman in conversation with her lover; but it is made clear that she is less a woman than a symbol of the imagination, music, and poetry, which he has forsaken in his pursuit of knowledge. Now he is woing her to "lose/ All this gay mastery of mind," and to return to the company of those who are votaries of the spirit and imagination. He speaks to her, not so much to express his love, as to "unlock the sleepless brood/ Of fancies from my soul," even though he warns her that her role in the confessional is dangerous, since she has only her "naked love" to guard her: ". . . whoso sucks a poisoned wound/ Envenoms his own veins!"

He straightway comes to the point—a point which, as we have seen, plagued Browning increasingly as he grew older: the limits of legitimate human knowledge and the relationship of mind and spirit. Having stifled his creative nature in his quest for forbidden knowledge, he knows that until he has confessed his sin "it were vain/ To hope to sing." He has committed hubris. He has "learned the spell which can call up the dead." His quivering lip has been bathed in nature's enchantments, and his brow burns "beneath the crown to which her secrets knelt." His pursuit of knowledge beyond sanctioned bounds, however, has not been like that of Faust, for abuse of power. One is reminded of Shelley, whom Browning addresses as "Suntreader" in the famous invocation. Indeed, like Shelley he has had only "wild dreams of beauty and of good" for mankind. He is

> . . . Made up of an intensest life,
> Of a most clear idea of consciousness
> Of self, distinct from all its qualities,
> From all affections, passions, feelings, powers;

---

5. Ll. 43-46.

> And thus far it exists, if tracked, in all:
> But linked, in me, to self-supremacy,
> Existing as a centre to all things,
> Most potent to create and rule and call
> Upon all things to minister to it;
> And to a principle of restlessness
> Which would be all, have, see, know, taste, feel, all—
> This is myself. . . .[6]

It would be hard to find in poetry a more complete statement of the principles of hubris than this: "to create and rule and call/ Upon all things to minister to it; . . . be, have, see, know, taste, feel, all. . . ." In short, to be Godlike in one's pride of mind and power.

Luckily he has been blessed with another faculty of great importance to Browning in 1833 and of increasing importance as he grew older: imagination, the shaping power which embraces or is identified with love.

> And of my powers, one springs up to save
> From utter death a soul with such desire
> Confined to clay—of powers the only one
> Which marks me—an imagination. . . .[7]

The effects of this imagination are nothing less than the finest piece of myth making and romantic imagery in Browning. Never again did he employ such haunting images of pure romantic imagination, of fiends "in darkness chained forever/ Within some ocean cave," of the fountain-heads "Long lost of some great river washing towns/ And towers," and "banks untrod of human foot." These bring echoes of "The Hesperides" and "The Kraken," Tennyson's loveliest examples of myth making, so pitiably rare after the century possessed him, and of Arnold's "The Forsaken Merman." One can only wonder why such imagery became less and less as Browning grew older and insisted more dogmatically on the value of the imagination.

The young lover tells of the shaping power of "the wisest ancient

---

6. Ll. 268-279.
7. Ll. 281-284.

books"—the six thousand volumes in the Browning library—and how
they became

> All halo-girt with fancies of my own;
> And I myself went with the tale—a god
> Wandering after beauty. . . .[8]

Into this imaginative paradise, when he looked on the "dim clustered
isles in the blue sea,/ The deep groves and white temples and wet
caves," came sin as he "learned to turn/ My mind against itself," a
breach in wholeness, or order, whence

> Came cunning, envy, falsehood, all world's wrong
> That spotted me. . . .[9]

Music, which is an earnest of heaven and which gives us emotions not
to be experienced through other media, calls up the aid of fancy to
bring the young sinner from his Carlylean Everlasting No to a Centre
of Indifference: "I had/ An impulse but no yearning—only sang." He
turns to the ancient vine of fable, the old myths which once fed his
soul when he was young and which gave him a measure of peace,
until the time when his intellect took the ascendancy and he fell
victim to the sin of pride.

> I dreamed not of restraint, but gazed
> On all things: schemes and systems went and came,
> And I was proud (being vainest of the weak)
> In wandering o'er thought's world to seek some one
> To be my prize, as if you wandered o'er
> The White Way for a star.[10]

His prize was Shelley, and like his idol he vowed himself to liberty
and to the task of making men like gods and earth like heaven. This
time was "an hour one fondly waits/ For a fair girl that comes a

---

8. Ll. 320-322.
9. Ll. 350-351.
10. Ll. 398-403.

withered hag!" Total disillusionment—the surest result of setting mind against love—made him resolve not to think. But such resolutions are more easily made than kept. His restlessness of passion meets head-on the craving after knowledge, a "sleepless harpy," which tempts him "to forego/ All happy ignorant hopes and fears to live,/ Finding a recompense in its wild eyes." Luckily he discovers in time that such a choice means death of the soul; and he again turns to "old delights," the ancient myths that nourish the heart but, in the spirit of the Victorian compromise, he keeps the urge for knowledge "a chained thing, still prompt/ To serve me if I loosed its slightest bond. . . ." And he adds in a spirit which makes one wonder whether he is really free of hubris: "I cannot but be proud of my bright slave." Perhaps the greatest error of man—an error that Browning insists upon ever more fervently—is to chain love by the "few truths" which reason has caught from its chainless wanderings. The concept of man's greatest gift—love, the spirit, and the imagination—chained like Prometheus by reason or by the false god that reason has created to tyrannize over man has its parallel in the Andromeda legend, the central myth in Browning.

It is an error to suppose that *Pauline,* the most romantic of the poet's works, is a denunciation of the mind as a viper lying in wait for the imagination as it innocently props tendrils in an Eden of love and innocence. Romantic as the poem is, it administers no bastinado to a villainous Urizen. Reason is treated as a genie kept in a bottle, a potent and indispensable adjunct to the imagination and love. Reason is "my bright slave," as he, upon entering the magic forest of the imagination with Pauline, is

> . . . loves' slave,
> Looking no farther than his liege commands.[11]

The heart has reasons which the reason understands not. The young man burns to see the "calm pure truth" of the heart "out-flash/ The brightest gleams of earth's philosophy"—which is a far different thing

---

11. Ll. 948-949.

from feeling that the mind yields no light at all. The intellect is an imperfect instrument, as is everything in the mortal state, but it is indispensable. Only if it tyrannizes over the heart or aspires to knowledge of the infinite is it a snake in the beautiful garden. "Reason's pedantry," it is true, fails to fathom "music's mystery," but it is for all that not in itself an evil.

The poem ends on a note of such romantic escapism into the forest of myth, "old stories of dead knights," and native song that the unwary may be betrayed into the conclusion that Browning is throwing out the reason entirely. Certainly it is impossible to conclude from the evidence that the invitation to Pauline to escape with him into the heart of the uninhibited forest is an invitation to rapturous sin. Never was a mistress in less danger, save from possible discomfort or filibuster. To purge himself of hubris, he resolves to flee with Pauline to a land of faery and impassioned recital of Ovidean myth

> . . . where nature lies all bare
> Suffering none to view her but a race
> Or stinted or deformed, like the mute dwarfs
> Which wait upon a naked Indian queen. . . .[12]

He seeks escape from festering thought "that tells of the past doubt," but a few lines later he adds that with the coming of spring —*i.e.,* the rebirth of love, imagination, and joy—

> . . . we will question life once more,
> Till its old sense shall come renewed by change,
> Like some clear thought which harsh words veiled before. . . .[13]

Mind, if kept in the benevolent servitude of the heart, leads to wholeness and clear thought,

> Feeling God loves us, and that all which errs
> Is but a dream which death will dissipate.[14]

---

12. Ll. 954-957.
13. Ll. 975-977.
14. Ll. 978-979.

The lover knows that he has been a law unto himself in defiance of God's plan. He has too much trusted his "own lawless wants," while seeking in pride to break the limitations of the mortal condition in his quest for infinite knowledge. The rewards of life are granted only to those who live it, fittting their finiteness to the rules and limitations of the finite in their journey toward the infinite.

II

Paracelsus (1835) continues Browning's exploration of the theme of hubris, the relation of mind and love, and the adjustment of each to the limitations of life. By the time of the composition of this remarkable and little-read poem, Browning had reflected upon John Stuart Mill's severe criticism inscribed in the margins of his review copy of *Pauline,* and had repudiated all public confession of lacerations from the thorns of life. That he was deeply embarrassed by his morbid self-revelation in *Pauline* is amply attested to by his resolution never again to disclose his heart directly to the public gaze. But it is an error to suppose that he suddenly applied the wisdom of showing only shop and not house. In his use of the historical Paracelsus may be seen a clear hedge against the autobiographical entanglements of the earlier poem; but, although Paracelsus has a new name and face, his garb is but little changed. He is, of course, not Browning;[15] but the similarities between the problems, frustrations, and failures of the sixteenth-century doctor and those of Pauline's less-than-ardent suitor are unmistakable.

The dramatis personae of the play are four: Aureolus Paracelsus, who represents the eternally restless mind; Aprile, a Shelleyan poet, who repudiates mind in his pursuit of love; and Festus and Michal, a married pair who together represent the balance between the extremes and complement each other to form a perfect whole. Even their hair,

---

15. On March 20, 1845, Elizabeth Barrett wrote (*The Letters of Robert Browning and Elizabeth Barrett Barrett, 1845-1846,* I, 42): "But I shall be afraid of you at first—though I am not, in writing this. You are Paracelsus, and I am a recluse, with nerves that have been all broken on the rack, and now hang loosely—quivering at a step and breath."

when mixed, is of one blended hue, more beautiful than the disparate shades unblended. Paracelsus, like Faust, feels set apart from other men by his commission to discover the answer to the riddle of life. Impatient and proud, he abjures traditional paths of study, the idle arts of pedants, even though the voice of conscience counsels him to beware the sin of seeing wisdom's countenance "no veil between." His presumptuous desire is

> . . . to comprehend the works of God,
> And God himself, and all God's intercourse
> With the human mind. . . .[16]

One hears faint echoes of Raphael's counsel to an earlier sinner:

> Heav'n is for thee too high
> To know what passes there; be lowly wise:
> Think only what concerns thee and thy being. . . .[17]

Paracelsus, who presumably shares Browning's Andromeda complex —his lifelong preoccupation with chivalrous rescues of damsels, often nude, from dragons—is selfless in his desire for forbidden knowledge, wishing only to have mankind partake of his largess, while he would reject their thanks like a knight who "frees a desert people from the tyranny of a dragon." He defends his excursion down forbidden paths of knowledge on the grounds that traditional lore has abated none of the suffering and evil of a groaning world. Thus Browning's treatment of hubris is tinged with nineteenth-century romantic sentimentalism; Paracelsus' sin is not only pride and desire for forbidden knowledge, but it is equally his scorn of human love and the limitations set upon man. Having no patience to follow the laws of life in his search for ultimate truth, he aspires to know by transcending the conditions of life, which are God's means of testing man. By scorning life's instrumentalities and the laws governing human aspiration, he seeks to circumvent God's divine plan. His pride, which forbids famil-

---

16. I, 533-535.
17. *Paradise Lost*, VIII, 172-174.

iarity with his fellow creatures whom he yearns to help, is, of course, hubris. To serve man is not enough if one in Godlike isolation seeks to be an elite corps of one.

Festus, who is always the voice of conscience counseling the proud doctor to love more and know less, fears to brood overmuch on the legitimate limits of study, lest he be corrupted by even this discreet inquiry: "I dare not thoroughly probe/ This matter, lest I learn too much." He merely knows that if he were happily numbered among the intellectuals, he would encircle himself with love and raise a "rampart" of his fellows against failure and sin. There are strange punishments for the sin of pride, but here Festus is more concerned with Paracelsus' undemocratic reluctance to be on terms of sweaty intimacy with man than he is with the medieval sin of aspiring to Godhead.

Michal, with womanly intuition, is more medieval in her fears of hubris:

> An angel warns me, too,
> Man should be humble; you are very proud:
> And God, dethroned, has doleful plagues for such![18]

Paracelsus defends his reckless search for knowledge in a curious melange of medieval and romantic thinking. "To know," he says, consists of opening a gateway through the "baffling and perverting carnal mesh" for the escape of truth, which lies within us, and is therefore ours to discover. How can man be guilty in probing the "inmost centre in us all,/ Where truth abides in fulness. . ."? One does not need to scale the ramparts of heaven to discover the Absolute, for God has made of man a repository wherein all truth is hidden, awaiting only him who can find the key and unlock the splendor within:

> . . . may not truth be lodged alike in all,
> The lowest as the highest? some slight film
> The interposing bar which binds a soul
> And makes the idiot, just as makes the sage

---

18. I, 701-703.

> Some film removed, the happy outlet whence
> Truth issues proudly?[19]

Here is a surprising extension of Miltonic right reason, the faculty granted to all men to know the will of God, right and wrong, the beautiful and the ugly. To Paracelsus, who shares Browning's bumptious exuberance, right reason becomes a romantic reservoir of all truth whatever—not just instinctual perception of God's will. What distinguishes the imbecile from the philosopher is a fleshly film which hides the inner light from the one but which can be breached by the other. Since the obscuring film is in no way the responsibility of its victim, as Omar's unstable pots were guiltless of the imperfect craftsmanship of their maker's palsied hands, Paracelsus gingerly approaches the position of modern psychiatry. Right reason, whereby each man has perfect knowledge and responsibility for making a moral choice, becomes through the sophistries of Paracelsus a much distorted faculty, which can be obscured by defects of the flesh in no way the fault of man. If the pituitary gland fails to make the secretion which regulates conduct, how is man morally responsible? The proud doctor, anticipating the pride of nineteenth-century science, is guilty of making the glands the seat of moral responsibility and justifying man's indifference to the effects of his conduct. No one could be more aware of the implications of this heresy than Browning, for it strikes at the center of his belief, everywhere disclosed in his poetry, that life is a moral gymnasium created for the purpose of testing man by the measure of his works, for which he alone has full responsibility. The moral irresponsibility of Paracelsus, who would pass the blame to a glandular imbalance, is revealed in his reckless challenge to God:

> See if we cannot beat thine angels yet!
> Such is my task.[20]

Part II of Browning's closet drama is set in the house of a Greek conjurer in Constantinople, 1521. Paracelsus is in a bitterly reflective

---

19. I, 754-759.
20. I, 784-785.

mood as, coming "to a pause with knowledge," he scans the heights he has attained. The backward vista is disheartening. His early resolution to become "the greatest and most glorious man on earth" led through "one vast unbroken chain of thought" to the middle distance of despair, where he sickens on a dead gulf streaked with light "from its own putrefying depths alone." The greatest wisdom he has learned is that

> God may take pleasure in confounding pride
> By hiding secrets with the scorned and base. . . .[21]

He has explored the murky depths of necromancy, looking for the philosophers' stone and the fountain of youth, not, as he now knows, to aid man but to satisfy the cravings of his ego. He faces the ignoble selfishness that has so long masqueraded as altruism when he confesses that if he fails he wants no luckier man to profit by his failure and so become man's new Prometheus. His hubris is now an inescapable reproach to him, not to be exorcised by sophistries, and he fears that God will visit him with the punishment he fears most, madness:

> "I crushed him, lest he should disturb
> My law. Men must not know their strength: behold
> Weak and alone, how he had raised himself!"[22]

Aprile, the poet, enters and disturbs these dark reflections with an annoying counterphilosophy: "I would love infinitely, and be loved!" It is a mistake to fancy that Aprile is intended as a perfect foil for Paracelsus—the unreflecting lover, in tune with God's purpose, contrasted with the eternally reflective and loveless outcast. Both are guilty of hubris, one of spirit, one of mind. The poet is as consecrated to love as the philosopher is to knowledge; and both share the contempt for God's test of man through imperfection and limitation. Paracelsus wants absolute knowledge; Aprile wants absolute love. Both seek an ideal that is unattainable on earth, and both scorn partial attainment.

---

21. II, 180-181.
22. II, 243-245.

Aprile's love is an idealization of perfection which admits of no stooping to the frailty of the flesh or the homely joys of earthly love. He is, in short, the romantic poet, in love with a love which would shiver asunder on the rock of actuality and would never survive a bad cold. He has spurned the realities of life and its test of man as fully as has Paracelsus. No mistake could more distort Browning's intention than to conclude that Aprile seeks the good and his bemused friend seeks the bad. Only the incompleteness which is the result of pursuing one—knowledge or love—is evil. Both men have impatiently sought to invade heaven to secure in its absolute form what the flesh can but struggle to attain in life. It is how man strives that tests him. Aprile takes all love to be his province—so long as it is not sullied by imperfection—and would build a world of art which is free of the flaws of this world. He would play God with his art, and so " 'create a world for these my shapes/ Fit to sustain their beauty and their strength!' " as the creator granted to each of his sprites " 'a sphere to be its world.' " He advances through the several arts, from the most material to the least, successively through the plastic arts, poetry, and ultimately to music, the least gross of the creations of man. His prayer indicates the egocentricity underlying his vision:

> He would approve my prayer, "I have gone through
> The loveliness of life; create for me
> If not for men, or take me to thyself,
> Eternal, infinite love!" [23]

Aprile, like Paracelsus, broods upon his sin of pride. It is as dangerous to probe too deep within the soul as within the mind. His hubris, like that of Paracelsus, has been compounded by his rejection of the imperfect instrumentalities God has granted man and his scorn of earth's limited love. His search for an impossible ideal, divorced from mind, has been as sterile as that sundered from love. Paracelsus moans:

> Love me henceforth, Aprile, while I learn
> To love; and, merciful God, forgive us both!

---

23. II, 484-487.

> We wake at length from weary dreams; but both
> Have slept in fairy-land: though dark and drear
> Appears the world before us, we no less
> Wake with our wrists and ankles jewelled still.
> I too have sought to KNOW as thou to LOVE—
> Excluding love as thou refusedst knowledge.
> Still thou hast beauty and I, power. We wake:
> What penance canst devise for both of us? [24]

The truth bursts upon them both. Each has equally shattered the order of creation by scorning the conditions of this world and seeking while in the mortal state the heavenly vision. Both have striven to be God-like. Both are twin fragments of the wholeness which is man's true goal.

> Are we not halves of one dissevered world,
> Whom this strange chance unites once more? Part? never!
> Till thou the lover, know; and I, the knower,
> Love—until both are saved. [25]

Readers who may discover in *Paracelsus* a gulf between the heart and the head of the poet's own contriving or who find the informing principle in his poetry to be rejection of knowledge might with profit read the poem again. So far is Browning from supporting anti-intellectualism in the downfall of Paracelsus, that he wrenches the ancient concept of hubris to link incompletion with the prime sin. Browning is well on the way to the concept of the triple soul. It is not the employment of mind that is the root of the philosopher's sin, any more than love alone is Aprile's. God, who is the perfect fusion of power and love, "is the perfect poet," Aprile finally understands, and only through wholeness can man aspire upward. This revelation exacts a high price: his immediate death.

In Part III Paracelsus perceives that only in death does man see absolute truth. In life it is better for man to comprehend why pansies, "eyes that laugh bear beauty's prize/ From violets, eyes that

---

24. II, 618-627.
25. II, 634-637.

dream . . ." than to marvel at the gray knowledge he has wrung from
a loveless existence. In his revulsion against learning, he asks why men
should strive to know what is beyond their powers of comprehension
and incapable of adding one jot to happiness. Knowledge, indeed,
can kill joy in simple people, and is widely mistrusted. He tells of his
cure of the prince in spite of the unlucky ministrations of a battery of
jealous quacks, who had brought their sovereign to the point of death.
For his pains Paracelsus was hounded out of town as an enemy of
established truth; and the gratitude of the recovered prince, who
burned a dozen heretics to mark the event, failed to allay his bitterness. Disillusioned, Paracelsus discovers the cardinal philosophical fact
in Browning: man is incapable on this side of the grave of attaining
ultimate truth. Not one veil stands between man and the Absolute,
but an infinite number of veils shield his eyes from the white light of
eternity. Man's duty is to make the most of his capacities within the
limitations of this life. Like Lucifer, Paracelsus has been thrust from
his proud eminence, in spite of apparently admiring crowds that attend his lectures at Basel. Men do not much admire learning, he discovers. Half of those who attend his discourses come from "sheer
amazement" or "mere novelty," and all but a few are moved by hatred
of established dogmas or institutions, to which his lectures may supply
a rationale; and some hope to discredit him. Most disillusioning of all,
he has found it impossible to impart his knowledge; man's capacity
for misunderstanding is illimitable—a conclusion that teachers less
learned than Paracelsus commonly discover in their early years of
teaching. He longs to end his mad quest for knowledge and "content
me/ With beauty for itself alone," but by now his imagination is
atrophied.

> And now the forest-creatures fly from me,
> The grass-banks cool, the sunbeams warm no more.[26]

Man can know only cause-and-effect relationships, as a doctor can
surmise the sick man's state by the pulse, the fevered brow, and the

---

26. III, 716-717.

languid eye. But this is God's plan: to conceal truth and to test man's fidelity to the search for it in spite of doubt, weariness, and despair. Were man all mind, he would be dehumanized: "love, hope, fear, faith—these make humanity." All the inferior spirits possess intelligence denied to man, "which casts our mind/ Into immeasurable shade." Many of man's proudest fruits of erudition are but cavils and petty attacks upon established doctrine. In his total despair he utters the astonishing doctrine that

> . . . mind is nothing but disease,
> And natural health is ignorance.[27]

These lines, taken from context, appear to supply conclusive evidence in support of Browning's supposed anti-intellectual espousal of the romantic virtues of garden-variety ignorance.[28] Paracelsus, however, is experiencing the aridity of knowledge unallied with love, and his reaction might be likened to a blacksmith's opinion of anvils after one has dropped on his toe.

> Thus: I possess
> Two sorts of knowledge; one,—vast, shadowy,
> Hints of the unbounded aim I once pursued:
> The other consists of many secrets, caught
> While bent on nobler prize,—perhaps a few
> Prime principles which may conduct to much:
> These last I offer to my followers here.[29]

To suppose that Browning's theme is the evil of knowledge or of the mind is like concluding that Captain Ahab's obsessional pursuit of Moby Dick illustrates the folly of hunting whales. Paracelsus sees the wisdom of the limitations God sets on man. Knowledge is blessed of God up to a point just short of the Absolute:

---

27. IV, 279-280.

28. One is bewildered to find Joseph E. Baker ("Religious Implications in Browning's Poetry," *op. cit.*, p. 445), who believes Browning to be wholly anti-intellectual, discovering essential agreement between Swift and Browning: "They agree in their contempt for man's use of his reason." Swift, it seems clear, scorned man for failing to follow reason, not for using it.

29. III, 922-928.

> Ah, the curse, Aprile, Aprile!
> We get so near—so very, very near!
> 'T is an old tale: Jove strikes the Titans down,
> Not when they set about their mountain-piling
> But when another rock would crown the work.[30]

That Paracelsus does not repudiate legitimate knowledge is made clear in his offer to impart to Festus the meager knowledge he possesses, to explain its "bounded nature," and to confess his insufficiency and pride. As he approaches the threshold of death, he gains a new and unearthly wisdom, which he turns upon old events; but he is forbidden to reveal what he sees behind the veil, for it is not lawful for man to pry into such mysteries. Festus, who cannot comprehend the glory of the dying man's vision into truth, asks whether the sum of wisdom were not to wait in patient ignorance, nor "fret themselves with what concerns them not." Paracelsus shouts in horror at his friend's misconception, which has certain resemblances to that of some of Browning's critics:

> No, no; mistake me not, let me not work
> More harm than I have worked![31]

Ignorance is not a virtue, nor does God command that men "lie down/ Content as God has made them." The knowledge and the love that man wrests from life are turned into "new strifes, new triumphs:— doubtless a strong soul"—the first instance in Browning of his philosophical defense of evil and failure as a test. Love and power (*i.e.,* knowledge) must work together in wholeness:

> I learned my own deep error; love's undoing
> Taught me the worth of love in man's estate,
> And what proportion love should hold with power
> In his right constitution; love preceding
> Power, and with much power, always much more love;

---

30. V, 122-126.
31. V, 581-582.

> Love still too straitened in his present means,
> And earnest for new power to set love free.[32]

Once he learned the great lesson of life—the finite cannot comprehend the infinite—"the secret of the world" was his, "save for that doubt" which keeps man upon the road, unblinded by the white radiance of eternity. The mind is an instrument which guides man well and far, but never to the end of the road. Browning, who cannot find it in his heart to suggest that God is niggardly even in ultimate things, has Paracelsus, speaking from the wisdom that approaching death has brought him, observe that where the mind becomes useless in the search for truth, the spirit ("perception unexpressed,/ Uncomprehended by our narrow thought") takes over the task of informing man of "what God is, what we are,/ What life is. . . ." Thus God grants man knowledge commensurate with his capacities, and capacities equal to his needs and the plan of life. As he climbs the evolutionary scale, led surely upward by love and mind, not serenely pure but "strong from weakness," he will grow nearer to God in love and power, for "man is not Man as yet." He will always remain limited and vexed, but these are the conditions of growth. The poem ends with the plea of Paracelsus that the sin of hubris of which both he and Aprile were guilty in their separate ways be taken as a lesson to the pride of man:

> Let men
> Regard me, and the poet dead long ago
> Who loved too rashly; and shape forth a third
> And better-tempered spirit, warned by both. . . .[33]

III

Sordello (1840) continues the themes of the two earlier poems—romantic isolation and social responsibility, mind and heart, pride and humiliation; but the central theme, of which these are a part, is the

---

32. V, 853-859.
33. V, 884-887.

adjustment of an aspiring poet to the demands of his craft, the world, God, and himself. Sordello may be considered to be a medieval Browning who lived, reflected much, suffered, and failed seven hundred years ago. To attest his new objectivity, Browning repudiates Shelley's spirit ("come not near/ Now—not this time desert thy cloudy place/ To scare me . . ."). His insistence that the poem is in no way autobiographical immediately arouses suspicions that he protests too much.

> Who will, may hear Sordello's story told:
> His story? . . .
>
> . . . .
> Only believe me. Ye believe? [34]

It is singular that he would go to such lengths to insist that the story of Sordello is truly Sordello's story, not somebody else's. The evidence of the two previous poems invites skepticism. One is inclined to suspect that the incidents in a human soul that are alone worth study may be incidents in Browning's soul.

Sordello, like Pauline's suitor, is a romantic escapist, living an idyllic life at Goito, a castle ringed by low mountains. Both young men are obsessed by a desire to flee from the world to a sanctuary where no eye can pierce and no foot follow. Goito is such a retreat. The main defiles are hidden by firs and larches to give added secrecy. The imagery used to describe the castle in its silent isolation would interest a psychiatrist probing the psyche of the introspective poet living there. The castle is like

> Some captured creature in a pound
> Whose artless wonder quite precludes distress,
> Secure beside in its own loveliness.[35]

The picture of artless innocence, symbolized by the castle, captured and yet free, with distress kept at bay, strikingly reminds one of the

---

34. I, 1-9.
35. I, 384-386.

young Browning immured within the double walls of his dream world
and of his father's magical library. But the full secrecy of Goito is yet
to be told. As one passes within, he finds a maze of corridors, dark
winding stairs, and dim galleries, leading to "the inmost chambers,"
within which is the most secret sanctuary of all, a maple-paneled room
of exceeding wonder. A golden haze floats magically upon the panels,
unfolding in graven characters the "Arab's wisdom everywhere." Significant of Browning's stress of soul, however, is the disturbing circumstance that the way to this fabled sanctum is through "corridors
contrived for sin" and that within the chamber itself the cabalistic
wisdom illuminated by golden light is marred for a "moment" by the
shadows of slim pillars,

> Cut like a company of palms to prop
> The roof, each kissing top entwined with top,
> Leaning together; in the carver's mind
> Some knot of bacchanals, flushed cheek combined
> With straining forehead, shoulders purpled, hair
> Diffused between, who in a goat-skin bear
> A vintage. . . .[36]

The fusion of bacchanalian sexuality, Arabic wisdom, and Godlike
isolation in this "drowsy paradise" is symbolic of the central psycho-
logical question for both Sordello and the young Browning: can an
aspiring poet build himself a lordly pleasure house and live without
sin in a world of his own imaginative or intellectual contriving? The
answer to the problem, as suggested by *Pauline* and *Paracelsus,* is a
ringing no.

In Goito there is a further retreat, more secret even than the maple
chamber, a vault—"the main wonder"—not lit by a golden haze but
darkened by thick black shade about the ceiling and lit fitfully by a
dim light that filters through fine slits across the buttress. In the center
of this doleful place is a dull, gray-streaked font upheld by a ring of
shrinking caryatides:

---

36. I, 399-405.

> Of just-tinged marble like Eve's lilied flesh
> Beneath her maker's finger when the fresh
> First pulse of life shot brightening the snow.[37]

Their postures reveal their guilt and sense of sin: some muse upon the ground with eyelids half closed; some meekly pine with arms resignedly held behind their backs; some veil their eyes as if in shame; some prop their "chins and cheeks so pale," and some

> . . . hanging slack an utter helpless length
> Dead as a buried vestal whose whole strength
> Goes when the grate above shuts heavily.[38]

The symbol of a young vestal (the young Browning, consecrated to poetry?) whose strength goes when the grate of self-indulgence clangs upon her sin becomes clearer in these lines:

> So dwell these noiseless girls, patient to see,
> Like priestesses because of sin impure
> Penanced forever, who resigned endure,
> Having that once drunk sweetness to the dregs.
> And every eve, Sordello's visit begs
> Pardon for them: constant as eve he came
> To sit beside each in her turn, the same
> As one of them, a certain space. . . .[39]

As he sits by each in turn "as one of them," the sunshine slants cheerfully through the buttress chinks, and in his fancy he sees each stone maiden smile as if his ministrations had lightened her burden. The identification of Sordello with each of the "sin impure" caryatides, on whom the grate of the inner sanctum of luxury, idleness, and sin has clanged shut, strongly suggests the nameless sins of the young lover in *Pauline,* whose yearning for a retreat from the world, if not to the womb, approaches the pathological. Like him, Sordello is sen-

---

37. I, 413-415.
38. I, 421-423.
39. I, 424-431.

sually alive to drink delight "at every sense." He feels set apart from other men and "framed for pleasure." In a passage remarkable for its sexual symbolism, he is compared to lands overlush with a "loose fertility," where "mere decay/ Produces richer life" and where day by day "still more labyrinthine buds the rose." He is, however, sterile in the midst of this purposeless, loose fertility, which may symbolize the selfish, egocentric lucubrations of the young poet whose overheated fancy prompts him to fear the clanging shut of the door of self. He is a man "haunted by the curse that haunts such natures," the curse of being unable to bring good to those they love; and thus he turns to isolation and the caryatides. His immediate problem, then, is whether to "dwell distinct" from man or to bury himself, "the whole heart wide and warm," in something outside himself. One is reminded of Browning's first letter to Elizabeth Barrett, in which he wrote excitedly:

> Since the day last week when I first read your poems, I quite laugh to remember how I have been turning and turning again in my mind what I should be able to tell you of their effect upon me, for in the first flush of delight I thought I would this once get out of my habit of purely passive enjoyment. . . .[40]

In the same letter he remarks upon the time when he paid a visit to her home in the company of John Kenyon:

> . . . you were too unwell, and now it is years ago, and I feel as at some untoward passage in my travels, as if I had been close, so close, to some world's-wonder in chapel or crypt, only a screen to push and I might have entered. . . ?[41]

Sordello belongs to a "regal class" whom nature has severed from the mass of men:

> For there's a class that eagerly looks, too,
> On beauty, but, unlike the gentler crew,

---

40. *The Letters of Robert Browning and Elizabeth Barrett Barrett, 1845-1846*, I, 1.
41. *Ibid.*, I, 2.

> Proclaims each new revealment born a twin
> With a distinctest consciousness within,
> Referring still the quality, now first
> Revealed, to their own soul—its instinct nursed
> In silence. . . .[42]

That *Sordello* is heavily autobiographical and thus of first importance in understanding the young Browning's spirit may be seen in
Stewart Walker Holmes' excellent study "Browning's *Sordello* and
Jung: Browning's *Sordello* in the Light of Jung's Theory of Types."[43]
It is beyond the scope of the present study to attempt to show the
extent to which the problems of Sordello were those of Browning, but
it is essential to see that in the introverted intuitive poet Browning is
dramatically describing his own dilemma.

Sordello soon learns that the peril of being numbered among the
regal class is morbid introversion, sterility, and pride. Homage turns
inward, he discovers, and the poet feeds upon himself. Gentler souls,
innocent of such perverse pride, cannot comprehend how such percip-
ience should deject the soul; but Browning gives in answer the resolution which he so painfully worked out for his own salvation. Since
the egocentric poet, gifted above the lot of man, finds a certain mood
which counsels him to slumber in the solitude, indifferent to mankind's good, the poet must break the bonds of self or die. The tertiary
stage of the disease is that already seen in the two earlier poems: the
desire to comprehend the Absolute:

> Or if yet worse befall,
> And a desire possess it to put all
> That nature forth, forcing our straitened sphere
> Contain it,—to display completely here
> The mastery another life should learn,
> Thrusting in time eternity's concern,—
> So that Sordello. . .[44]

---

42. I, 523-529.
43. *PMLA*, LVI (September, 1941), 758-796.
44. I, 561-567.

The three ellipsis dots, which are Browning's, and the reluctance to complete the sentence suggest that Sordello—as well as Browning, perhaps—has been guilty of luxurious self-indulgence and the desire to wrest from eternity the knowledge and power that are the concern of the infinite alone. Remembrance of the autobiographical confession in *Pauline* strengthens one's conviction that the youthful Browning, like Sordello, "spied the mark of leprosy, violet dark" upon himself as he sought to evolve a satisfactory *Weltanschauung*. Leprosy, "ruinous to spirit," Sordello discovers, demands some pyx to screen the pest, "some lid to shut upon/ The goblin!" Holmes believes that *Sordello* was the lid which Browning slammed upon the goblin haunting his youth.

So lives the neurotic Sordello, unto himself the center of all creation, hanging like a spider in the middle of its web of fancies. Browning condemns such sloth: the world is pledged tacitly to destroy such a spangled fabric in the dust, whether at a blow or through the erosion of time. Sordello experiences doubts of the virtue of his selfish life and, as a first step toward a cure, cultivates love for his woodland companions, bird, beast, and flower, until he feels that even the poppy communes with him. His experiment with Wordsworthian pantheism, though better than sloth, is not enough. His next step is to study man hungrily and to "blend" himself with mankind as he learns to blend with tree and flower, "—nay more entirely else/ 'T were mockery. . . ."

Seeking to know mankind, he journeys to the walls of Mantua, outside of which a court of love is being held by Palma, the more fleshly counterpart of Pauline. Eglamor, the court minstrel, sings imperfectly of love, and on impulse Sordello sings, wins the contest, is made Palma's minstrel (Eglamor dies with convenient promptness), and as a final reward his neck is encircled by Palma's scarf, "her neck's warmth and all." The warm scarf, symbolic of life and love, so stirs his desire that he is stricken with amnesia and comes to his senses back in Goito, many leagues away, the scarf still around his neck. He experiences a rebirth and awakening of dormant faculties. He begins "to think now; hitherto he had perceived," but unfortunately his tri-

umph increases his pride and contempt for mankind. Like Paracelsus,
he sees no reason to "square his course/ By any known example."
With the awakening of his faculty of thought, he fancies himself as
"wise, and restricted to becoming wise," and in his pride of intellect,
he cannot stoop to love. He will, rather, demand that the world bow
down before him, who, Godlike, will contemplate the blisses of life but
will not taste of them himself. "Be mine mere consciousness," he begs.
He fears the grossness of the flesh and scorns the body with a vehemence that is striking evidence of his inhibitions, stimulated by the
touch of a scarf warm from a woman's neck. Indeed so traumatic is
his experience that he prefers "the song's effect" to the song itself. His
first contact with the outside world frightens him into even more pronounced introversion and pride. Bitter years pass, during which the
poet and the man, the spirit and the body, love and fear are at strife
that tears him "incessantly piecemeal." He is "sundered in twain" as
he ponders which is the proper course:

> . . . to pursue
> This course, still leap o'er paltry joys, yearn through
> The present ill-appreciated stage
> Of self-revealment, and compel the age
> Know him—or else, forswearing bard-craft, wake
> From out his lethargy and nobly shake
> Off timid habits of denial, mix
> With men, enjoy like men.[45]

Sordello is not yet ready to learn the great lesson which life alone
can teach the poet: if you would have your songs endure, "Build on the
human heart." In Goito he resumes his old self-indulgence, the visionary dreams enwrapping him wholly, as he cools his hot brow symbolically on the cold marble shelf beside the ring of caryatides. In this
suspended life, his eyes, once bright with exploring, grow dim from
receiving; but he is still at war with himself. His heart tells him that
his minstrel's trade is "to behold mankind," but his "own concern
is just to bring my mind/ Behold. . . ." He has never found whole-

---

45. II, 699-706.

ness—the perfect fusion of body, mind, and soul, the poet's and man's proper goal.

Browning, in one of his revelations *in propria persona,* tells of his musing on the steps of a ruined palace in Venice, which is the symbol of life, with good and evil inextricably mixed. He sees a brown beggar maid, the type of suffering humanity, who incites him to utter one of his noblest statements of sympathy for the hurt and the poor, and indirectly a description of the stuff of poetry.

> Warped souls and bodies! yet God spoke
> Of right-hand, foot and eye—selects our yoke,
> Sordello, as your poetship may find!
> So, sleep upon my shoulder, child, nor mind
> Their foolish talk; we'll manage reinstate
> Your old worth; ask moreover, when they prate
> Of evil men past hope, "Don't each contrive,
> Despite the evil you abuse, to live?—
> Keeping, each losel through a maze of lies,
> His own conceit of truth? to which he hies
> By obscure windings, tortuous, if you will,
> But to himself not inaccessible;
> He sees truth, and his lies are for the crowd
> Who cannot see; some fancied right allowed
> His vilest wrong. . . ."[46]

Earthly truth, far from being absolute, is always relative, each losel being his own judge of what he considers to be truth.

> "All men think all men stupider than they,
> Since, save themselves, no other comprehends
> The complicated scheme to make amends
> —Evil, the scheme by which, thro' Ignorance,
> Good labors to exist."[47]

This statement may lead one to the conclusion that Browning is extolling ignorance as a positive virtue, that the greater the ignorance

---

46. III, 781-795.
47. III, 800-804.

the greater the good. Nothing could be more in error. Ignorance, a tool of evil, is thus an evil itself, the essential test which gives life meaning. Life is an obstacle course to try man's strength and spirit and thus to nurture his growth as preparation for the next life. Of all the tests, the greatest is to stretch man's faith on the rack of doubt, and doubt is another name for ignorance. His philosophical view of ignorance was precisely that which he had of all other evils: recognize their function in the scheme of things as a test for man, but fight them while there is life, for only in this struggle lies the test. Browning says that it were "a slight advance,—/ Merely to find the sickness you die through/ And naught beside!" But this is not at all the same as saying that it is useless to achieve a medical discovery, even though it be only the naming of a malady. The figure, of course, clearly means that one gains little if he learns only the name of the disease that is killing him, but he does learn something. To know that our period of struggle, suffering, growth, and death is called life is not to know life. There is no talismanic significance in nomenclature, but, on the other hand, he does not say that there is positive virtue in ignorance of the word.

Browning next illustrates his favorite doctrine of the impossibility of finite man to comprehend the infinite plan of God. To the man born blind the sound of a trumpet may seem to embrace the whole of the concept we call "red," but the man gifted with more accurate perceptions will immediately recognize with a smile the childlike inaccuracy of the supposition. Man must seek truth with the faculties he has at hand, and it is better for the blind man to fancy red to be like a trumpet blast than to fancy nothing about the unknown. A greater sin than to fail the test of life is not to take the test at all. We can marvel at life and its wonderful plan—or "office"—but can we in life comprehend this office? No, says Browning; in life we can only discern the "what" and not the "how":

> What do we here? simply experiment
> Each on the other's power and its intent
> When elsewhere tasked,—if this of mine were trucked
> For yours to either's good,—we watch construct,
> In short, an engine: with a finished one,

> What it can do, is all,—naught how 't is done.
> But this of ours yet in probation, dusk
> A kernel of strange wheelwork through its husk
> Grows into shape by quarters and by halves;
> Remark this tooth's spring, wonder what that valve's
> Fall bodes, presume each faculty's device,
> Make out each other more or less precise—
> The scope of the whole engine's to be proved;
> We die: which means to say, the whole's removed,
> Dismounted wheel by wheel, this complex gin,—
> To be set up anew elsewhere, begin
> A task indeed, but with a clearer clime
> Than the murk lodgment of our building-time.[48]

It is important to remember that Browning does not counsel man to ignore the machine, its valves and wheels and springs, even though he knows all along that the ultimate secret of the machine is inscrutable to man. Quite the contrary, man is eminently right in employing his imperfect faculties in discovering whatever of truth he can find. This must be recalled as one reads the following lines, which have the appearance of establishing at least partial anti-intellectualism in Browning. He says that since the ultimate "how" of the machine cannot be learned, "it behoves forget/ How 't is done. . . ." Mrs. Sutherland Orr discovers in this passage evidence of Browning's supposed opposition to science. "What science teaches us," she says, "is made useless by the shortness of human existence; it absorbs all our energy in building up a machine which we shall have no time to work."[49] Her basic misconception is that the machine is a creation of man, to which he devotes attention and energy without reward. The engine is not man's, but God's. It is the cosmos, the divine plan, the watch made by the master watch maker, which man from birth to death must contemplate and study within the limitations set by life, even though the beginning of wisdom is to know that absolute truth can never be man's. Clearly he says that the machine, "this complex

---

48. III, 837-854.
49. *Handbook of the Works of Robert Browning* (5th ed.; London, 1890), pp. 41-42.

gin," is to be set up again in the afterlife for man's further study and greater knowledge. If it were a machine of man's contriving, it would be unlikely to be set up elsewhere. Her second error lies in a failure to understand what he meant by the "how" of the machine. Browning was a good pragmatist who believed that man should attempt the possible and let the impossible alone. The impossible is the "how," the answer that remains after the final veil is ripped asunder and man beholds the white light which he must not gaze upon steadily. Leave to life the business of life, and leave to eternity the business of eternity. Science has its role in life and is good if not misused; but, like Matthew Arnold, Browning knew that science is but a tool in a larger scheme of things. He knew that he would be mistakenly accused of obscurantism, for he imagines his readers "turning upon their heels" in contempt for his principle that science should deal with the matters proper to science.

Browning saw the growth of scientific materialism in his age, the encroachment of physics upon metaphysics, and the threat to man's spirit. Science, which seemed bent upon elevating man, or at least his ductless glands, to the throne of God, was invading an area outside its province; and Browning sought to act as a corrective. Science's main task is to prevent man from being "blind and dumb," to let him see "somewhat of man's state." Ignorance is not a virtue, but neither is it wise or fruitful to postulate too freely on what one is not equipped to understand.

If in *Sordello* Browning set limits to the role of the scientist, he also set them to the function of the artist. For the least creative artists it is given

> . . . to say they so have seen;
> For the better, what it was they saw; the best
> Impart the gift of seeing to the rest:
> "So that I glance," says such an one, "around,
> And there's no face but I can read profound
> Disclosures in; this stands for hope, that—fear,
> And for a speech, a deed in proof, look here!
> 'Stoop, else the strings of blossom, where the nuts

> O'erarch, will blind thee! Said I not? She shuts
> Both eyes this time, so close the hazels meet!
> Thus, prisoned in the Piombi, I repeat
> Events one rove occasioned, o'er and o'er,
> Putting 'twixt me and madness evermore
> Thy sweet shape, Zanze! Therefore stoop!'. . . ."[50]

If one searches too far into forbidden knowledge of the Absolute, his eyes will be scratched out. Love is life's greatest shield against such hubris.

Since life is the business of the living, the world is right in preferring Salinguerra (the general of the Ghibelline cause in the conflict with the Guelf, or Papal cause, which supports the people) to the poet Sordello. Here may be seen the first development of the theme that life is always greater than its arts, which flourish only to subserve it. The General is the man of unreflecting action; Sordello is the poet of reflecting inaction:

> Alack,
> Not so unwisely does the crowd dispense
> On Salinguerras praise in preference
> To the Sordellos: men of action, these!
> Who, seeing just as little as you please,
> Yet turn that little to account,—engage
> With, do not gaze at,—carry on, a stage,
> The work o' the world, not merely make report
> The work existed ere their day! In short,
> When at some future no-time a brave band
> Sees, using what it sees, then shake my hand
> In heaven, my brother![51]

Salinguerra is not a blind activist. He is always on the alert for the practical in life, watching "For men, to read their hearts and thereby catch/ Their capabilities and purposes. . . ." It would be the height of unwisdom to believe that Browning's love of action implies a corresponding anti-rationalism. It is not so much Sordello's paralysis of

---

50. III, 866-878.
51. III, 916-027.

reflection as his selfish desire to exploit mankind that is reprehensible.
He cares only to use his fellows to draw forth himself, as a flint to
steel; but once their function is complete, he scorns them, "Eager for
cause to stand aloof from men. . . ." It is true that to Salinguerra
thoughts are "caprices in the course of deeds," but he is nowhere pictured as a romantic or mystical follower of intuition to the exclusion
of mind.

Rome is the symbol in *Sordello* of man's aspirations, his desire to
build and to know: the visible form of "the scheme to put mankind/
Once more in full possession of their rights," and the struggle between
the Guelfs and Ghibellines is the struggle of man in small. In the
rebuilding of Rome, Browning sees the vision of life. Man desires
the fruits of his labor without the labor. He aspires to perfection by
leaping over the steps leading to it; in short, he would deny life and
gain heaven while yet on earth. Rome was built step by step, brick
by brick, by workmen fit for the task, but not "too fit," for Rome in
all its glory is not of as much importance as the trial of each workman
as he matches his imperfect talents with the day's small tasks:

> Use thy wit!
> The work marched: step by step,—a workman fit
> Took each, nor too fit,—to one task, one time,—
> No leaping o'er the petty to the prime,
> When just the substituting osier lithe,
> For brittle bulrush, sound wood for soft withe,
> To further loam-and-roughcast-work a stage,—
> Exacts an architect, exacts an age:
> No tables of the Mauritanian tree
> For men whose maple log's their luxury!
> That way was Rome built. "Better" (say you) "merge
> At once all workmen in the demiurge,
> All epochs in a lifetime, every task
> In one!"[52]

There is no first or last: each step by however imperfect a workman
is essential to the fulfilment of the divine plan. Rome will never be

52. V, 49-62.

completed, and in this certainty lies the meaning of life, for it is the striving for perfection, not perfection itself, that is essential. Full of these reflections, Sordello hears a voice telling him of his great sin:

> "Sordello, wake!
> God has conceded two sights to a man—
> One, of men's whole work, time's completed plan,
> The other, of the minute's work, man's first
> Step to the plan's completeness: what's dispersed
> Save hope of that supreme step which, descried
> Earliest, was meant still to remain untried
> Only to give you heart to take your own
> Step, and there stay, leaving the rest alone?
> Where is the vanity? Why count as one
> The first step, with the last step? What is gone
> Except Rome's aëry magnificence,
> That last step you'd take first?—an evidence
> You were God: be man now! Let those glances fall!
> The basis, the beginning step of all,
> Which proves you just a man—is that gone too?"[53]

No clearer figure appears in Browning's early works than this important statement of the uses of intellect. Man is divinely commissioned to use his wit, together with all other gifts, in furthering his daily tasks in the restoration of Rome, earth's glory; but he is denied the attainment before the task. He is granted a dim prevision of the completed whole, for in the very imperfections of life may be perceived the perfection of the infinite; but the cardinal command of life is not to play God by attempting to build Rome from the roof down. Lucifer before the fall was of surpassing brilliance, no witless grinning romantic; only through aspiring to Godhead—a misuse of the intellect—did he fall. "Let these glances fall!" means exactly what the comforting angel meant in desolate Eden: "Be lowly wise," in which the last two words are of equal importance. Man must pursue legitimate knowledge, but beware the tree of forbidden knowledge.

---

53. V, 84-99.

Man's job is to build Rome, not to fashion a tower of Babel with which to scale the ramparts of heaven.

The concept of wholeness—the "order" of earlier centuries—is explicit in *Sordello*. As each man's tasks are indispensable to the whole, and each step must be taken before the road ends, so each of man's gifts—body, mind, and spirit—is a part of a whole, as the microcosm is but the macrocosm seen through the wrong end of a telescope. All creation, if properly seen from the perfect perspective which life denies man, is a unity, which wisdom may comprehend by analogy with the world, properly understood, and by flashes of insight when the veil between life and death parts for a fleeting moment. In search for wholeness, man must not reject the parts as lowly or imperfect, just as the poet must accept the possible tasks of the world as essential to the whole of life, and reject the unattainable dreams of working good for man by refusing life's offices. Life must not be handled with tongs. If the world is a realm of sweat and tears, minister to the sweaty and tearful, not by turning over schemes of human restoration within the hygienic isolation of Goito, but by entering into the houses and the hearts of man.

Browning uses Charlemagne as a symbol of strength (the Ghibelline cause) and Hildebrand as a symbol of knowledge (the Guelf, or Papal cause). The former sharpened his "strength by stress of strength"; the latter, "of the huge brain-mask," waged a grim warfare of thought with thought. By using one gift at the expense of the other, neither man was whole. Work knowledge "by stress of Strength":

> Knowledge by stress of merely Knowledge? No—
> E'en were Sordello ready to forego
> His life for this, 't were overleaping work
> Some one has first to do, howe'er it irk,
> Nor stray a foot's breadth from the beaten road.
>
> . . . .
>
>   Much done—and yet
> Doubtless that grandest task God ever set
> On man, left much to do: at his arm's wrench,

> Charlemagne's scaffold fell; but pillars blench
> Merely, start back again—perchance have been
> Taken for buttresses: crash every screen,
> Hammer the tenons better, and engage
> A gang about your work, for the next age
> Or two, of Knowledge, part by Strength and part
> By Knowledge! Then, indeed, perchance may start
> Sordello on his race—would time divulge
> Such secrets![54]

Man's wisdom is to fuse strength and knowledge, for the whole is greater than the sum of its parts taken separately. The image of man's need to keep to the road of life, leading from birth to death, reappears many times in Browning's later works, for hubris he pictured more and more as an illegal shortcut off the King's Highway, which is not merely a limited access road, without branch or fork, but a road with access only at one end and egress at the other.

> If one step's awry, one bulge
> Calls for correction by a step we thought
> Got over long since, why, till that is wrought,
> No progress![55]

Sordello learns that he must renounce Goito, the symbol of his romantic evasion of life, and speed to Ferrara, the symbol of the real world. In a life devoted to the self, a man in "free fancy" may glut his sense and yet write no verses. Dreams must yield to life, and this happens "the moment you descry/ Mankind as half yourself. . . ." Carlyle said much the same thing in *Sartor Resartus*. *Selbsttödung*—annihilation of self—is the first step out of the Everlasting No. When a poet discovers that he is involved in mankind, Sordello finds, then fancy's trade stops forever, for "how may half evade/ The other half? Men are found half of you." Before one concludes that Browning substituted an "intuitional psychology" for mind as man's guide in life, he might recall Sordello's words of bitter

---

54. V, 211-230.
55. V, 230-233.

recrimination for his years wasted in romantic search for the over-
soul at Goito:

> Then a flash of bitter truth:
> So fantasies could break and fritter youth
> That he had long ago lost earnestness,
> Lost will to work, lost power to even express
> The need of working! Earth was turned a grave. . . .[56]

He embraces the Guelf cause—the cause of the people—as an
earnest of his new wisdom that even the finest mind is in no way
"diverse in kind" from other minds, however imperfect or earthy.
Browning, of course, does not mean that minds are equal in capacity
or acumen, for one mind, he says, may climb beyond its fellows,
step by step, " 'by just ascent sublimed.' " The rule of life is to keep
to the road, but there are no speed limits. That Browning entertained
no anti-intellectualism may be seen in his words: " '. . . divest/ Mind
of e'en Thought, and, lo, God's unexpressed/ Will draws above us!' "
How can man understand God's will without mind? Of all men the
artist most needs to be on guard against the sin of pride, but he must
never renounce the intellect. It is his duty to show how the parts
united make for wholeness, in man as well as in the world. He must
show man how the white light of eternity, when

> ". . . thwarted, breaks
> A limpid purity to rainbow flakes,
> Or shadow, massed, freezes to gloom: behold
> How such, with fit assistance to unfold,
> Or obstacles to crush them, disengage
> Their forms, love, hate, hope, fear, peace make, war wage,
> In presence of you all!"[57]

The artist's task—Sordello's task—is to reweave—imperfectly, in accord with life's limitations—the rainbow flakes into a prefiguration of
the white light of God. From this knowledge, he discovers the corollary that as light on earth is broken into its imperfect colors to spare

---

56. V, 363-367.
57. V, 605-611.

man from blindness, so man himself is broken into imperfect pieces which yearn for wholeness; and this too is the job of the artist: to help man toward this goal. His contemplation of the broken light and the poet's duty leads to his resolution to " 'cast external things away/ And natures composite, so decompose/ That' . . ." After these ellipsis dots, which were inserted by Browning, he adds one of the most revealing asides in the poem: "Why, he writes *Sordello!*" The pronoun *he* seems to refer equally to Sordello and to Browning. The meaning is clear that Browning identified himself with his medieval troubadour and thus wrote the long poem to resolve in his own mind the means and the ends of the artist, which are the study of perfection through life's imperfection, through the agency of mind, body, and spirit—the triple soul, although he had not yet enunciated the figure.

Sordello beseeches Salinguerra, the Emperor's General, to forsake the Ghibellines and embrace the democratic cause of the people, but the General is persuaded that Sordello and he together can "break up Hildebrand" (*i.e.,* knowledge, the Guelf cause) and rebuild Charlemagne. Thwarted, Sordello threads his way through a maze of casuistry. Desiring to be faithful to his painfully learned truth, he is still unable to take the final step of open defection from the Ghibellines. He wants to believe but not act upon belief; there is still the old gulf between head and heart which prevents wholeness. Perhaps, he argues, he can best serve mankind by serving his own selfish interests; but he knows that his sophistry is a symptom of his riven soul. Most disturbing of all, in spite of his new vision of the artist's function, he yearns to seize absolute truth by swerving from the only road life permits man to travel, the road of trial and failure and sweat and frustration to the very end. His mind tells him that in life one should "Amass the scintillations, make one star . . ."—a perfect figure for Browning's concept of wholeness. Man's wholeness, he warns, is a unity within the self and between the self and God's will; it is not the pride in self-sufficiency which tempts man to become "a law to his own sphere." Truth must be "veiled/ Helpfully to weak vision. . . ." Otherwise man in his pride of life becomes "drunk with truths

and wine/ Grown bestial, dreaming how become divine." Can truth
be seized and settled forthwith, he asks? Vain, most vain!

> . . . a life to spend ere this he chain
> To the poor crowd's complacence: ere the crowd
> Pronounce it captured, he descries a cloud
> Its kin of twice the plume; which he, in turn,
> If he shall live as many lives, may learn
> How to secure: not else.
>
> .   .   .   .
>   Hence
> Must truth be casual truth, elicited
> In sparks so mean, at intervals dispread
> So rarely, that 't is like at no one time
> Of the world's story has not truth, the prime
> Of truth, the very truth which, loosed, had hurled
> The world's course right, been really in the world
> —Content the while with some mean spark by dint
> Of some chance-blow, the solitary hint
> Of buried fire, which, rip earth's breast, would stream
> Sky-ward![58]

It is of the first importance that this key passage in the poem not
be misunderstood. Browning does not say that truth and wine infallibly make men drunk with aspirations not unlike Lucifer's, nor
that since the truth which man may perceive is "casual" and imperfect man should abandon thought as unprofitable. Browning is
not denigrating the role of the intellect in the slightest by saying that
today's truths are tomorrow's errors. Indeed, his belief seems remarkably open-minded and scientific. The average life of even "scientific
truth," so it is said, is but a paltry twenty years, and no one would
think of accusing a scientist of anti-intellectualism because of his
admission of this surprisingly high infant mortality rate of the mind.
John Stuart Mill, the great rationalist, based his whole belief in freedom of thought on the concept that no "truth," however wide or
old its dissemination, should be immune from examination and re-

---

58. VI, 170-194.

jection if it were found to be error. Mill, unlike Browning, is rarely
called anti-intellectual. How could Browning not believe in perpetual
inquiry into truth, since he believed that man's truth is inevitably
and eternally tinged with falsehood on this side of death? Instead of
shirking the search for truth and throwing over the test of life, he
quite naturally advised man to remain "content the while with some
mean spark" until, through application of mind and soul, the buried
fire will stream skyward.

> . . . for Mankind springs
> Salvation by each hindrance interposed.
> They climb; life's view is not at once disclosed
> To creatures caught up, on the summit left,
> Heaven plain above them, yet of wings bereft:
> But lower laid, as at the mountain's foot.
> So, range on range, the girdling forests shoot
> 'Twixt your plain prospect and the throngs who scale
> Height after height, and pierce mists, veil by veil,
> Heartened with each discovery; in their soul,
> The Whole they seek by Parts—but, found that Whole,
> Could they revert, enjoy past gains? The space
> Of time you judge so meagre to embrace
> The Parts were more than plenty, once attained
> The Whole, to quite exhaust it: naught were gained
> But leave to look—not leave to do: Beneath
> Soon sates the looker—look Above, and Death
> Tempts ere a tithe of Life be tasted. Live
> First, and die soon enough, Sordello![59]

Browning speaks with a clarity that is rare in the tortuous and
obscure *Sordello* when he enunciates, in his own person, his secret
of life: joy comes to man when the proper amount of soul is wreaked
in time on matter; and sorrow comes when the soul attempts to sublime matter beyond the earthly scheme. The great message, then,
is to fit our infinity to the finite and thus to proceed in due degree
forever.

---

59. VI, 274-292.

Sorrow how avoid?
Let the employer match the thing employed,
Fit to the finite his infinity,
And thus proceed forever, in degree
Changed but in kind the same, still limited
To the appointed circumstance and dead
To all beyond.[60]

It is better for man not to meditate too much on God's morning cluster-chord of beauties, if his aim is to explore to its source the mystery of the celestial diapason; for while attempting this impossible task, he will discover that his finger, which was fitted to pluck strings in the mighty orchestra, is palsy-struck. Music is to be enjoyed and made more beautiful, not sifted for its mysteries.

Henry Charles Duffin, in his sympathetic revaluation, *Amphibian, a Reconsideration of Browning,* finds Browning's warning to Sordello perplexing. "Eternity's concern," he says, "may be alien to the soldier, the lawyer, or the stockbroker, but it is surely the very business of the poet."[61] The poet did not mean what Duffin thinks he meant. To say that eternity's concern is not for the poet—or for anyone else on earth, for that matter—is not at all the same as saying that the poet is not to concern himself with eternity. The very business of every man, but most especially the poet, is to do just this; but it is no man's business to seek out the knowledge which eternity hides from man behind the veil of death. This misunderstanding lies at the root of the whole misconception of Browning's supposed theory of nescience.

In the end of the poem, Sordello dies, spurning under foot the badge of office that Salinguerra has given him. He fails through his contempt for life and love. His selfish scorn of mankind and the body, his impatient desire for knowledge and power that are denied man, and, above all, his failure to employ the instrumentalities of body, mind, and soul to achieve wholeness—all these together destroy him.

---

60. VI, 497-503.
61. P. 231.

Browning's first three published works afford no evidence of the poet's distrust of the mind and certainly no hostility toward it. At no point does he state or imply that ignorance in itself is a positive good, any more than some other evil is good. He does not say that because there are certain realms of knowledge proper to the next world alone that man should cultivate ignorance of the things that are proper to this world. Nor does he even suggest that since the intellect always leads man into error, he should rely almost wholly on intuition. Because the mind can never fully separate error from truth, man is challenged from birth till death to climb upward toward truth on the steps of half-truths that are his only means of ascending. To expose man to the white light of absolute truth would be like removing evil and pain and stress from life: life would be without function; or, to put it another way, it would no longer be life: it would be heaven.

CHAPTER IV

BROWNING'S INNOCENTS AND
SUPPOSED INNOCENTS

—Rustic simplicity, uncorrupted youth,
Ignorant virtue!
                              —"The Pope"

E. D. H. Johnson, writing in *The Alien Vision of Victorian Poetry*, discovers that Browning's delineation of uncorrupted and unreflecting innocent characters owes much of its conviction and tenderness to his belief that "the intellectual faculties are self-corrupting," that "he endorsed the unconscious as the true wellspring of being," and that "to Browning . . . flesh and the spirit seemed natural allies against the insidious distortions of the intellect." None of these charges, as I trust I have made clear, is supported by the works of Browning published between 1833 and 1889. As an inevitable corollary, Johnson finds that Browning's innocents, by reason of their dependence on intuition and larval intellects, demonstrate in the simple beauty of their lives the poet's endorsement of Romantic primitivism as the proper way of life for man threatened with the machinations of mind. He notes that in Browning the lovers, artists, and constructive activists are never "primarily" remarkable for powers of intellect. Instead of a triple soul, there is only a dualism in which "fleshly and spiritual well-being are bound up together." The number of persons in Browning's gallery who perceive truth through a flash of inspiration, he notes, and who act instinctively, without reflection to spoil their fine spontaneity, illustrate his exuberant praise of intuitionism and vitalism as guides to right conduct.

No one could seriously doubt that Browning hailed the intuition or heart as a prime source of insight, that he believed in action instead of inaction (even though sin were involved in the action, as in "The Statue and the Bust"), or that the warm heart is preferable to the cold intellect, if a choice must be made between them. In a moment of crisis, the promptings of the intuitions usually have precedence, as we know. Pedestrians who seek to avoid death under the wheels of passing cars through the guidance of syllogistic reasoning are admittedly rare, for they have long since been killed off, while those who leap mightily for safety without pausing to discover the rationale for their act live to leap again. All of this, of course, is not to say that a state of cheerful idiocy is the secret of safe and full living, either on or off the highway. Browning found no antagonism between the flesh and spirit on one side and the mind on the other, prompted by "insidious distortions." Distortions, yes, but not insidious, since man's progress upward to truth is by a stairway of partial truth. It remains to be seen whether Browning's alleged innocents are always blessed with the unfurnished mind and whether, if they are admirable, they are so because of their uncomplicated state.

I

The first of Browning's supposedly simple innocents is Pippa, Pauline being the merest whiff of myth. Pippa is without formal education, of course, but ignorance and stupidity are not to be confused. Far from being an unintellectual child of nature, reacting solely on an intuitive and emotional level, she is perhaps the most cerebral child of eleven years in all of English literature.[1] Her wisdom and ability to reason from facts to logical conclusions are astonishing. Her

---

1. See Margaret E. Glen, "The Meaning and Structure of *Pippa Passes*," *University of Toronto Quarterly*, XXIV, No. 4 (July, 1955), 411: "She is far too often treated more as a fairy than as a human being, because of an undue emphasis upon her lyric outbursts. But her real humanity, as well as her complexity, becomes apparent in her first speech and more especially in her last. Browning's suggestive depiction of Pippa . . . her shrewdness and humour, represents one of the triumphs of his narration."

ecstasy on her holiday need not be interpreted as proof of an over-emotional nature or susceptibility to visions. Her words upon arising at dawn of New Year's Day are full of hardheaded resolution and earnest conviction not to waste a mite of her twelve hours' treasure. I think that few children of eleven years of age would plot their steps and the philosophical purpose of their day with such reasoned care.

If *Pauline, Paracelsus,* and *Sordello* are studies in pride and malaise, *Pippa Passes* is an examination of humility and the workings of the unconscious on man. The protagonists in the three early poems are all spiritually crippled, in their several degrees, and cannot accept life with a conviction of purpose and joy. Little Pippa, a foil to their imperfections, eagerly embraces life and resolves to wring the last drop of experience from each of her twelve hours. She perfectly accepts life's limitations and is aware of the necessity of evil as a test. With sage wisdom uncommon among children, she does not seek pleasure solely on New Year's Day; rather she welcomes equally the tasks, the labor, the "fitful sunshine-minutes," and the intervening shadows that the day may bring. She is a natural spirit, but certainly not unreflecting:

> —My day, if I squander such labor or leisure,
> Then shame fall on Asolo, michief on me![2]

She does not, however, suggest that her holiday might ultimately prove more beneficial if it should bring more pain rather than less. On the contrary, although she recognizes that acceptance of whatever her day brings is the essence of wisdom, she is humanized by her prayer that the day "prove gentle" so that she may gain strength to withstand the sorrows that the new year will bring. She feels that her day may best serve as an earnest of heaven if she will live out in fancy the lives of the four happiest ones in Asolo. She is unaware that each of the four is in crisis, each hesitating at a crossroads, unable to reason out the proper course of action.

---

2. Introduction, 11, 19-20. Cf. Glen, *op. cit.,* p. 414: "But Pippa shows a shrewd power of discrimination when she in fancy chooses her lot," and (p. 424): "Pippa's innocence does not automatically imply helplessness. Her shrewdness becomes apparent. . . ."

Ottima and her paramour, Sebald, are discussing their illicit love and their murder of her husband, whose body lies unburied. Sebald feels the prick of conscience and wishes the deed undone; Ottima seeks to deaden his conscience by plying him with wine, displaying her naked charms, and stirring his concupiscence by recounting their first night of love in imagery remarkable for its sexual storm symbolism, which, unfortunately, is reduced to bathos by one of the lamentable figures in poetry:

> Sebald, as we lay,
> Rising and falling only with our pants. . . .[3]

Her erotic imagery nevertheless works its powerful charm upon him until he is at the point of forgetting his remorse in a resurgence of sexuality:

> Ottima: . . . .
> Crown me your queen, your spirit's arbitress,
> Magnificent in sin. Say that!
> Sebald: I crown you
> My great white queen, my spirit arbitress,
> Magnificent . . .[4]

From without Pippa is heard singing the most controversial lines in Browning:

> The year's at the spring
> And day's at the morn. . . .
> God's in his heaven—
> All's right with the world!

The effects of the song are instantaneous: Sebald intuitively sees his crime and means of expiation illuminated as by a flash of lightning. Neither he nor Pippa fancies the lines to mean that whatever is, is right and sin is but a name. Evil is yet evil, though it may yield fruit of

---

3. I, 207-208.
4. I, 217-220.

good; otherwise Sebald would have found in the words justification of his sins and comfort in pursuing the sin his flesh was incited to. God is in his heaven precisely because the creation is divinely planned, with a balance of evil and good; the voice of Sebald's conscience is stimulated by the happy song to inform his will when the intellect fails, to the end that the test may be completed and justice prevail. The song has proved embarrassing to many Browning lovers, who have been forced to remind the unwary that a little ignorant girl, under the stimulus of her solitary holiday during the year, is uttering such fatuous optimism.

Bennett Weaver believes that Pippa's song is satiric, for it is sung by Pippa "as she passes the Shrub-house of Lucca, where all's wrong with the world," and he adds: "To say that these verses from Pippa's song, which has a special dramatic function, are the epitome of Browning's philosophy is as dull and wrong as to say that Shakespeare's philosophy is summed up in Ophelia's verse, 'Hey non nonny, nonny, hey, nonny.' "[5]

Others, however, affirm that Browning, as well as Pippa, is voicing this Leibnitzian cheerfulness. Properly understood, in the light of Browning's philosophy of the function of evil, the words are as much his as Pippa's, and certainly they are not satiric. Sebald sees the whole divine plan, which is precisely what Pippa's song reveals, and the moral decay in both himself and his mistress is horribly illuminated in the radiant purity of the little girl:

> My God, and she is emptied of it now!
> Outright now!—how miraculously gone
> All of the grace—had she not strange grace once?
> Why, the blank cheek hangs listless as it likes,
> No purpose holds the features up together,
> Only the cloven brow and puckered chin
> Stay in their places: and the very hair,
> That seemed to have a sort of life in it,
> Drops, a dead web![6]

5. "A Primer Study in Browning's Satire," *College English,* XIV, No. 2 (November, 1952), 76-77.
6. I, 239-247.

His reason has failed him, blinded by lust and greed; and another faculty becomes the instrument of truth. He sees beyond the physical with the eye of intuitive perception. To the physical eye Ottima would appear unchanged, but to the inward eye of awakened intuition, she is the visible symbol of moral rottenness. A few lines before the arrival of Pippa, he refers to her "splendid shoulder, both those breasts of yours" in glowing admiration; and while his new perception sees her as hideous, his eye still tells him of her "olive faultless shoulder-blades." Ottima, the voluptuous woman of rounded flesh, and Ottima, the woman of hanging cheeks and pinched chin, are both "true," but there is a truth to which the eye and brain may be blind. The intellect is wholly good—only its abuse is bad—but the intuitive faculty often perceives depths of truths beyond the power of mind, and, to Browning, the faculty which apprehends moral and spiritual truths is the supreme faculty. Sebald, who has all the facts with which to reason his way to repudiation of evil, could not conquer by mind the forces within him working for evil; but with Pippa's words he sees not merely his sin but God's moral plan:

> That little peasant's voice
> Has righted all again. Though I be lost,
> I know which is the better, never fear,
> Of vice or virtue, purity or lust,
> Nature or trick! I see what I have done,
> Entirely now! Oh I am proud to feel
> Such torments—let the world take credit thence—
> I, having done my deed, pay too its price!
> I hate, hate—curse you! God's in his heaven![7]

After stabbing himself, he feels that death first "drowns" his brain, but he still retains the other perceptive faculty:

> My brain is drowned now—quite drowned: all I feel
> Is . . . is, at swift-recurring intervals,
> A hurry-down within me, as of waters

7. I, 261-269.

> Loosened to smother up some ghastly pit:
> There they go—whirls from a black fiery sea![8]

The second scene, like the first, concerns the intuitive apperception of truth through the agency of Pippa's second song. A group of art students are playing a vicious practical joke on Jules, a young French sculptor. Improbably enough, they have through forged love letters tricked him into marriage with an accomplice, a model of imperfect moral development, named Phene. The climax of the monstrous business will come when she undeceives her bridegroom by reading a set speech to him, something

> "To hold Jules long in doubt, yet take his taste
> And lure him on until, at innermost
> Where he seeks sweetness' soul, he may find—this!
> —As in the apple's core, the noisome fly:
> For insects on the rind are seen at once,
> And brushed aside as soon, but this is found
> Only when on the lips or loathing tongue."[9]

When Jules is told of the cruel deception, he reacts as reason dictates, following the way of the world. He flings his gold to her cynically, announcing that he has lost all hope or care or need of it. Vowing to root out the guilty gang and exact justice, he hears the song of Pippa, who is innocent of the tremendous force which for one day she wields in men's lives. He sees in a flash of revelation beneath the visible surface and recognizes the pathos and moral worth of Phene:

> Here is a woman with utter need of me,—
> I find myself queen here, it seems!
>   How strange!
> Look at the woman here with the new soul,
> Like my own Psyche,—fresh upon her lips
> Alit, the visionary butterfly,
> Waiting my word to enter and make bright,
> Or flutter off and leave all blank as first.

---

8. I, 277-281.
9. II, 169-175.

> This body had no soul before, but slept
> Or stirred, was beauteous or ungainly, free
> From taint or foul with stain, as outward things
> Fastened their image on its passiveness:
> Now, it will wake, feel, live—or die again!
> Shall to produce form out of unshaped stuff
> Be Art—and further, to evoke a soul
> From form be nothing? This new soul is mine![10]

This is perhaps the most extreme and memorable example in Browning of the convulsive power of intuition to tear away in one bright moment the veil hiding truth. The intellect, good as it is, could never on this planet discover in a moment of vision the virtue of a common drab whose rudimentary moral sense would permit her to marry an unsuspecting and trusting man out of cruelty. Indeed, the typical reaction to the story is that it is not "reasonable," which is Browning's point in the first place. Jules hears God's voice and sees truth beneath the painted surface of life; his new wisdom makes his course clear: he will sail "to Ancona—Greece—some isle," where he can "begin Art afresh." Life, properly looked at, is art, the supreme art; but it "takes pains to know" what one wants to do with life. Pippa's song gives him the new truth and the splendid vision.

In the third scene, Luigi and his mother, inside the Turret on the hill above Asolo, are discussing Luigi's plan to assassinate the Austrian emperor and so free Italy of the oppressor. The boy, frightened and indecisive, tells his mother of his special qualifications for committing the bloody deed. In reply to his mother's reasonable suspicion that he will be unable to cross the palace threshold, much less get close enough to kill the royal person, Luigi, in a fine enunciation of Browning's philosophy of the imperfect, replies that he would have great trouble had he conspired; but his qualities, especially his imperfections, admirably fit him for the work:

> Every one knows for what his excellence
> Will serve, but no one ever will consider

---

10. II, 285-300.

> For what his worst defect might serve: and yet
> Have you not seen me range our coppice yonder
> In search of a distorted ash?—I find
> The wry spoilt branch a natural perfect bow.
> Fancy the thrice-sage, thrice-precautioned man
> Arriving at the palace on my errand!
> No, no![11]

The implication is not that thought is bad and unrehearsed instinctual action is always good. Luigi, indeed, immediately says that he has thought much about his plan: "I have rehearsed it all/ Inside the turret here a hundred times," but all the same, the pale cast of too much thought can destroy the will and becloud the moral sense. Again Pippa passes, singing her song of a king who lived "In the morning of the world/ When earth was nigher heaven than now," an indication that sapient little Pippa, in her joy, is aware that the world has declined from an earlier golden age when things were a little better than just "all right" with the world. Luigi, like Sebald, is electrified into action by his sudden vision of truth: " 'T is God's voice calls: how could I stay? Farewell!" He leaves to do a deed presumably worth doing and thus unwittingly escapes the police who are closing in on the tower to arrest him.

In the fourth scene, inside the palace by the Duomo, the Monsignor likewise faces a moral crisis in his life. He has connived at the basest of crimes, including the planned murder of Pippa, who as the daughter of his brother stands in the way of the inheritance the man of God lusts after. He has received a letter from Jules, the sculptor who has now turned painter, saying that "He never had a clearly conceived Ideal within his brain till to-day." Since he first took up a chisel, he says that he has imitated the art of others and has attained such dexterity that he foresees certain failure ahead; and therefore, in the light of his new insight, he has renounced the chisel for the brush—the clearest instance in Browning's early works of the doctrine of apparent failure. It is interesting to note Browning's insistence that the new

---

11. III, 96-104.

light which entered the soul of the young sculptor was not a false light. The Monsignor admires the young man who has dared to break the bonds of convention:

> Foolish Jules! and yet, after all, why foolish? He may—probably will—fail egregiously; but if there should arise a new painter, will it not be in some such way, by a poet now, or a musician (spirits who have conceived and perfected an Ideal through some other channel), transferring it to this, and escaping our conventional roads by pure ignorance of them; eh, Ugo? [12]

Browning's belief that ignorance of traditional techniques in art may be the salvation of one's artistic soul was to grow upon him with age.

The resolution of the Monsignor to arrest his fellow conspirator and to face retribution is made at the moment when he hears Pippa, his intended victim, singing:

> *Overhead the tree-tops meet,*
> *Flowers and grass spring 'neath one's feet;*
> *There was naught above me, naught below,*
> *My childhood had not learned to know:*
> *For, what are the voices of birds*
> *—Ay, and of beasts,—but words, our words,*
> *Only so much more sweet?*
> *The knowledge of that with my life begun.*
> *But I had so near made out the sun,*
> *And counted your stars, the seven and one,*
> *Like the fingers of my hand:*
> *Nay, I could all but understand*
> *Wherefore through heaven the white moon ranges;*
> *And just when out of her soft fifty changes*
> *No unfamiliar face might overlook me—*
> *Suddenly God took me.* [13]

Pippa's communion with the birds and the beasts to gain the wisdom of nature is close to the theme of Wordsworth's immortality ode.

---

12. IV, 60-67.
13. IV, 218-233.

Significantly Pippa was born with innate knowledge and even as a child eleven years old she could "all but understand" the significance of creation. The secret of why the moon ranges the vault of heaven and shows man her fifty changes symbolizes the ultimate mysteries that man cannot look steadily upon.

The Monsignor, like the other of the "happiest four," is visited with a revelation upon hearing the song, and orders the arrest of his villainous accomplice.

Little Pippa returns to her chamber at the end of the day, tired and emotionally wrung from her long day of "fooling." She wonders whether in some way she might ever approach the happiest four "so as to touch them," never suspecting that for one day she has been God's emissary in Asolo.

On the surface Pippa may seem to be childhood innocence and perfection, untroubled by sickly intellectuality, informed by an intuition uncorrupted by the sordid world, a sunny and joyous natural being who is unaware of the pain and suffering that encompass her about, as her first song may seem to suggest. This interpretation is imperfectly supported by the evidence, for if life has taught her anything it is the prevalence of pain, sadness, weariness, and suffering—those realities with which she lives all the year. It is significant that on her holiday she wants to project herself out of her body and to live other lives, for to live one more day as Pippa, with her memories of the drudgery behind her and the desolation that lies before her, is insupportable. Another possible view is that she knows the world to be dark with evil, but that she refuses to think of such reality on her one day of freedom; at all costs she will pretend that God is where he should be and all is therefore well—in short, tomorrow she will repudiate the song as she wearily winds silk. Yet a third interpretation—that she is voicing Browning's philosophical rationale for evil—may appear untenable on the grounds that such an ignorant and uninformed girl would be unable to arrive at Browning's philosophy. But Pippa is a young girl only in body; she perfectly understands the divine uses of evil and the import of her words would not escape her whatever the day. She is most mature and observant, as is everywhere apparent: her remarks upon the nature of sexual love ("Lovers grow cold, men learn to hate their wives. . ."), mother love (Luigi and his mother "talk/ Calmer than lovers, yet more kind than friends"), and God's love ("God's puppets, best and worst,/ Are we; there is no last nor first") are alarmingly percipient for a girl of eleven. Her wise, tolerant views of human nature are not unworthy of comparison with the most mature reflections of the Pope in passing sentence on Guido.

Pippa may be taken as the type of wholeness possible in life. She is limited in all three faculties: body, mind, and spirit, as all men are; but all three function together. Her single day is an example of what life might be if man achieved oneness with self and God. She is an almost perfect being, not because she is ignorant, but because she is whole. Browning uses the four separate scenes to illustrate the wisdom of her famous song and the communion with truth possible to one whose triple soul is not fissured. At the end of her tiring day she is granted no flash of revelation into the extent of her influence in the lives of the four. Rather she is humanized by weariness and a vague sense of discouragement as she wonders whether she might touch their lives.

II

Brother Lawrence in the "Soliloquy of the Spanish Cloister" is one of Browning's most engaging, if hastily sketched, innocents. It is impossible to speculate with profit upon the uses and development of his mind, other than to observe that his sweet simplicity is striking evidence of the wholeness of his soul. It is to strain the sense of the lines to find him vacuous, nourished by sense and revelation alone, and properly illustrating the principle that to be good one must be ignorant or simple. Furthermore, in passing, one might observe that the sadism of his brother monk, who surely has the smallest soul in villaindom, does not afford clearer evidence of the dangers of intellectuality than do the planned machinations of Shylock.

The last duchess of the proud duke in Ferrara is Browning's most famous innocent.[14] We can know little about the poor duchess, of course, except by reflection from the personality of the duke. Her naïve acceptance of the obvious flattery of Frá Pandolf, who calls the blush to her cheeks as much for perverse sexual pleasure as for art, is hardly to be construed as a revelation of the poverty of her intellect. Perhaps she was aware of the imperious decree of her husband that the painter finish the portrait in a single day as a means of occupying hands suspected of dexterity in the art of love as well as of painting. If this surmise is correct, her blush might be appropriate to a much more worldly woman than she is. Her heart was too easily impressed and too soon made glad, the duke feels, for he is the type of heartless calculation who despises the signs of common humanity in others. Like another duchess in Browning, also an innocent, she doubtless felt a kinship with creation and its divine plan:

> You know God Almighty granted
> Such little signs should serve wild creatures
> To tell one another all their desires,
> So that each knows what his friend requires,
> And does its bidding without teachers.[15]

"The Boy and the Angel" illustrates God's love of his simple, natural children like Theocrite, who sing "the little human praise" which God loves. Theocrite is one whose heart is clearly the guiding instrument, who sings his love of God from instinctual promptings. He is cheerful beyond the common lot of mortal flesh, content to live either on earth or on the sun, so long as it is God's will. He is no stranger to angelic visitations, and he dreams dreams. He is, in fine, as fully instinctual as any of Browning's creations, so far as the evidence permits of conclusion; but God loves him for his love and praise, not for his undeveloped mind. Both Robert Browning and his God love a gentle and worshipful heart and loathe a cunning, contriving head. Similarly the man of faith, oppressed cruelly by

---

14. For a balanced and judicious interpretation of the poem, see B. R. Jerman's "Browning's Witless Duke," *PMLA*, LXXII (June, 1957), 488-493.

15. *The Flight of the Duchess*, ll. 727-730.

the tyrant in "Instans Tyrannus," is clad in the triple brass of faith
and love which puts him beyond the infamous powers of the king;
but the mark of his character is obscurity, "minuteness, to wit," not
untutored, unreflecting intuition.

The fugitive Italian in England puts his whole faith and fate into
the hands of a woman because

> . . . I saw that woman's face,
> Its calm simplicity of grace,
> Our Italy's own attitude
> In which she walked thus far, and stood,
> Planting each naked foot so firm,
> To crush the snake and spare the worm—
> At first sight of her eyes, I said,
> "I am that man upon whose head
> They fix the price, because I hate
> The Austrians over us. . . ."[16]

That his faith is well placed is, presumably, evidence that women
who dare to crush snakes with their bare feet are built of heroic
stuff and are to be trusted by those running for their lives; but we
are not told whether his decision was a suprarational reflex or whether
the experiences of his lifetime, thoroughly sifted by the mind, came
into play. Certainly one cannot pronounce with finality that he acted
by intuition alone any more than one can tell that the brave woman
nursed a lifelong grudge against all cerebral effort whatever. Ever
since the Romantic conception of the noble savage, there has been
a tendency to associate goodness, cheer, and trust with primitive
types, the poor, and the uneducated. In attributing virtue to the rich
and cultivated, Dickens, as is everywhere attested, found much the
same difficulty as the scriptures assure us camels find in passing
through the eyes of needles. But Browning, who was no primitivist,
loved goodness because it was good, not because it was uniformed,
and he recognized evil whatever its dress.

The dying man in "Confessions" perhaps may not properly be

---

16. Ll. 57-66.

numbered among the true innocents in Browning, except as he places reliance on the impulses of the heart as a sure guide to conduct. The father confessor, dutifully seeking to wring from the dying man a confession that the world is a vale of tears, is shocked, we assume, by the spirited account of the illicit love affair "By the rim of the bottle labelled 'Ether.'" Intellectually the dying man knows that it was "bad and mad," but his heart informs him "how it was sweet." There can be no doubt that Browning regarded this love as the supreme moment in the man's life—good then, now, and forever, whatever the disapproval of the priest or the intellect; for no one seriously questions that all of his philosophy, from first to last, is in a sense a subhead of love.

III

In *Balaustion's Adventure,* the young Rhodian girl, whom Douglas Bush properly identifies as "Ba," Browning's affectionate name for his wife, is one of the most admirable and fresh in all the gallery of girls the poet left us: intelligent, poetic, resourceful—the antithesis of the ignorant primitive.[17] Balaustion, living during the second phase of the Peloponnesian War, sets sail from Rhodes to Athens, after the defeat of the Athenian fleet at Syracuse. Rhodes, resenting the defeat, has defected to the side of the Peloponnesian League against Athens, but Balaustion remains loyal to her mother city. Pursued by a pirate ship, her vessel makes for the nearest port—the rowers exhorted to greater efforts by the song of the valiant girl—and she finds that it has sought safety in the hostile port of Syracuse. They are about to be denied sanctuary, when the Syracusans, who have watched the pursuit across the waters, remark upon the "veritable" Aeschylus they heard inspiriting the rowers. They ask whether she knows any verses of "the newer and not so famous Euripides." She not only knows

17. See Hoxie N. Fairchild, "Browning's Pomegranate Heart," *Modern Language Notes,* LXVI, No. 4 (April, 1951), 266: "It is universally accepted that Balaustion, delightful champion of 'Euripides the human,' is none other than Elizabeth."

some verses from the newer bard; she is prepared to recite from memory, from first to last, that "strangest, sweetest song," the *Alcestis*. Her intelligence and taste in poetry are attested by the fact that the play came to her island only within the year. If one recalls Browning's love for Euripides, he is compelled to accept her love for the Greek tragedian as an index to her character and intelligence. Euripides, a favorite also of E. B. B., was of all the Greek dramatists the most intellectual, realistic, and fearless critic of contemporary opinions and morals. Like Browning, he was a psychologist of souls, searching the motives and hearts and minds of men—in short, he was, as Bush remarks, "an Athenian Browning." It is not sufficiently remembered from time to time that Browning's admiration for the intellectual searcher of souls is incompatible with an assumption that the poet admired the naïve, unreflecting singer of happy songs who parades an arrested mentality. Ranking with Pippa and Pompilia as admirable females, Balaustion shares Browning's views precisely:

> I soon was at the tragic house, and saw
> The master, held the sacred hand of him
> And laid it to my lips. Men love him not:
> How should they? Nor do they much love his friend
> Sokrates: but those two have fellowship:
> Sokrates often comes to hear him read,
> And never misses if he teach a piece.
> Both, being old, will soon have company,
> Sit with their peers above the talk. Meantime,
> He lives as should a statue in its niche;
> Cold walls enclose him, mostly darkness there,
> Alone, unless some foreigner uncouth
> Breaks in, sits, stares an hour, and so departs,
> Brain-stuffed with something to sustain his life,
> Dry to the marrow 'mid much merchandise.[18]

Her percipient admiration of Socrates and Euripides, the intellectual critics of Athenian mores, is matched by her mature insight into the function and nature of poetry:

---

18. Ll. 289-303.

What's poetry except a power that makes?
And, speaking to one sense, inspires the rest,
Pressing them all into its service; so
That who sees painting, seems to hear as well
The speech that's proper for the painted mouth;
And who hears music, feels his solitude
Peopled at once—for how count heart-beats plain
Unless a company, with hearts which beat,
Come close to the musician, seen or no?[19]

Her tribute to the role of poetry, "that brave/ Bounty of poets, the one royal race . . . ," marks her as uncommonly sensitive and intelligent. Poetry is the language of wholeness, for it evokes all of man's senses at once, as it leads man to see "Deeper into the seeming dark of things." In Balaustion there is no hint of obscurantist distrust of mind.

Pompilia is widely considered to be Browning's supreme triumph in characterization of the artless, natural spirit of womanhood. She is quite illiterate, innocent as Pippa: pure soul and song in a world crowded with evil. It has followed naturally that her beauty and charm have been alleged to stem directly from her diminished mind and fully developed intuition, and the further corollary has been urged that Browning intends for us to believe that the unfurnished intellect is a condition of right thinking and noble feeling.[20] It is forgotten that Pompilia's speech is a masterpiece of both mind and spirit working in harmony in a reading of life that reveals a depth of wisdom granted only to the dying. It may be objected that her ratiocinative philosophy is not "really" hers, but Browning's, for she could not have spoken so well in full health, and certainly not under the disability of twenty-two wounds from a hook-edged Genoese dagger. The objection to her eloquence in the final extremity of pain is well taken and may be explained only through artistic license or dramatic necessity. Operatic arias demanding full resources of power

19. Ll. 318-326.
20. See E. D. H. Johnson's interpretation of the dangers of the intellect in *The Alien Vision of Victorian Poetry.*

and control are regularly written for sopranos supposedly dying of tuberculosis, and the applause for the achievement of a ringing high *C* is undiminished because of the infrequency of such evidence of vigor in terminal cases. Pompilia's words must be understood to be hers as fully as Guido's are Guido's. Her personality shines through every word, lifting it above mere "gray argument" in its luminous sincerity. She is no undeveloped primitive. In her unsuccessful appeal to the cynical archbishop, she corrects his assumption that she is ignorant of a wife's duties: "I am not ignorant,—know what I say. . . ." She is unaware of many things, but, being whole, she is wise and clear eyed, the perfect woman clad in the shining whiteness of virtue.

Browning's appraisal of primitivism may safely be adduced from Guido's description of himself as a primitive religionist:

> I think I never was at any time
> A Christian, as you nickname all the world,
> Me among others: truce to nonsense now!
> Name me, a primitive religionist—
> As should the aboriginary be
> I boast myself, Etruscan, Aretine,
> One sprung,—your frigid Virgil's fieriest word,—
> From fauns and nymphs, trunks and the heart of oak,
> With,—for a visible divinity,—
> The portent of a Jove Aegiochus
> Descried 'mid clouds, lightning and thunder, couched
> On topmost crag of your Capitoline. . . .[21]

Guido shares almost precisely the beliefs of Caliban, another primitive, on the nature of the deity. He says:

> Why should we do our duty past the need?
> When the sky darkens, Jove is wroth,—say prayer!
> When the sun shines and Jove is glad,—sing psalm![22]

Browning's view of the natural man and his likely lines of un-

---

21. XI, 1910-1921.
22. XI, 1946-1948.

savory development may be seen when the Pope sadly reflects upon the easy corruptibility of the four innocent rustics whom Guido seduced into complicity in the slaughter:

> 'T is done:
> Wherefore should mind misgive, heart hesitate?
> He calls to counsel, fashions certain four
> Colorless natures counted clean till now,
> —Rustic simplicity, uncorrupted youth,
> Ignorant virtue! Here's the gold o' the prime
> When Saturn ruled, shall shock our leaden day—
> The clown abash the courtier! Mark it, bards!
> The courtier tries his hand on clownship here,
> Speaks a word, names a crime, appoints a price,—
> Just breathes on what, suffused with all himself,
> Is red-hot henceforth past distinction now
> I' the common glow of hell.[23]

The Pope is no Wordsworth defending the incorruptibility of rustics, preserved against the seductions of evil by the double shield of poverty and ignorance.

Perhaps the most direct evidence that Browning, unlike Matthew Arnold, nursed no lifelong yearning for a return to an earlier time when in the morning of man's day he might live instinctively in unreflecting joy is seen in the "Parleyings with Girard de Lairesse," in which, as has been noted, he counseled the painter to eschew Greek myths and accept the modern world. By the law of life everything today must be better than formerly, for growth makes life meaningful. To believe that he made an exception of primitive barbarians is to ignore one of his basic beliefs. The first and last time that Browning seemed to counsel romantic flight to the forest of primitivism and irresponsible repudiation of life appears in the conclusion of *Pauline,* a poem which plagued him with embarrassment for the rest of his life. Jules in *Pippa Passes* hopes to fly to a Greek island, it is true, but there he intends to find clay with which to work and develop, not an escape to a forest of Arden.

---

23. X, 772-783.

CHAPTER V

BROWNING'S INTUITIONAL PSYCHOLOGY

"It had to be:
I could no other: God it was, bade 'Act for me!' "
—*I。。。

—Ivàn Ivànovitch

A commonplace of criticism is that as Browning degraded the intellect he placed ever greater faith in the intuition as a mystical guide to knowledge and conduct. As Browning grew older, E. D. H. Johnson discovers, he relied more and more on "intuitional psychology," or flashes of truth wholly short-circuiting the mind. It will prove interesting to examine more fully Browning's reliance on intuition to see whether it follows that one must make a choice between intuition and intellect, or whether they are inherently antagonistic. As has been noted earlier, the sudden moment of intuitive certitude is one of the frequent occurrences in Browning's poetry which have led his most responsible critics to conclude that he believed the brain is so unreliable that it is best by-passed if a vital decision is demanded.

The rider in "Through the Metidja to Abd-el-Kadr" is one of Browning's most complete mystics, mesmerized by the galloping of the horse and visited by visions in profusion. As he rides madly to join his adored chief, he sees witnesses and cohorts in the vast desert and hears heavenly voices. He is a man possessed, reality having quite disappeared behind the fantastic visions and the voices. His state is comparable to only one other in Browning: that of David after the great revelation, as he staggers home through the night filled with the new life. Both men are in trance-like states of ecstasy, in which the barrier between life and death is pierced by the overheated fancy.

The experience of David, however, one is confident, is no delusion and has whatever validity such an experience affords. But it seems equally certain that the experience of the visionary rider borders on dementia. I doubt that Browning had a more settled conviction of what constitutes the boundary between reality and vision than did Keats when the word "Forlorn!" called him back from one of the most notable suprasensory experiences in English poetry.

That Browning was no stranger to such experiences may be gathered from the famous scene in *The Ring and the Book* in which he describes his discovery of the "Old Yellow Book" in Florence:

> . . . when a Hand,
> Always above my shoulder, pushed me once,
> One day still fierce 'mid many a day struck calm,
> Across a Square in Florence, crammed with booths. . . .[1]

The interesting assertion that he was always conscious of God's hand above his shoulder is doubtless not to be taken literally, but it is significant nevertheless. Early in his correspondence with Elizabeth Barrett, April 16, 1845, he promised that "One of these days I shall describe a country I have seen in my soul only, fruits, flowers, birds and all." Whether this country is the mystical land revealed only to the psyche or whether it is merely the imaginative land created by a poet applying his craft with mind and spirit, no one can tell. What is remarkable about these letters is the almost total absence of anything that could be construed as mystical. She, on the other hand, has far more expressions of reliance upon intuition than he does:

> Surely I believe in you and in 'mysteries.' Surely I prefer the no-reason to ever so much rationalism . . . (rationalism and infidelity go together they say!).[2]

> Well—and do you know that I have, for the last few years, taken quite to despise book-knowledge and its effect on the mind—I mean when

1. I, 39-42.
2. *Letters*, I, 348.

people *live by it* as most readers by profession do, . . . cloistering their souls under these roofs made with heads, when they might be under the sky. Such people grow dark and narrow and low, with all their pains.[3]

It will be clear that her objection to rationalism is more apparent than real. Like Browning, she objects to the stultifying of souls by mind, not to mind itself. Indeed, her basically rationalistic spirit is seen in her letter about her father: "The bitterest 'fact' of all is, that I had believed Papa to have loved me more than he obviously does: but I never regret knowledge . . . I mean I would never *un*know anything . . . even were it the taste of the apples by the Dead Sea— . . . ." It is small wonder that Browning found much in common between himself and the enchanting invalid, for her words are almost precisely the words that he might have written. He too never regretted knowledge, for life and its meaning were his meat and drink.

The rejected suitor in "Cristina" experiences by elective affinities the revelation of love as the young queen looks at him. He is aware that such love at first sight is supremely binding, though no word is uttered to solemnize the union, and he assumes that she too should have recognized the contractual nature of the look she gave him. Like Browning, he knows that the dark of life is fitfully lit by flashes of truth:

> Oh, we're sunk enough here, God knows!
> But not quite so sunk that moments,
> Sure tho' seldom, are denied us,
> When the spirit's true endowments
> Stand out plainly from its false ones,
> And apprise it if pursuing
> Or the right way or the wrong way,
> To its triumph or undoing.
>
> There are flashes struck from midnights,
> There are fire-flames noondays kindle,
> Whereby piled-up honors perish,
> Whereby swollen ambitions dwindle,

---

3. *Ibid.*, I, 172.

> While just this or that poor impulse,
> Which for once had play unstifled,
> Seems the sole work of a life-time
> That away the rest have trifled.[4]

Cristina is one of the many who miss their infinite moments; such a soul, Browning says, "loses what it lived for." Perhaps she felt the flash of revelation, but

> The world's honors, in derision,
> Trampled out the light forever:
> Never fear but there's provision
> Of the devil's to quench knowledge
> Lest we walk the earth in rapture![5]

Here knowledge is primarily what is gleaned in moments of mystical insight, but it is also knowledge of our infinite purpose, however gained, by head or by heart.

Perhaps the most beautiful instance in Browning of the insight into truth by channels other than intellect is in "A Toccata of Galuppi's," one of the poetical triumphs of the world. The scientist in England hears the music of Galuppi and suddenly is aware that his soul or imaginative life has been atrophied through disuse. He has lived on the level of mind so long that as the music speaks to him, he becomes profoundly disturbed, for the notes tell him of the warmth, frivolity, and love of old Venice—a whole world alien to his life and thinking. His vision of young love in May on the Grand Canal is at first shocking to his severe sensibilities, and he feels that he must chide the lovers for their butterfly lives. But as the music plays on he becomes less sure that his world of the mind is not incomplete and sterile:

> But when I sit down to reason, think to take my
>   stand nor swerve,
> While I triumph o'er a secret wrung from nature's
>   close reserve,

---

4. Ll. 17-32
5. Ll. 50-54

> In you come with your cold music till I creep
> through every nerve.[6]

His dormant emotional life glows into fire at the end when he thinks of the "dear dead women, with such hair, too. . . ." It is important to recognize that the failure of the scientist is not that he has used his mind, but that he has abused it. He has become a logic-chopping machine, without capacity to love or feel, and the visions the music brings into his newly awakened soul do not tell him of the evils of mind, but rather of the sins of partial development.

An example of the power of love to communicate is seen in "By the Fire-side," one of the world's great love poems. By an effort of mind that breaks the bonds of the "flesh-stuff," the lovers are perfectly aware of each other's thoughts:

> When, if I think but deep enough,
> You are wont to answer, prompt as rhyme;
> And you, too, find without rebuff
> Response your soul seeks many a time
> Piercing its fine flesh-stuff.[7]

The mind, operating with soul, effects thought transference between lovers to achieve a wholeness between two souls, an extension of Browning's concept of wholeness within the soul:

> Think, when our one soul understands
> The great Word which makes all things new,
> When earth breaks up and heaven expands,
> How will the change strike me and you
> In the house not made with hands?[8]

"New depths of the divine" can be seen if "brain prompt mine." The power of love, being at its best wholeness of souls and wholeness between two souls, gives mystical insight into creation:

---

6. Ll. 30-32.
7. Ll. 116-120.
8. Ll. 131-135.

> . . . hands unseen
> Were hanging the night around us fast;
> But we knew that a bar was broken between
> Life and life: we were mixed at last
> In spite of the mortal screen.
>
> The forests had done it; there they stood
> We caught for a moment the powers at play:
> They had mingled us so, for once and good,
> Their work was done—we might go or stay,
> They relapsed to their ancient mood.[9]

Mystical insight beyond the capacity of the mind is attributed to love between two unified souls; but the most remarkable characteristic of this poem is not its mystical intensity but its consistently intellectual detachment. The emotion is carefully concealed behind the extended metaphysical conceit of his poring over "a great wise book" —the symbol of his love—as in old age he sits in reminiscence before the fire. The ingenious subtlety of the image is only adumbrated at first; we are told that it beseems age to read the wise book, for Greek opens a vista far and wide, "And I pass out where it ends." Love leads to a widening of perceptions, at the end of which is eternity. The intellectual symbolism is made quite clear only in the last lines of the final stanza:

> So, earth has gained by one man the more,
> And the gain of earth must be heaven's gain too;
> And the whole is well worth thinking o'er
> When autumn comes: which I mean to do
> One day, as I said before.

"The Statue and the Bust" is one of the poems cited with regularity as evidence of the sinister powers of mind to inhibit the intuitive heart. At the moment of elective affinities, the bride and the Great-Duke Ferdinand fall in love by a sudden flash of insight. The effects of

---

9. Ll. 231-240.

instant love are indeed a tonic. The Duke, heretofore an empty sheath of a man, becomes "straightway brave and wise." The lady, dressing for her wedding, "looked at him, as one who awakes;/ The past was a sleep, and her life began." No one can doubt from the context either of the poem or of all the poet's works that their intuitive love is the white light, which they unfortunately do not heed. Their resolutions to defy the world and elope come from the heart and are right; their procrastination is wrong. Their irresolution is offered in evidence of the evils of reflection, but the theme of the poem is clearly not the evils of mind but the evil of refusing to play the game of life. To Browning the supreme sin is to evade life, to refuse to take the test that alone gives earth purpose. Browning, it is clear, would have regarded as the saddest of all obituaries the jingle:

> He led a quiet, blameless life;
> For him death had no terrors.
> St. Peter wrote upon his score:
> No runs, no hits, no errors.

It is true that the bride temporizes and rationalizes away her resolution to put on the coat of a page and escape with her lover; but Browning emphasizes her infirm faith—"the unlit lamp and the ungirt loin." If one fails to follow the promptings of the heart because of their failure to compel action, it seems strange to urge the failure as proof of the enervating effects of the intellect. The sin committed by both the lady and the Duke is the sin of being fragmentary: body, mind, and soul are in conflict.

Joseph E. Baker, however, interprets the poem to mean very candidly that "the force of Original Sin is not to be resisted but obeyed." The intellect, because it tends to stimulate reflections upon the consequences of sin, is inhibitory and thus evil. Browning, he believes, steadily held this interesting ethical code of misconduct. Baker affirms that Browning "gave his public what so many of them wanted: he used religious phrases to justify an indulgent complacency toward evil that, in the Bible, had been censured by all the prophets; and he claimed all the promises of Christianity without the rigors of the ancient creed."[10] This judgment is on all fours with the bracing notion that St. Paul advocated adultery.

Two poems that are important in the study of Browning's attitude toward intuition are those remarkable studies in psychic disorder "Johannes Agricola in Meditation" and "Porphyria's Lover." Both poems offer the clearest kind of evidence that Browning placed no implicit faith in the certain trustworthiness of intuition as opposed to mind. Johannes Agricola (1494-1566), a founder of the Antinomian heresy, believed that a Christian under the new dispensation was absolved of responsibility which prevailed under the Mosaic law and hence could not be guilty of sin, however heinous his acts might be. Only the unregenerate, who still were under the stern moral code, could sin. In the *Monthly Repository* Browning prefaced the poem with an explanatory note:

> Antinomians, so denominated for rejecting the Law as a thing of no use under the Gospel dispensation: they say, that good works do not further, nor evil works hinder salvation; that the child of God cannot sin, that God never chastiseth him, that murder, drunkenness, etc. are sins in the wicked but not in him, that the child of grace being once assured of salvation, afterwards never doubteth . . . that God doth not love any man for his holiness, that sanctification is no evidence of justification, etc. Potanus, in his Catalogue of Heresies, says John Agricola was the author of this sect, A.D. 1535.—*Dictionary of all Religions,* 1704.[11]

Antinomianism, akin as it was to Calvinism in its belief in election, was repugnant to Browning, because its bigotry and cruelty struck directly at the root of his belief in the function of life. If life is a test, it must be a test for all alike, with no special privilege for a few; and no process of thought or intuition could reconcile a contrary scheme of things with a moral creator. Johannes illustrates the dangers of sole reliance on intuition. He has the firmest inner con-

---

10. "Religious Implications in Browning's Poetry," *op. cit.,* pp. 443-452.
11. Quoted in DeVane, *A Browning Handbook,* p. 112.

viction that he cannot sin; indeed, his unreflecting bigotry is the mark of his madness. He entertains no doubt that he can blend all sins together and gulp them down in absolute safety, for the dispensation under which he lives will convert "The draught to blossoming gladness fast." To Browning he is not an inspired mystic, seeing with special powers into truth; he is a madman, vicious and detestable in his egotism:

> There's heaven above, and night by night
> I look right through its gorgeous roof;
> No suns and moons though e'er so bright
> Avail to stop me; splendor-proof
> I keep the broods of stars aloof. . . .[12]

Perhaps the most repellent of Johnnes's beliefs, which was shared by St. Thomas Aquinas, is that among the beatific pleasures awaiting the saved in heaven are the fierce joys of watching in comfort the damned eternally writhing in their fiery torment:

> I gaze below on hell's fierce bed,
> And those its waves of flame oppress,
> Swarming in ghastly wretchedness. . . .[13]

One wonders whether Johannes does not share the dubious distinction of the Pardoner in Chaucer: the one damned soul in the lot.

"Porphyria's Lover," a companion study of aberration, shows the workings of a diseased imagination and the tragic effects of obeying without question the dictates of the inner voice. Maddened by the weakness and indecision of Porphyria, the young man suddenly "knows" that she really loves him and wants him to protract her moment of strength and resolution eternally in death. As if he has heard the direct command of God, he finds "a thing to do," and without the least remorse or qualm he strangles her with her hair to preserve for eternity a moment of beauty and truth/In his madness

---

12. Ll. 1-5.
13. Ll. 43-45.

he is sure that she is now happy, her doubts and vacillation put behind her:

> The smiling rosy little head,
> So glad it has its utmost will,
> That all it scorned at once is fled,
> And I, its love, am gained instead![14]

The concluding lines, in which the murderer relates how he has been sitting all night with the dead body drooping on his shoulder, while he awaits a word from God, may be introduced as evidence that Browning held little belief in the unfailing truth of intuitive insight.

Similarly I vàn Ivànovitch, after beheading Dmitri's wife, calmly cites the expressed will of God as justification for his act:

> "It had to be:
> I could no other: God it was, bade 'Act for me!' "[15]

"Abt Vogler" is one of Browning's most successful poems on the intuitive process, operating under the influence of music. Under the spell of music, man receives a vision of God's plan and attains a conviction of unity with creation:

> Novel splendors burst forth, grew familiar and dwelt with mine,
> Not a point nor peak but found and fixed its wandering star;
> Meteor-moons, balls of blaze: and they did not pale nor pine,
> For earth had attained to heaven, there was no more near nor far.[16]

Nor is the vision of the plan and sense of union all: the intuitive revelation of music evokes visions of those "who walked in the glare and glow,/ Presences plain in the place. . ." and of the dead and those yet unborn.

Even more important than Abt Vogler's intuitive vision into truth is his instinctive apperception of the limitation that denies man steady

---

14. Ll. 52-55.
15. "Ivan Ivanovich," ll. 255-256.
16. Ll. 29-32.

vision of the whole truth, which would destroy the wonder of becoming, "the process so wonder-worth." He knows that such fitful
glimpses into the Absolute are permitted only in Platonic moments
when the dome of many-colored glass is briefly riven. It is man's
task to take these moments of partial vision, these notes of music,
each of which in itself is nought, and "out of three sounds" to make
"not a fourth sound, but a star." Each glimpse of truth is to be used
by the whole person: "I mix it with two in my thought. . . ." Even
in such an ecstatic moment, mind has its role to play.

The poem "Tray" includes one of Browning's clearest contrasts
between the heartless intellect and the warm instinctual nature. Three
bards recite their stories of heroism, the first two stories concerning
stock accounts of chivalric valor, the third being a story of a beggar
child who falls off a quay into the stream:

> "Bystanders reason, think of wives
> And children ere they risk their lives.
> Over the balustrade has bounced
> A mere instinctive dog, and pounced
> Plumb on the prize. 'How well he dives!' "[17]

The dog rescues the child and plunges in again to retrieve the child's
doll. While the dog is yet in the water the onlookers are more inter-
ested in observing the motives and instincts of the animal than they
are in the plight of the child or of its frantic mother:

> " 'How strange we saw no other fall!
> It's instinct in the animal.
>
> . . . .
>
> " 'Here he comes, holds in mouth this time
> —What may the thing be? Well, that's prime!
> Now, did you ever? Reason reigns
> In man alone, since all Tray's pains
> Have fished—the child's doll from the slime!' "[18]

---

17. Ll. 16-20.
18. Ll. 26-35.

The final irony occurs when a scientist, alive in mind but dead in spirit, yearns to dissect the noble creature's brain as a contribution to knowledge of the soul:

> "And so, amid the laughter gay,
> Trotted my hero off,—old Tray,
> Till somebody, prerogatived
> With reason, reasoned: 'Why he dived,
> His brain would show us, I should say.
>
> " 'John, go and catch—or, if needs be,
> Purchase—that animal for me!
> By vivisection, at expense
> Of half-an-hour and eighteenpence,
> How brain secretes dog's soul, we'll see!' "[19]

The heartless scientist, "prerogatived with reason," reasons his way to villainy, but who would conclude that he does so because he is intelligent? Browning shows open scorn of the man whom God has given the gift of intellect and who uses it without heart to injure a selfless and loving dog. The depth of his scorn may be surmised from the statement he once made against vivisection: "I would rather submit to the worst of deaths, so far as pain goes, than have a single dog or cat tortured on the pretense of sparing me a twinge or two."[20] His hatred of vivisection reflects an aversion to heartlessness, not to intelligence; and similarly his loathing of the scientist in "Tray" cannot be taken as evidence of his opposition to science. For right reason, as Milton understood the term, Browning had nothing but praise—ever.

An interesting parallel between the gullibility of mind and intuition is described in the "Parleyings with George Bubb Dodington." Intuitions are not always the direct word of God, however convinced one may be of their authenticity and reliability. Man has infinite capacity for error, if not for truth; and this is the weakness that a

---

19. Ll. 36-45.

20. *The Poems and Plays of Robert Browning* (The Modern Library: New York, 1934), p. 1064.

shrewd and unscrupulous politician like Disraeli uses to seize and hold power over men. Originally rule began with strength alone, Browning observes to Dodington; later strength gave way to deception and lies. But now people are so skilled in "lies of superior fashion" that they detect dishonesty altogether too readily. The last and best stratagem to awe the populace is the use of the supernatural:

> Well,
> The last expedient, which must needs excel
> Those old ones—this it is,—at any rate
> To-day's conception thus I formulate:
> As simple force has been replaced, just so
> Must simple wit be: men have got to know
> Such wit as what you boast is nowise held
> The wonder once it was, but, paralleled
> Too plentifully, counts not. . . .[21]

In short, the formula for the modern politician is to go beyond flesh and mind to the supernatural:

> "Perpend
> My key to domination! Who would use
> Man for his pleasure needs must introduce
> The element that awes Man. Once for all,
> His nature owns a Supernatural
> In fact as well as phrase—which found must be
> —Where, in this doubting age? Old mystery
> Has served its turn—seen through and sent adrift
> To nothingness: new wizard-craft makes shift
> Nowadays shorn of help by robe and book,—
> Otherwise, elsewhere, for success must look
> Than chalked-ring, incantation-gibberish."[22]

Not being shrewd enough to impose by means of "Man's despot, just the Supernatural," Dodington, unlike Disraeli, is a transparent failure. The Victorian statesman, whom Browning detested, imposes

---

21. Ll. 170-178.
22. Ll. 187-198.

successfully even on those who detect the wires that activate his puppets, and although their reasons are undeceived, their credulity is stronger than mind:

> "Can it be—this bold man, whose hand we saw
> Openly pull the wires, obeys some law
> Quite above Man's—nay God's?" On face fall they.
> This was the secret missed, again I say,
> Out of your power to grasp conception of,
> Much less employ to purpose. Hence the scoff
> That greets your very name: folk see but one
> Fool more, as well as knave, in Dodington.[23]

The true political villain seeks to impose, not upon the mind, but upon the superstition, the belief in the supernatural, the intuitive life. To have the duped intuitions overcome reason is almost unique in Browning.

Perhaps no more telling evidence in Browning's words of his respect for truth and for the mind's role in arriving at truth, even when such application of mind was in conflict with the great love of his life, is supplied in a letter to Isa Blagden, September 19, 1867. He lists seven Greek letters and adds:

> There! Those letters indicate seven distinct issues to which I came with Ba, in our profoundly different estimates of thing and person: I go over them one by one, and must deliberately inevitably say, on each of these points I was, am proved to be, right and she wrong. And I am glad I maintained the truth on each of these points, did not say, "what matter whether they be true or no?—Let us only care to love each other."

As if in refutation of those who maintain that Browning believed that pure and innocent natures see into the heart of truth intuitively, he adds:

> If I could ever have such things out of my thoughts, it would not be to-day—the day, twenty years ago, that we left England to-gether. If I

---

23. Ll. 338-345.

ever seem too authoritative or disputative to you, dearest Isa, you must remember this, and that only to those I love very much do I feel at all inclined to lay down what I think to be the law, and speak the truth,— but no good comes of anything else, in the long run,—while as for *seeing* the truth, it seems to me such angelic natures don't—and such devilish ones *do:* it is no sign of the highest nature: on the contrary, I believe the very highness blinds, and the lowness helps to see.[24]

---

24. *Letters of Robert Browning Collected by Thomas J. Wise,* pp. 121-122.

CHAPTER VI

BROWNING'S CASUISTS

Why take the artistic way to prove so much?
Because it is the glory and good of Art,
That Art remains the one way possible
Of speaking truth, to mouths like mine at least.
—"The Book and the Ring"

Browning's casuistical writings have very properly received a substantial share of criticism, for they have been recognized from their inception as paradoxical and even embarrassing. The problem, very simply, is that into the mouths of some of the slipperiest knaves in literature Browning put the sagest and most enlightened views side by side with the most consummate rationalizations of villainy. The question is not so much which of the beliefs the poet shared, for the whole of his writings makes this clear, but why he allowed scoundrels to confuse the true and the false with such slick urbanity that the reader feels unable to separate true from false values. One ends in distrust of human capacity to distinguish right from wrong and is forcibly reminded of the great debate in hell, in which the fallen angels in discourse sweet

. . . reason'd high
Of Providence, Foreknowledge, Will, and Fate,
Fixt Fate, free will, foreknowledge absolute,
And found no end, in wand'ring mazes lost.[1]

Richard D. Altick alleges that the purpose of the casuistical poems

---

1. *Paradise Lost*, II, 558-561.

is simply to denounce the mind and to subvert faith in intellectual processes:

> His famous and seldom-read casuistical poems, "Mr. Sludge, the Medium," "Prince Hohenstiel-Schwangau," "Bishop Blougram's Apology," "Fifine at the Fair," doubtless were intended to expose the hollowness and futility of mere mental gymnastics; but it is impossible to read them without feeling that Browning experienced an unholy joy in writing them. His acrobatic mind revelled in such exercises. And when he came to the end of such a poem, he realized that he had done his job too thoroughly, for, as Professor Hoxie N. Fairchild has pointed out, he hastened to tack on a "giveaway" to warn the reader that all that had gone before, despite its often attractive appearance, was sophistry pure and simple, and that the truth lay elsewhere: not in the head but in the unsophisticated heart that responded only to the promptings of God. He was a born dialectician, yet he was bidden by his deeper self to deny the efficacy of all reason . . . He was obliged to load the dice against every speaker in his poems who chose to vindicate himself by reason rather than by intuition.[2]

It has been urged similarly by Raymond that the purpose of the casuistical writings is to demonstrate the dangers of intellectualism as snares to the moral sense. All of his casuists share one characteristic: an agile if not profound intellect, and it is tempting to conclude that since they share equally intelligence and knavery, the first characteristic bore fruit in the second. This cause-and-effect relationship, as I hope to show, is at best dubious. It seems immediately obvious that if Browning's purpose is to demonstrate the pitfalls into which the mind leads man, he would have been somewhat careful not to entrust his most cherished philosophical beliefs to the mouths of men who are in the process of demonstrating the unwisdom of their intellects. No better statement of Browning's purpose, I feel, could be found than that in which Milton assesses the reason for the wandering of the fallen host in "mazes lost": "Their song was partial. . . ." Raymond in his discussion of "Browning's Casuists" comments:

---

2. "The Private Life of Robert Browning," *op. cit.*, pp. 260-261.

I turn now to the particular consideration of the casuistry of *Bishop Blougram's Apology* in its relation to the basic dualism of the poet's thought—a gulf between love and reason involving a profound distrust of the latter faculty. I have drawn attention to the fact that an agnostic rejection of knowledge is the seedling of casuistry. . . .[3]

In earlier chapters I have cited evidence in some abundance to show that a dualistic gulf between love and reason is precisely what Browning deplored. The gulf often exists, it is true, but this is man's tragedy, not his salvation. The mischief which results from this dualistic gulf is everywhere shown in the tortuous speeches of the casuists, who pervert everything they touch because the triple soul is sundered and intellect is unguided by heart, and their song is partial. What Browning set about to do in these sinuous speeches is to show that the mind, unguided by heart, is an organ gone wild. A man without a mind but with consummate love would be an idiot, perhaps not inferior as a being to the man of intellect alone with no heart at all, a condition leading as directly to viciousness as the reverse to madness. The reader is very naturally confused by the involved ratiocination of Blougram, Prince Hohenstiel-Schwangau, Sludge, and Don Juan; for Browning expects to lose us in the twistings and turnings of heartless intellect. We are expected to end the discourses confused, frustrated, and suspicious of our most cherished values. We doubt the ability of the mind to make a valid moral choice, for we have been led by intellectual perversion to a view of moral chaos.

When we are most confused, the heart intervenes and puts an end to the matter by asserting that "this is right and that is wrong because I know in my heart the difference between the two in whatever guise they may be concealed." Browning in this way forcefully emphasizes his belief that the heart is the highest tribunal, which must ever be vigilant to cut the Gordian knot tied by intellect untempered by heart. He intends no condemnation of the mind, any more than a biopsy report of the finding of cancer cells is a condemnation of healthy tissue. Giantism and deformity result from imbalance of the

---

3. *The Infinite Moment and Other Essays in Robert Browning*, p. 137.

pituitary gland, as everyone knows, but where is the man who would conclude that the gland itself is evil? Without it we would die, and only when it functions in harmony with the rest of the body can we live without disaster.

I

Bishop Blougram's rationale of his religious principles and conduct has understandably perplexed the reader. Of all the major casuists in Browning, he is the least odious and, I believe, the most convincing. He is thoroughly the urbane man who has accepted the world's values while enjoying the cloth as well. He sees that the world is largely made up of half-truths: frauds, small and great; temporizing, equivocating, rationalizing. Expediency, masquerading as principle, is the god whom no man acknowledges, except for advantage—and who is therefore his true Lord of Hosts. So speaks his mind in its isolation.

Blougram's opening words with Gigadibs reveal his character. He is a sensualist and worldling with excellent taste in art, architecture, and wine—and with an eye for the spurious. Furthermore he is disarmingly honest in his dishonesty. In open candor, which grows as he warms to his discourse, he admits that he is aware of the contempt of Gigadibs for him and assures his companion that he will sift truth to the bran. His knowledge of human frailty is consummate. He is fully aware that Gigadibs, while sitting in luxurious surroundings after an excellent dinner—the visible marks of the world's approval—cannot wholly despise him. The bishop's first and greatest argument is that possession is nine-tenths of the moral law and that the odor of sanctity which accompanies success is a judgment which admits of no higher appeal. Principles, after all, are serviceable to beat an opponent with, but they are edgy and uncomfortable as constant companions. Gigadibs, whose superior honesty has brought only pain and poverty, is condemned by the testimony of his condition. As a subtle and ingeniously unkind preface to his argument, Blougram predicts that in later years the correspondent will treasure the memory of this evening with the bishop and will confess the wisdom of accommodating principle to the world, which values only appearances.

Born into such a world, the bishop argues, man is on the horns of a dilemma: to be "honest" and throw overboard dogma, which no one can accept fully, and along with it all hope of preferment; or to recognize man's limitations, conceal his doubts behind a feigned acceptance, and so gain the world's praise and fruits, with the added possibility of learning to believe through the habit of feigning to do so. Since the world is the realm of "the grand Perhaps," man is well advised to make profession of faith rather than of doubt, for both embrace error with truth in a ratio beyond man's power to assess. The main difference between them is that one gains the approval of the world and its products as well, whereas the other gains nothing. Doubt being a test of faith, man has two choices: "a life of doubt diversified by faith" or "one of faith diversified by doubt." Since the validity of each is the same, the test of advantage must tip the beam.

It should be apparent that Blougram's argument is not markedly inconsistent with Browning's known anti-asceticism, love of good living, and faith in the function of doubt as a test. Indeed, Lord Dunsany affirms with confidence that the identification between Browning and Blougram is complete, an affirmation which is surely questionable.[4] When the bishop says that everyone at times feels the gnawing ulcer of doubt, we hear Browning speaking; but when he adds smoothly that no man can really believe at all, we see that a tenable principle has been extended to outrage the moral sense operating with mind. Blougram utters one of Browning's cherished principles:

> "But try," you urge, "the trying shall suffice;
> The aim, if reached or not, makes great the life. . . ."

And he immediately adds an application of the principle for which Browning would have had contempt:

> Spare my self-knowledge—there's no fooling me!
> If I prefer remaining my poor self,

---

4. "Browning Is Blougram," *Nineteenth Century and After,* CXXXIX (April, 1946), 175-177.

> I say so not in self-dispraise but praise.
> If I'm a Shakespeare, let the well alone;
> Why should I try to be what now I am?
> If I'm no Shakespeare, as too probable,—
> His power and consciousness and self-delight
> And all we want in common, shall I find—
> Trying forever? while on points of taste
> Wherewith, to speak it humbly, he and I
> Are dowered alike—I'll ask you, I or he,
> Which in our two lives realizes most?
>
> . . . .
>
> We want the same things, Shakespeare and myself,
> And what I want, I have. . . .[5]

The doctrine that a man's reach should exceed his grasp is perverted to "a man's reach should grasp all it can get."

Blougram takes the concept dear to Browning that the validity of religion is based on proofs of the heart, not on historical evidence in the Bible:

> All's doubt in me; where's break of faith in this?
> It is the idea, the feeling and the love,
> God means mankind should strive for and show forth
> Whatever be the process to that end,—
> And not historic knowledge, logic sound,
> And metaphysical acumen, sure!
> "What think ye of Christ," friend? when all's done and said,
> Like you this Christianity or not?[6]

He straightway proceeds to pervert this belief to the notion that if a little unbelief is good, "perpetual unbelief" is better: "With me, faith means perpetual unbelief. . . ." He accepts Browning's concept that the white radiance of absolute truth is hidden from man, lest he be blinded by its purity; and he extends this truth by cold logic to include the opinion, repugnant to Browning, that creation's function is to conceal God entirely—"to hide him all it can. . . ." The beliefs which

---

5. Ll. 494-540.
6. Ll. 620-627.

Browning felt are to spur a man to greater heights of belief or works
are reduced to absurdity through an apparently valid extension to
afford a rationale for his true faith, in which all other belief is
included:

> How we may lead a comfortable life,
> How suit our luggage to the cabin's size.[7]

He takes Browning's principle that the strivings of man in his
world are the earnest of his strivings in the next; and he promptly
perverts it to a reasoned justification of total worldliness:

> Let us concede (gratuitously though)
> Next life relieves the soul of body, yields
> Pure spiritual enjoyment: well, my friend,
> Why lose this life i' the meantime, since its use
> May be to make the next life more intense? [8]

It is an ingenious stretching of Browning to argue that since life is
to be lived fully and not discounted, the more worldly a bishop is
the greater will be his reward of spiritual enjoyment in the next life.

Blougram examines the well-springs of religion to show that they
are inadmissible to the mind. Natural religion, he says, stemmed
from prohibition and fear; hence man, like Caliban, "saw the use
of going out of sight/ In wood or cave to prosecute his loves. . . ."
All moral law, if sufficiently examined by logic, is on much the same
level as this, and as ugly:

> Does law so analyzed coerce you much?
> Oh, men spin clouds of fuzz where matters end,
> But you who reach where the first thread begins,
> You'll soon cut that!—which means you can, but won't,
> Through certain instincts, blind, unreasoned-out,
> You dare not set aside, you can't tell why. . . .[9]

---

7. Ll. 762-763.
8. Ll. 775-779.
9. Ll. 834-839.

On the premise that absolute truth is hidden from man, he pursues the principle to his conclusion that the mind must reject all religious law.

Another belief of the poet—that man, being midway between angel and brute, must accept the conditions of life—Blougram distorts to justify acquiescence in things far more brutish than angelic. Perhaps the secret of the whole work is included in the line: "He said true things but called them by wrong names." Blougram is an intellectual whose mind, lacking the balance of the spirit, has twisted words until they mean much the opposite of their original intent. The noblest principles, if pushed to their extreme without the spirit to leaven the lump, can become vicious.

Gigadibs's reaction to the sophistries of the bishop is not recorded directly, but his setting sail the following week for Australia to become a settler-farmer suggests that he feels the need of a fresh start in a new country where the word is not yet perverted beyond all recognition.

C. E. Tanzy, in his essay "Browning, Emerson, and Bishop Blougram," maintains that Blougram is evil only on the surface level: "on the 'real' level he is good," for he forces Gigadibs to abandon his paralyzing idealism and to accept the conditions of earthly imperfection and to work in the world as it is, an example of Browning's theme that evil works for good.[10] It is true that Blougram is more to be admired than the negative Gigadibs, who unmistakably finds the evening's discussion instructive and corrective, but it is dangerous to pronounce Blougram good, whatever the level. He is a fusion of both truth and error, principle and expediency, and thus is a fine example of Browning's concept of the shattered triple soul.

F. E. L. Priestley believes that Gigadibs is so systematically demolished that he perforce sees the shallowness of his own thinking and sets sail for Australia to pursue an ideal, the ideal of following those things in Blougram's career he formerly despised:

---

10. *Victorian Studies,* I, No. 3 (March, 1958), 255-266.

But Gigadibs has been more successful than he had expected. Gigadibs, seized with a "sudden healthy vehemence," renounces his ambitions of power and place, of literary eminence, and sails for Australia. He has presumably found an ideal, and is preparing to follow it. Moreover, he is apparently intent on the study of the Gospels. He has in fact turned away from precisely those things in Blougram's career which he formerly valued, and is seeking that which he formerly despised; he who doubted above all the possibility of the life of faith is now pursuing it. The victory, unexpected to be sure in its scope, is Blougram's.[11]

Mr. Raymond discovers Browning to be as confused and enmeshed in the toils of casuistry as Gigadibs himself:

> I have dwelt on Browning's intellectual scepticism, because of its intimate connection with his casuistic poems. For a nescient theory of knowledge is the very soil in which casuistry breeds. If reason, self-tricked and deluded, is always involved in a "vile juggle," casuistry must be constantly attendant upon it and, indeed, inherent in its nature. Browning escapes the fogs of sophistry when he invokes the sunlight of love to dispel the mists that becloud the mind. The emotions of the heart are in intuitive touch with truth. But when the poet descends to the arena of reason, he is unavoidably entrapped in casuistry. Hence it becomes an interesting question, how far his hand is dyed by the medium in which he works. To what extent is he above his casuists, and to what extent is he at one with them?[12]

His conclusion is that once Browning allowed his elusive villains the key to his chest of sacred principles to use in their own defense, he discovered that a Pandora's box had been opened. In short, the casuists so rifled the arsenal, to change the figure to fit Raymond's, that "It is difficult to avoid the conclusion that Browning's casuists are never really routed from the standpoint of reason."

The dying bishop in St. Praxed's was not routed, either, nor was Andrea or Cleon or Karshish. In fact, I am not sure that Browning

---

11. "Blougram's Apologetics," *University of Toronto Quarterly*, XV, No. 2 (January, 1946), 147.

12. *The Infinite Moment and Other Essays in Robert Browning*, p. 133.

routed anyone, for the reason that it is not the business of a poet to do so.[13] Browning was the great observer, the student of the soul; and his enduring power and charm are that he was the largest-souled poet of his age, who would not stoop to parade the obvious worth of virtue or the unworth of villainy. These things he left to his readers— with a hope, I am sure, that they would share something of his breadth of vision and his love. To suppose that Browning was trapped by the casuistical twists and turns of his own creation is unbelievable. In the first place, the whole of Browning reveals firmness of belief and artistic integrity that are almost unique. Like Milton, he gives every evidence of knowing what he is about. If specific proof of this should be necessary, *The Ring and the Book* alone is sufficient. If ever there was an opportunity to lose sight of one's aim, it is in that vast quarry which yielded so many imperishable monoliths; and yet at no time did he lose his way or become lost in the maze of testimony. The reader may get lost and fancy that Guido in his opening speech is the manly, long-suffering defender of the home he hopes to convince the court that he is, but Browning was not deceived. It is to mis-understand the spiritual, mental, and artistic solidity of the man to suppose that he groped in error and darkness through the casuistry of his own characters, hoping that by chance light would shine and he would find contrivance enough to extricate himself somehow from the web that he had made. Browning was too much consecrated to his craft and to truth to send to the publisher works that demonstrate that he did not know how to shape a poem or end it without uphold-ing himself to the public gaze as a bungler, trapped by his own principles and freely showing that they really do not bear application or examination. We know that he never swerved from faith in the basic tenets that inform his poetry; we also know that he would never permit in print a poem which, properly understood, would undermine faith in those tenets or convict him of being one who could not hold from first to last the vision of artistic purpose.

---

13. For a differing opinion, see Hoxie N. Fairchild's "Browning the Simple-Hearted Casuist," *op. cit.*

II

Mr. Sludge, the pettiest of all Browning's casuists, has the fewest redeeming qualities and the least regard for rectitude in Browning's gallery. That the poet detested the man may be safely assumed from his attitude toward Daniel Home, the original of Sludge, who occasioned one of the rare misunderstandings between the poet and his wife. Home's crude impostures Browning resented because they were a mockery and perversion of everything spiritual, but even more important, because the medium dared to impose upon E. B. B.'s credulity, Sludge is discovered in the perpetration of a gross deception and faces his wrathful host. Like Guido, fresh from his tortures before the court, Sludge wheedles and flatters, blaming his indiscretion on the good champagne, which triumphed over judgment and probity ("I took it for Catawba, you're so kind. . . ."). While confessing his charlatanry, he seeks to implicate "a thick/ Dusk undeveloped spirit" which owes him a grudge—he is unable to speak truth, and lies by reflex, while promising a full revelation of his tricks as the price of ship's passage which will allow him to go where he will "cheat no more." The underlying principle of his whole argument is that of all the casuists in Browning. He

> Will lay down spiritual laws, read wrong things right
> By the rule o' reverse.[14]

Like Blougram, Sludge forces Browning's most cherished principles into the devil's service. His mind is unhampered by any shred of scruple or sign of soul, which would have impeded the ready formation of seemingly unimpeachable corollaries in support of knavery. His main defense is based on Browning's belief that man's finite mind cannot comprehend total truth, but he quickly perverts it to mean that the truth is absolutely shut from man, that nescience is man's lot, and that since one falsity is not demonstrably superior to another,

---

14. Ll. 308-309.

the liar in no wise compounds error. Indeed, he has the analogy of
God's plan to comfort him in his impostures:

> Why, of old,
> Great men spent years and years in writing books
> To prove we've souls, and hardly proved it then:
> Miss Stokes with her live coal, for you and me!
> Surely, to this good issue, all was fair—
> Not only fondling Sludge, but, even suppose
> He let escape some spice of knavery,—well,
> In wisely being blind to it! Don't you praise
> Nelson for setting spy-glass to blind eye
> And saying . . . what was it—that he could not see
> The signal he was bothered with? [15]

Life is such a fusion of truth and error that one may push the idea
a little further to the point where both terms become names for something which does not exist. It is absurd to speak of falsehood, he
concludes:

> "In so many tales
> Must be some truth, truth though a pin-point big,
> Yet, some: a single man's deceived, perhaps—
> Hardly, a thousand. . . ." [16]

The principle is pushed to the extreme when Sludge reasons that
since God fused truth and error, man might be well advised to aid
the divine plan by superadding a little extra falsehood here and there
by way of precaution that the wishes of the deity not miscarry:

> Don't let truth's lump rot stagnant for the lack
> Of a timely helpful lie to leaven it!
> Put a chalk-egg beneath the clucking hen,
> She'll lay a real one, laudably deceived,
> Daily for weeks to come. I've told my lie,
> And seen truth follow, marvels none of mine;
> All was not cheating, sir, I'm positive! [17]

---

15. Ll. 683-693.
16. Ll. 718-721.
17. Ll. 1305-1311.

Sludge unintentionally gives a fine picture of the cold, intellectual skeptic, among whom he must be numbered:

> Men emasculate,
> Blank of belief, who played, as eunuchs use,
> With superstition safely,—cold of blood,
> Who saw what made for them i' the mystery,
> Took their occasion, and supported Sludge
> —As proselytes? No, thank you, far too shrewd![18]

These are the men—emasculate and cold of blood—whose dualism has riven a gulf between head and heart.

The next step in Sludge's logic is that since truth and error are really but names for what does not exist, one can argue that his fake seances have a share in the truth-error complex:

> I cheated when I could,
> Rapped with my toe-joints, set sham hands at work,
> Wrote down names weak in sympathetic ink,
> Rubbed odic lights with ends of phosphor-match,
> And all the rest; believe that: believe this,
> By the same token, though it seem to set
> The crooked straight again, unsay the said,
> Stick up what I've knocked down; I can't help that
> It's truth! I somehow vomit truth to-day.
> This trade of mine—I don't know, can't be sure
> But there was something in it, tricks and all![19]

Sludge uses the argument that in all creation there is a certain testation of the infinite power visible to the perception of him who sees, a valid belief which he distorts to justify the grossest superstition and imposture.

> I've sharpened up my sight
> To spy a providence in the fire's going out,
> The kettle's boiling, the dime's sticking fast
> Despite the hole i' the pocket. Call such facts

---

18. Ll. 734-739.
19. Ll. 800-810.

> Fancies, too petty a work for Providence,
> And those same thanks which you exact from me
> Prove too prodigious payment: thanks for what,
> If nothing guards and guides us little men? [20]

His rejection of the belief that God would not concern himself with such trifling matters or reveal to insignificant people the hidden meaning in small events is an extension of Browning's belief that in God's eyes there is no first or last. Because God cares for the lowliest creature and sees the fall of every sparrow, it follows that all things are signs and omens for the discerning; and thus, by logical implication, God sanctions mediums.

The medium distorts Browning's doctrine of apparent failure to justify his fraudulent seances. Poor blundering man is doomed to fail and fail again, is he not? And yet he must attempt the heights in spite of failure. Similarly the medium fails often, very often indeed, but there is always the chance that he might make contact with the spirit world:

> Man's still man,
> Still meant for a poor blundering piece of work
> When all's done; but, if somewhat's done, like this,
> Or not done, is the case the same? Suppose
> I blunder in my guess at the true sense
> O' the knuckle-summons, nine times out of ten,—
> What if the tenth guess happen to be right? [21]

To attempt to communicate with the spirits is no worse than any other undertaking which has its allotted failures and perhaps no success at all. In all things there is a minute chance of success that no one can deny. Indeed, since failure and blundering are the law of life, he notes, his form of fraud may be as legitimate as employment of the latest findings of science:

> Oh, be sure,
> You, everybody blunders, just as I,

---

20. Ll. 961-968.
21. Ll. 1017-1023.

> In simpler things than these by far! For see:
> I knew two farmers,—one, a wiseacre
> Who studied seasons, rummaged almanacs,
> Quoted the dew-point, registered the frost,
> And then declared, for outcome of his pains,
> Next summer must be dampish: 't was a drought.[22]

His neighbor, scorning science, prognosticated accurately because one brindle heifer stiffened her tail in the evenings, a sure sign of drought.

Sludge, not Browning, reveals himself as the true intellectual skeptic. "I tell you, sir, in one sense, I believe/ Nothing at all. . . ," he says as a corollary to another thinly stretched principle:

> . . . every cheat's inspired, and every lie
> Quick with a germ of truth.[23]

The final refinement on his extension of principle is that since the world is made meaningful by evil to test man, he meets evil with evil. The world is to challenge man to better it; truth is to be pursued, not found on a silver platter; and when Sludge gets through he has abetted the scheme of things by increasing the evil and confusing the truth!

> I cheat in self-defence,
> And there's my answer to a world of cheats!
> Cheat? To be sure, sir! What's the world worth else?
> Who takes it as he finds, and thanks his stars?
> Don't it want trimming, turning, furbishing up
> And polishing over? Your so-styled great men,
> Do they accept one truth as truth is found,
> Or try their skill at tinkering?[24]

His final application of mind, after his host has upheld his part of the bargain, is to mature a devilish plot to ruin the reputation of his host and to practice his deceptions elsewhere.

---

22. Ll. 1043-1048.
23. Ll. 1324-1325.
24. Ll. 1345-1353.

III

Prince Hohenstiel-Schwangau, the most dated of the casuistical
pieces, is a monologue of the recently deposed Louis Napoleon, then
in exile at Chislehurst, England, in defense of his policy of inaction
and expediency. Unlike his wife, who placed an unreasonable trust
in the judgment and rectitude of the rascally emperor, Browning
detested him for his temporizing and opportunistic policies which
led to the overthrow of France in the war with Prussia and which
blocked the unification of Italy. His letter to Isa Blagden, January
23, 1871, expresses his detestation of the emperor and all his works:

> I daresay we are altogether, you and I, in sympathy, about Paris:
> mine begins, however, at the point when Paris renounced the wretched
> imposter and all his works: we all, in our various degrees took the man
> on trust, believed in his will far too long after the deed was miserably
> inadequate to what we supposed the will; but when the mask fell and
> we found a lazy old and worn-out voluptuary had neglected every duty,
> ignored every necessary, engaged in this awful war because his wife
> had plagued him and "something" must be done to brighten matters
> at the end of his life, just as when, at the Fair in my young days, Rich-
> ardson the showman, at any crisis of his tragedy found the action halt,
> he set the blue fire burning and ended the scene with éclat.[25]

Of the three slick casuists so far noticed, Louis Napoleon alone is
proved before the world to be a scoundrel and a failure. Blougram is
eminently successful and respected; Sludge is admired by the cred-
ulous and still not found out. Napoleon is failure itself, branded by
the Assembly of Bordeaux on March 1, 1871, as "responsible for the
ruin, invasion and dismemberment of France."[26] Browning permits
this detested blackguard to say "what I imagine the man might, if
he pleased, say for himself."

The deposed emperor is defending his conduct to a young woman
he has met in Leicester Square. With a reference to the medium

---

25. *Letters of Robert Browning to Miss Isa Blagden,* ed. A. Joseph Armstrong (Waco, Texas,
1923), p. 186.
26. DeVane, *A Browning Handbook,* p. 320.

Home, the original of Sludge, he launches into a sophisticated discourse on "the law by which I lived." Knowing that lethargy and reaction are the two most damaging charges the world lays at his doorstep, he immediately pictures himself as horrified by inaction. A confirmed activist, he is compelled by his nature to do something—anything—rather than nothing, in proof of which fiction he idly connects two dots of ink on a scrap of paper before him. It may be purposeless to connect two random dots, but it is less purposeful to do nothing—a view in which the perceptive will see one of Browning's views somewhat distorted for the occasion. The two dots and his connecting line symbolize his whole life:

> Analyze with me
> This instance of the line 'twixt blot and blot
> I rather chose to draw than leave a blank,
> Things else being equal. You are taught thereby
> That 't is my nature, when I am at ease,
> Rather than idle out my life too long,
> To want to do a thing—to put a thought,
> Whether a great thought or a little one,
> Into an act, as nearly as may be.
> Make what is absolutely new—I can't,
> Mar what is made already well enough—
> I won't: but turn to best account the thing
> That's half-made—that I can. Two blots, you saw
> I knew how to extend into a line
> Symmetric on the sheet they blurred before—
> Such little act sufficed, this time, such thought.[27]

He is like a courier, he adds, who is charged by the emperor to deliver a message. The delivery is all-important; the route taken—whether across fields and hedges or along the footpath—is of no concern to the emperor. In other words, he argues by analogy the doctrine of dictators that the end justifies the means. These principles lead him to a defense of man's taking the world as he finds it and

---

27. Ll. 76-91.

living by the rule of least change. Browning's doctrine that man must accept the law of life, which is implicit here, is pushed into service as a justification of doing nothing about the state of the world, an extension diametrically opposed to the central theme of the poet. To Napoleon to accept life and its conditions means to accept the comfortable *status quo* of special privilege. What is, he argues, was arrived at over much time and at the expenditure of much thought and energy, and man is well advised to preserve what he finds, for the good outweighs the evil, and, as everybody knows, evil is necessary to the plan and should not be overmuch tampered with!

Perhaps the most subtle piece of rationalizing in Browning occurs when the bland emperor extends the theory to include the belief that man's relationship with the purpose of creation demands that he not thwart God's design by attempting to become something more sublime than God intended him to be:

> Such is the reason why I acquiesced
> In doing what seemed best for me to do,
> So as to please myself on the great scale,
> Having regard to immortality
> No less than life—did that which head and heart
> Prescribed my hand, in measure with its means
> Of doing—used my special stock of power—
> Not from the aforesaid head and heart alone,
> But every sort of helpful circumstance,
> Some problematic and some nondescript:
> All regulated by the single care
> I' the last resort—that I made thoroughly serve
> The when and how, toiled where was need, reposed
> As resolutely at the proper point,
> Braved sorrow, courted joy, to just one end:
> Namely, that just the creature I was bound
> To be, I should become, nor thwart at all
> God's purpose in creation. I conceive
> No other duty possible to man. . . .[28]

28. Ll. 231-249.

This outrageous *reductio ad absurdum* of a principle dear to Browning must have been written in cold fury, and I doubt not that it reveals his contempt not only for the emperor but for the critics who attempted to reduce his philosophy to absurdity by similar cynicism. Napoleon uses Browning's idea of imperfection—"good i' the germ"— to supply an excuse for his tolerance of evil:

> I recognize, contemplate, and approve
> The general compact of society,
> Not simply as I see effected good,
> But good i' the germ, ...
>
> . . . .
>   all results, in short,
> For better or worse. . . .[29]

It need not be emphasized that Browning keenly resented having his philosophy of functional evil masquerade as a justification of evil. He was hurt by having "The Statue and the Bust" interpreted as a hymn to the bracing values of adultery. One can imagine his reaction to Joseph E. Baker's thesis that much of Browning's popularity resulted from his lusty justification of sin, Original and otherwise. Napoleon sees that "evil never means part company/ With mankind . . ." and he is much too filial a child of God to set himself against the Father. God planned infinite diversity in his creation and different circumstances for each of us, and the emperor therefore boasts that he has never been guilty of treading the world into a paste to make a smooth, uniform mound by misguided alleviation of inequity and oppression. Especially loathsome is his distortion of Browning's belief that man should not seek to attain the conditions of the infinite while on earth, a view which he uses to condemn all change for the betterment of the people.

Thanking God that he was made "a little lower than/ The angels," with imperfections, he misapplies the meaning: imperfections are to exploit, not remedy. Like the poet, he phrases the noblest sentiments; he knows that life is to teach us "how set foot/ Decidedly on

---

29. Ll. 360-365.

some one path to Heaven . . . ," but a ruler's prime duty is to "save society!" And the way to save it is to preserve it intact through refusal to adopt reforms. Houses have been known to fall when new foundations are being built under them, and society is always tottering. The one sacred thing to Napoleon is the *status quo,* for it gave him all that life offers. If one detects flaws in the construction of a temple, he asks, is the torch the remedy?

> This bad world, I experience and approve;
> Your good world,—with no pity, courage, hope,
> Fear, sorrow, joy,—devotedness, in short,
> Which I account the ultimate of man,
> Of which there's not one day nor hour but brings,
> In flower or fruit, some sample of success,
> Out of this same society I save—
> None of it for me![30]

One can dimly discern behind these words Browning's central doctrine, which is phrased in "Rabbi Ben Ezra," but with what a difference!

> Then, welcome each rebuff
> That turns earth's smoothness rough,
> Each sting that bids nor sit nor stand but go![31]

It is absurd, he insists, for man to attempt to use powers which God did not grant him—a good doctrine of Browning's. Acquiesce! The question for man is "Did I work aright/ With powers appointed me?" But the emperor finds this principle serviceable to justify the untenable conclusion that man should therefore live according to his bent. A man born greedy should be greedy, and a slothful emperor may reveal the workings of God's order through his slothfulness.

Not content with this absurdity, Napoleon seizes upon the concept that the intellect should be applied to the practical things of life, not to the Absolute, and uses this premise to justify his repudiation of

---

30. Ll. 639-646.
31. Ll. 31-33.

the lofty political platform he stood on before coming to power. When he was a voice without authority he promised unfettered commerce, freedom of speech and press, rights for labor, "with much beside"; but the words one speaks in the air have little relation to acts upon earth. When he promised the impossible, he was not of this earth, his words being carried by air, symbolizing the fitness of the promises for fulfillment only in the next world:

> "Hence you stand
> Proved and recorded either false or weak,
> Faulty in promise or performance: which?"
> Neither, I hope. Once pedestalled on earth,
> To act not speak, I found earth was not air.
> I saw that multitude of mine, and not
> The nakedness and nullity of air
> Fit only for a voice to float in free.
> Such eyes I saw that craved the light alone,
> Such mouths that wanted bread and nothing else,
> Such hands that supplicated handiwork,
> Men with the wives, and women with the babes,
> Yet all these pleading just to live, not die![32]

Napoleon accepts the new doctrine of evolution eagerly, for in it he finds a perfect rationale for his ignoble actions. If man developed over eons of time "Through fish and insect, reptile, bird and beast,/ Till he attained to be an ape at last/ Or last but one," man is still evolving. The backward view through time awes a man into a conviction of the inevitablity of growth and the futility of tampering with the grand design. Change will come in its own good time, without the meddling of misguided philanthropists and reformers. The course of all mankind may be seen, he finds, in his progress from a nobody to emperor. He was not born in full possession of his powers of emperorship, but gained them through struggle. A man is the better king, he says, if he was a cobbler once, for while sitting on the throne the cobbler-turned-king will know how life tastes to the man who

---

32. Ll. 899-911.

sweeps the doorway. Browning's concept that a knowledge of evil is essential to an understanding of good may be seen hidden in this conviction behind suitable change. Johannes Agricola, likewise, counted among the blisses of heaven the ability to contemplate the torments of the damned from comfortable bleacher seats.

> God takes time.
> I like the thought He should have lodged me once
> I' the hole, the cave, the hut, the tenement,
> The mansion and the palace. . . .[33]

An emperor is not to play God by substituting

> . . . his knowledge, will and way, for God's:
> Nor change the world, such as it is, and was
> And will be, for some other, suiting all
> Except the purpose of the maker. No!
> He saw that weakness, wickedness will be,
> And therefore should be. . . .[34]

This speech is perhaps the most outrageous distortion in the casuistic writings of Browning's belief that the world should not be perfect, like the Star of my God Rephan. To alleviate suffering becomes the rough equivalent of the unpardonable sin.

At the end of his long discourse, the emperor is aware of the emptiness of his words and, one suspects, is sick of himself. The rationalizations, which have revealed him as a heartless intellectual, seem self-evident before they are spoken, but in words they ring somewhat hollow:

> But, where one ceases to soliloquize,
> Somehow the motives, that did well enough
> I' the darkness, when you bring them into light
> Are found, like those famed cave-fish, to lack eye
> And organ for the upper magnitudes.[35]

---

33. Ll. 1011-1014.
34. Ll. 1313-1318.
35. Ll. 2105-2109.

Prince Hohenstiel-Schwangau has been toying with words and ideas and has given a dazzling performance in distortion of truth, the false analogy, and the *non sequitur*. There is at no time a glimmering of moral sense in his words, once they pass beyond the premise which he is intent on perverting. He is the soulless mind, the serpent in Eden, sitting

> Squat like a toad, close at the ear of Eve
> Assaying by his Devilish art to reach
> The Organs of her Fancy, and with them forge
> Illusions as he list. . . .

Browning is condemning, not mind, but the abuse of mind which destroys the spirit.

IV

Don Juan, the last of Browning's great casuists, continues the display of consummate perversity in *Fifine at the Fair*. He justifies infidelity first by stretching the credo that man should obey the law of life and of his own being. Since his being craves promiscuity and his heart "fires up for lawlessness," he claims as a right the gratification of his needs. Losels after indulgence, he observes, "seem to relish life the more," and everyone knows that Browning believed heartily in relishing life. To justify extravagant villainy he applies the poet's idea that the opposite of every good is essential to the growth of man toward the good. He extends to each losel an equivalent of the dispensation which Johannes Agricola boasted of:

> Now, what is it?—returns
> The question—heartens so this losel that he spurns
> All we so prize? I want, put down in black and white,
> What compensating joy, unknown and infinite,
> Turns lawlessness to law, makes destitution—wealth,
> Vice—virtue, and disease of soul and body—health? [36]

------

36. Ll. 138-143.

He pushes the point even beyond this—to convince Elvire that his infidelities are a requisite to her happiness. If her sky is overcast by the clouds of his faithlessness, the landscape but glistens more when the sun comes out. This is a sufficiently flimsy enlargement of Browning's idea, but it is massively sturdy compared with the outrageous extension of another principle which he links with it. He presses into malign service Browning's principle of the triple soul, the inter-relation of body, mind, and spirit, and urges that, since this relation-ship exists, it follows that in his search for mind, he must make full use of bodies. This hypothesis, as every campus dean will testify, was not originated by Don Juan, nor did it die at his death. The mere flesh, Juan adds, is of course nothing; it is the "inward grace" that allures through "the outward sign":

> I have not vexed in vain
> Elvire: because she knows, now she has stood the test,
> How, this and this being good, herself may still be best
> O' the beauty in review; because the flesh that claimed
> Unduly my regard, she thought, the taste, she blamed
> In me, for things extern, was all mistake, she finds,—
> Or will find, when I prove that bodies show me minds,
> That, through the outward sign, the inward grace allures,
> And sparks from heaven transpierce earth's coarsest covertures,—
> All by demonstrating the value of Fifine![37]

A further theory—that in the sight of God all creatures have both good and evil, and if properly understood evil only subserves good— he urges in extenuation of his use of the bedroom as a laboratory:

> No creature's made so mean
> But that, some way, it boasts, could we investigate,
> Its supreme worth. . . .[38]

Since in God's sight, there is no first or last, surely Don Juan can

37. Ll. 329-338.
38. Ll. 339-341.

be equally democratic in his investigations of the worth of Fifine, so he reasons.

One of the clearest proofs of his heartless intellectual toying with truth is seen in his question:

> Well then, thus much confessed, what wonder if there steal
> Unchallenged to my heart the force of one appeal
> She makes, and justice stamp the sole claim she asserts?
> So absolutely good is truth, truth never hurts
> The teller, whose worst crime gets somehow grace, avowed.[39]

It must be kept in mind that his entire confession of his sins is an exercise in how an unscrupulous mind can distort words to hide evil behind a mask, so that his worst crimes will get "somehow grace, avowed."

Don Juan reveals his method of argumentation and also his real contempt for women when he says that few families would be racked by self-inflicted torture if nature had only granted to women what it gave men: the power to "comprehend mental analysis!" This is the secret of *Fifine at the Fair*. Don Juan is conducting a most tortuous "mental analysis" without a tincture of heart by way of leaven. He uses an analogy of his painting of Raphael, which he recently secured to glorify his wall. For a week his heart palpitated with the pride of possession, and for a fortnight longer he remained in a paradise of rapturous contemplation; but a mortal cannot live for long in the rarefied air of paradise. Man sets himself against life's limitations by attempting to comport himself as if he were not a mortal, he argues. He must turn his eyes from his great treasure and pore over Doré's latest picture-book: "One chamber must not coop/ Man's life in. . . ." But if the house should burn, even if he were engaged in Doré "elbow-deep," he promises, to comfort his flesh-and-blood Raphael, that he would rescue the great painting and let all else burn. Women may or may not be primarily remarkable for their powers of "mental analysis," but few wives would feel warmly

---

39. Ll. 392-396.

secure in being assured that their husbands would rescue them first from the fire even though such heroism entailed the abandonment of a faithful mistress to the flames.

One of the brazen extensions of valid principle is his sophistry, first seen in *Paracelsus,* that one finds wholeness through complementary attributes. Contraries seek out contraries to form perfection from the joining of imperfections. Should he deny Fifine the right of combining her imperfections with his perfections, or his faults with her virtues? Can one justify his contempt for the moral plan of life if he fails to so fulfill himself?

> I find it in the fact that each soul, just as weak
> Its own way as it fellow,—departure from design
> As flagrant in the flesh,—goes striving to combine
> With what shall right the wrong, the under or above
> The standard: supplement unloveliness by love.
> Ask Plato else! And this corroborates the sage,
> That Art,—which I may style the love of loving, rage
> Of knowing, seeing, feeling the absolute truth of things
> For truth's sake, whole and sole, not any good, truth brings
> The knower, seer, feeler, beside,—instinctive Art
> Must fumble for the whole, once fixing on a part
> However poor, surpass the fragment, and aspire
> To reconstruct thereby the ultimate entire.[40]

It might be noted in passing that this tortuous defense of promiscuity as selfless sacrifice to the fulfillment of women has seldom deceived a woman, and it does not deceive Elvire. In the argument is clearly seen Browning's belief that man approaches perfection through stages of imperfection, which Don Juan interprets as adequate sanction for fulfilling all women whatever. By implication man should take care to subserve the moral plan by progressing from the least perfect women to the most perfect, for growth is the law of life, and everyone knows that Browning never wavered in his belief that man approaches the absolute vision only through his struggle for perfection. Don Juan

---

40. Ll. 679-691.

waxes rapturous in his vision of the time to come when "to love" will mean that each will "dispense" his gain upon another:

> What joy, when each may supplement
> The other, changing each as changed, till, wholly blent,
> Our old things shall be new, and, what we both ignite,
> Fuse, lose the varicolor in achromatic white! [41]

When man is "wholly blent" with all women, or with all other women who appeal to him sufficiently after a period of apprenticeship, he is

> Exemplifying law, apparent even now
> In the eternal progress,—love's law. . . . [42]

Elvire, whose patience is almost pathological, breaks her silence to ask:

> "Who is it you deceive—
> Yourself or me or God, with all this make-believe?" [43]

He feigns despair of the power of words to convey truth: "Words struggle with the weight/ So feebly of the False. . . ." In truth he is at the moment engaged in an almost clinical examination of how far words can be distorted to make the false seem true.

He employs another analogy to further his deception: a man floating in the sea (one of Browning's favorite sports in his middle years) must lie deep in the water, with just his nose out of the grosser element. To reach into the air is to upset the balance and to sink; but to reach into the depths is to elevate the face. It is clear, then, that to rise toward heaven one must seek the murky depths with his body:

---

41. Ll. 894-897.
42. Ll. 898-899.
43. Ll. 940-941.

> I liken this play o' the body,—fruitless strife
> To slip the sea and hold the heaven. . . .[44]

As a floater gains confidence by daring to submerge and test his skill at rising once again, so he spends a good deal of time down with the slime. "By practice with the false," he reaches the true. In defense of the pain he has caused Elvire, he argues that love flourishes as much through pruning limbs as by "lavishing manure," a figure as remarkable for its ineptness as for its ambiguity.

Near the conclusion, he perverts Browning's philosophical theories, not singly, but in batches:

> Are we not here to learn the good of peace through strife,
> Of love through hate, and reach knowledge by ignorance?
> Why, those are helps thereto, which late we eyed askance,
> And nicknamed unaware![45]

Because man should not seek to know the hereafter, he discovers that "Somehow the proper goal for wisdom was the ground/ And not the sky. . . ."

If the reader of *Fifine* is sick of the parade of lies by the end of the book, he is better enabled to understand the nausea Elvire experiences. Her husband's distortions of truth, together with his brutal "pruning" of her limbs, has revealed him as a man without a heart, who perverts truth through ingenious sophistries to lead man backwards to falsehood. Don Juan is thus the enemy of God's plan of progress from dark to light through the uncorrupted use of all faculties. His casuistry has one aim: to so obscure principle that evil masquerades as virtue and lies wear the face of truth. In man's journey from ignorance to knowledge, no greater test of his fortitude lurks in wait for him than such perversion of the truth.

One of the perplexing characteristics of the casuistic pieces is that Browning never refutes his villains directly, and one may reasonably

44. Ll. 1039-1040.
45. Ll. 1782-1785.

find that they give an embarrassingly good account of themselves. They do, indeed. Evil flourishes like the green bay tree, as Browning was aware, and these men illustrate the principle very well. Life is a test of our ability to see evil in whatever disguise it may present itself, and to detect falsehood whatever the words of apparent wisdom in which it may justify its misdeeds. Nowhere in Browning is the reader so directly tested as in these pieces in which evil is permitted to use every office of good in its own defense. One looks in vain for Browning to tip his hand and help the reader in forming his judgment of what is evil and what it not, in discovering the invisible line separating the lofty principle from its subtle misapplication in support of vice. This objectivity is part of the firm art of the poet, and because of it one can reread these difficult pieces endlessly and never exhaust their subtlety. Every reader must determine for himself where Browning would draw the line, for he does not tell us. One thing is entirely certain: Browning loathed villainy, and the more devious and subtly dishonest it is the more he loathed it. His detestation of the medium Home is well known, as also of Napoleon III. That he felt similarly toward Bishop Blougram may be surmised from his hatred of double-talk and distortion of truth in a bad cause. The bishop is almost devoid of spirit—the triple soul is now reduced to the double soul of mind and body—and he speaks as a man would speak in this condition.

It is interesting to reflect upon the feelings that come upon one severally when reading Browning. One is forcibly reminded of what a vigorous, healthy man he was. How he delighted in the sheer joy of living! A man who could dine on a pint of mayonnaise, indeed! At other times one is equally amazed by his vitality of mind, the tireless energy of his searching intellect. And yet again, one is struck with admiration for his spiritual health, because he was a happy man who never doubted for long that right would triumph and all would yet be well. In short, he was the example of the harmonious triple soul, which his casuists are not.

It should not be necessary to emphasize that Browning was a great moralist, both in his poetry and in his life. We know that he always sought to spare his wife the embarrassment or contamination of meeting with rakes. We know also how shocked he was when he discovered the facts in the sad case of Shelley's abandonment of Harriet Shelley and her suicide later in the Serpentine. It is impossible to believe that Browning countenanced evil, found vice attractive, or wavered in his respect for rectitude—that he really found his casuists engagingly attractive in their daring. The evidence which may be drawn from "The Statue and the Bust," with its conclusion that it is better to commit adultery than to do nothing at all, must not blind one to his real morality, which at times approaches prudery. The Lady Ashburton case might repay study; and one should reread "St. Martin's Summer" to see the lengths to which a man can carry the concept of fidelity—even to the dead. The greatest error in studying the casuist pieces is to assume that because Browning did not refute his villains he really was at one with them and approved, at least in theory, if not in practice, of kicking over the traces and having a refreshing go at sin.

Joseph E. Baker discovers clear evidence of Browning's delight in evil and his injunction to his age to go forth and sin some more: "The force of Original Sin is not to be resisted but obeyed":

> He would not like to see eliminated the disease, sorrow, hate, greed and lust that rage in the world. These are weeds, but only a simpleton would pull weeds out of a garden, he argues, in his "Parleying with Barnard de Mandeville". . . . The wise farmer (or perhaps the smart city man) would keep all the weeds in his garden to strengthen the other plants! The figure of speech Browning is using here to defend his position betrays, of course, the weakness of his whole philosophy. Whatever the suburban poet may think, it is shrewd for the farmer to pull weeds.[46]

It need hardly be emphasized further that Browning meant no such thing. He knew well enough that weeds grow in gardens, as sin flourishes on earth, to test man's fidelity to the ideal of endless struggle against wrong. It should be recalled that Prince Hohenstiel, to justify his sloth, similarly argued that since to eliminate evil, which is put

---

46. "Religious Implications in Browning's Poetry," *op. cit.*, pp. 446-448.

here by God for a purpose, would be to thwart God's plan, the moral man should acquiesce in the existence of evil and do nothing to combat it. Browning detested Napoleon, he hated evil, and his whole message is to pull the weeds from the garden of life with all one's strength.

All of the casuists illustrate the same principle: the warped and twisted ugliness of heartless villainy and the results of the shattering of the triple soul. Each is a fine example of the triumph of intellect and the atrophy of spirit. This fact alone makes it inconceivable that Browning did not know what he intended to show by permitting them the use of his philosophical treasures or that he secretly admired the brave knavery of his characters. This conclusion would be the twin of the belief that he nurtured an advanced case of hero worship for Guido and deplored the action of the Pope for his imperception in sentencing the rascal to the block.

All these casuists, then, may be considered as examples of Browning's lifelong belief that chaos and evil result when man violates God's purpose, scorns God's gifts, and violates order. They are the enemies of truth, which is a reproach to them; and so they pervert it at every chance. By the function of opposites they show that the whole man is formed of three souls operating in harmony: "What Does, what Knows, what Is. . . ." This is the heart of Browning's theory of knowledge—and of life as well.

CHAPTER VII

CONCLUSION

The poetry of Robert Browning, together with his letters and the facts in his life as we know them, afford weighty evidence of the intellectual cast of his mind and of his respect for intellect as a God-given tool for man to use in fulfilling the demands of this life. One of the earliest themes in his poetry—appearing in *Paracelsus* and *Sordello* directly and in *Pauline* less directly—is the theme of whole-ness as man's chief means of meeting the test, which to Browning is the reason for man's earthly existence. This concept was later to grow into the mature philosophy of the triple soul of man, most clearly seen in Browning's magnificent reading of life, "A Death in the Desert." Man has a three-fold soul of body, mind, and spirit making one soul; and man's surest duty is to keep the three in healthful cooperation in meeting the issues of life. There appears to be no real evidence that he deplored at any time the use of intellect, degraded the role of thought, or counseled man to throw out the mind as an evil power inherently inimical to love and the intuitive life. There is an abundance of evidence throughout the poet's works to prove beyond doubt that "Love is best" and that in the scheme of things on earth love is both the supreme value and the final arbiter in matters important to man. No one could seriously question for long that Browning preferred the loving worm upon his leaf to the loveless, heartless intellectual in his laboratory or in his study; but the intellectual is not necessarily without love. Browning no more counseled man to depreciate the mind than he urged him to flagellate the body, which, like the mind, has a way upon occasion of impeding the progress of spirit. He had no patience at all with asceticism, which denies the body and thus one-third of the soul of man. The hair shirt and the emaciated rib cage he deplored as contrary to God's plan of wholeness. Similarly he decried the rejection of mind, which in *Christmas-Eve* he labeled as the "clue" God gives man to follow his path through the world.

The many beautiful and innocent spirits in Browning's hall of women, as I hope I have shown, are not to be lightly urged as evidence of his distrust of mind. Close examination reveals Pippa and Pompilia, like most of their delightful sisters in innocence, to be conspicuous for their sound and active minds. Elizabeth Barrett Browning, who I am sure shaped the general character of Browning's Pompilia, was herself one of the cerebral women in English literary history. Her verse may not appeal widely to our generation, but her letters reveal a woman of active mind and spirit. Indeed, her correspondence with her ardent suitor has greater vitality and is more closely reasoned than his. And we know that Browning loved her for all three of her souls which made up the soul most beautiful in his eyes. He did not attempt to make her less intellectual than she was, nor did he submerge his mind in deference to hers. He held no sickly belief that love is so fragile that it would shatter before the collision of ideas.

It is important to understand Browning's conception of the role of thought, for if his most respectable critics persist in the opinion that he pushed Romantic distrust of reason to the conclusion that love is not merely best but is in sturdy opposition to the brain, his reputation as a thinker must remain tarnished, and since Browning is widely held to be a poet of thought, his reputation as a poet will continue to suffer as well. Furthermore, his view of the mind explains his central belief in the role of doubt and ignorance (both of which are forms of evil) in the test of man's fortitude and faith through uncertainty.

A most unjustifiable assumption is that because Browning found evil and ignorance and doubt essential in life, he therefore justified illimitable evil, ignorance, and doubt. Browning was not so naïve.

If a little castor oil is good, a great deal is not infallibly better. A father may punish his erring child, but he does not tear his flesh with red-hot pincers in the belief that if a little pain is helpful, torment is a specific remedy. Henry Charles Duffin, whose *Amphibian, a Reconsideration of Browning* reveals his love of Browning, finds his affection strained to the breaking point by the poet's "glib apologies for evil" and his "assumption that whatever is is right." He fancies that Browning seriously believed that since evil and ignorance are functional to test man and to let him catch glimpses of their opposite, "we should do nothing to save people from pain"—on the theory, apparently, that the more pain the better. The truth of the matter, of course, is that God set these unpleasant things before us precisely to see what we would do about them. One need not fear that to overcome evil is to thwart God through elimination of evil. If a child is given a painful problem in algebra to solve, he is supposed to solve it as best he can, not shirk the task in the mistaken notion that a headmaster so brutal as to confront a boy with algebra would surely be annoyed by the boy's triumph. Of one thing Browning was sure above all: there will be no end to the problems for man to pit himself against. It is impossible to define the limits to be set upon evil, for they are self-limiting. God fits the test to the individual in a way obscure to man. Can one assess how much frustration and opposition spurs a man to greater efforts and how much destroys the spirit and nurtures the ulcer?

Browning's explanation of the function of evil and ignorance, I believe, is only partially acceptable, if acceptable at all. But one should not reject his beliefs on the basis of a misunderstanding of what he meant. Perhaps there is no completely satisfactory explanation for the existence of evil in a morally conceived and guided universe. Certainly it seems doubtful that there is an explanation markedly superior to Browning's. Many men after a lifetime of reflection share Albert Schweitzer's honest appraisal that no explanation of the problem of evil can ever satisfy both the intellect and the moral sense; for each explanation ends in a fuzz of sophistry designed to deaden man's consciousness of the pain around him—and this ultimate cruelty

Browning would not countenance. I find Browning's explanation as good as the next and perhaps better.

A final misconception of Browning's central belief, as I have tried to show, is that Browning, having no faith in man's ability to attain real knowledge or to do anything more than to pursue an unattainable goal because of his limitation, championed blind activism. It is demonstrably true that he believed the pursuit, wherein man is tested, is more important than the attainment. Man's reach should indeed exceed his grasp if heaven is to have a meaning and a function; but it is wholly contrary to Browning's belief that since man cannot reach the goal in this life, the nature of the goal is of no importance and activism is everything. Quite the contrary, the goal is of supreme importance, for the test of man is to see whether he will follow the difficult path leading to the worthy goal or whether like Cuthbert and Giles he will lose heart and give up the quest leading to the Dark Tower. Hoxie N. Fairchild concludes that because ultimate attainment is forbidden man in this life, the goal must therefore be of no great concern, so long as man actively pursues something. "If the chase resulted in catching anything," he writes, "man would become that most pitiable of objects, a 'faultless painter.'" And he adds, apparently without seeing that Andrea is a pitiable thing, not because he attained something (technical perfection) but because he pursued and attained the wrong thing: "So far as our mortal existence is concerned, at all events, we are exhorted to lead lives of dauntless activity," which, he continues, neither can nor should "bear fruit in any final accomplishment. The nature of the goal is therefore relatively unimportant; what matters is the vigor and courage of the attaining. . . ."[1]

Similarly, it has been urged by others that "The Statue and the Bust" affords evidence of Browning's belief that it is always better to do something than to do nothing, even though evil is the deed and wicked are the consequences. The poem means no such thing. It does mean that it is better to follow one's heart and love—the

---

1. "Browning's 'Whatever Is, Is Right,'" *College English, op. cit.,* p. 379.

supreme value for Browning—than to deny the heart and to shilly-shally, even though ideally it is poor form to break up another man's home. So far as I have discovered no one has yet found in Browning's elopement with Elizabeth Barrett dark signs of his belief in the bracing joys of breaking up a father's home and darkening his life, even though to do so one may have to run off with his daughter, but I remain on guard against the unhappy disclosure.[2] It is clear that when principles collide, a choice must be made, and these are among life's most painful tests. The test is surely not to see whether one will merely do something, but rather whether he will do the right thing, the thing that will show that his values are straight, that he can put first things first, even though to do so may cause pain. To fail to see that all of Browning's philosophy is premised on values is to reduce his belief in progress to a faith simply in motion itself, whatever its direction, and it is to empty his works of both dignity and meaning. This fate to an alarming extent has already overtaken Browning. Whether he will again take his place in the hearts and minds of men only time can tell; but the world, as never before, needs Robert Browning. If his reading of life ever again becomes a living force among men, men must first understand what his reading of life is.

---

2. Lionel Stevenson ("The Pertinacious Victorian Poets," *University of Toronto Quarterly*, XXI, No. 3 [April, 1952], 238) believes that the poem "was not written to condemn a Florentine duke for failing to elope with Count Riccardi's incarcerated wife, but to justify Robert Browning for having eloped with Mr. Barrett's incarcerated daughter." I cannot believe that Browning felt compelled by guilt to so justify the one truly formative and beautiful act of his life.

SELECTED BIBLIOGRAPHY

Altick, Richard D., "Browning's 'Karshish' and Saint Paul," *Modern Language Notes,* November, 1957, LXXII, 494-496.

————, "The Private Life of Robert Browning," *Yale Review,* 1951, XLI, 247-262.

Armstrong, A. Joseph, ed., *Letters of Robert Browning to Miss Isa Blagden,* Waco, Texas: Baylor University Press, 1923.

Bagehot, Walter "Wordsworth, Tennyson and Browning," *Literary Studies,* ed. R. H. Hutton, London: Longmans, Green, 1895.

Baker, Joseph E., "Religious Implications in Browning's Poetry," *Philological Quarterly,* October, 1957, XXXVI, No. 4, 436-452.

Brockington, A. A., *Browning and the Twentieth Century,* London: Oxford University Press, 1932.

Browning, R. B., ed., *The Letters of Robert Browning and Elizabeth Barrett Barrett, 1845-1846,* 2 vol., New York: Harper and Brothers, 1898.

Burdett, Osbert, *The Brownings,* London: Constable and Co., 1928.

Charlton, H. B., "Browning as Poet of Religion," *Bulletin of the John Rylands Library,* 1942-43, XXVII, 271-307.

————, "Browning's Ethical Poetry," *Bulletin of the John Rylands Library,* 1942-43, XXVII, 36-39.

Chew, Samuel C., "The Nineteenth Century and After," in *A Literary History of England,* ed. Albert C. Baugh, New York: Appleton-Century-Crofts, 1948.

Cook, A. K., *A Commentary on Browning's "The Ring and the Book,"* London: Oxford University Press, 1920.

Corrigan, Beatrice, trans. and ed., *Curious Annals: New Documents Relating to Browning's Roman Murder Story,* Toronto: Toronto University Press, 1956.

Curle, Richard, ed., *Robert Browning and Julia Wedgwood. A Broken Friendship as Revealed by their Letters,* New York: Frederick A. Stokes Co., 1937.

DeVane, William C., *A Browning Handbook*, New York: Crofts, 1935; 2nd ed., Appleton-Century-Crofts, 1955.

————, *Browning's Parleyings, the Autobiography of a Mind*, New Haven: Yale University Press, 1927.

————, and Kenneth Knickerbocker, eds., *New Letters of Robert Browning*, New Haven: Yale University Press, 1950.

Duckworth, F. G. R., *Browning: Background and Conflict*, New York: E. P. Dutton, 1932.

Duffin, Henry Charles, *Amphibian: A Reconsideration of Browning*, London: Bowes and Bowes, 1956.

Dunsany, Lord, "Browning Is Blougram," *Nineteenth Century and After*, April 1946, CXXXIX, 175-177.

Fairchild, Hoxie N., "Browning's 'Whatever Is, Is Right,' " *College English*, April, 1951, XII, 377-382.

————, "Browning the Simple-Hearted Casuist," *University of Toronto Quarterly*, April, 1949, XVIII, No. 3, 234-240.

————, "*La Saisiaz* and the *Nineteenth Century*," *Modern Philology*, August, 1950, XLVIII, No. 1, 104-111.

Fotheringham, James, *Studies in the Poetry of Robert Browning*, London: Kegan Paul, Trench Co., 1887.

Glen, Margaret E., "The Meaning and Structure of *Pippa Passes*," *University of Toronto Quarterly*, July, 1955, XXIV, No. 4, 410-426.

Griffin, W. H. and H. C. Minchin, *The Life of Robert Browning, with Notices of his Writings, his Family, and his Friends*, New York: The Macmillan Co., 1910.

Hartle, Robert W., "Gide's Interpretation of Browning," *University of Texas Studies in English*, 1949, XXVIII, 244-256.

Hilton, Earl, "Browning's *Sordello* as a Study of the Will," *Publications of the Modern Language Association*, December, 1954, LXIX, 1124-34.

Holmes, Stewart Walker, "Browning's *Sordello* and Jung: Browning's *Sordello* in the Light of Jung's Theory of Types," *Publications of the Modern Language Association*, September, 1941, LVI, 758-796.

Hood, Thurman L., ed., *Letters of Robert Browning, Collected by Thomas J. Wise*, New Haven: Yale University Press, 1933.

Jerman, B. R., "Browning's Witless Duke," *Publications of the Modern Language Association*, June, 1957, LXXII, 488-493.

Johnson, E. D. H., *The Alien Vision of Victorian Poetry*, Princeton, N. J.: Princeton University Press, 1952.

Jones, Henry, *Browning as a Philosophical and Religious Teacher*, New York: Macmillan and Co., 1891.

Kenyon, F. G., ed., *Robert Browning and Alfred Domett,* London: Smith, Elder and Co., 1906.

Knickerbocker, Kenneth L., "Greek Wisdom and Browning: a Reply," *Classical Journal,* May, 1950, XLV, No. 1, 393-394.

Langbaum, Robert, *"The Ring and the Book:* a Relativist Poem," *Publications of the Modern Language Association,* March, 1956, LXXI, 131-154.

McAleer, Edward C., *Dearest Isa: Robert Browning's Letters to Isabella Blagden,* Austin, Texas: Texas University Press, 1951.

Miller, Betty, *Robert Browning, a Portrait,* London: John Murray, 1952.

Orr, Mrs. Sutherland, *Handbook to the Works of Robert Browning,* 5th ed., London: George Bell and Sons, 1890.

Priestley, F. E. L., "Blougram's Apologetics," *University of Toronto Quarterly,* January, 1946, XV, No. 2, 1939-47.

————, "A Reading of *La Saisiaz,*" *University of Toronto Quarterly,* October, 1955, XXV, No. 1, 47-59.

Raymond, William O., *The Infinite Moment and other Essays in Robert Browning,* Toronto: University of Toronto Press, 1950.

————, "Truth in *The Ring and the Book,*" *Victorian News Letter,* Autumn, 1956, No. 10, 12-13.

Santayana, George, *Interpretations of Poetry and Religion,* New York: Scribners, 1900.

Smalley, Donald, *Browning's Essay on Chatterton,* Cambridge: Harvard University Press, 1948.

Stevenson, Lionel, "The Pertinacious Victorian Poets," *University of Toronto Quarterly,* April, 1952, XXI, No. 3, 232-245.

Thompson, William L., "Greek Wisdom and Browning," *Classical Journal,* May, 1950, XLV, No. 1, 246-248.

Weaver, Bennett, "A Primer Study in Browning's Satire," *College English,* November, 1952, XIV, No. 2, 76-77.

Wenger, C. N., *The Aesthetics of Robert Browning,* Ann Arbor, Michigan: George Wahr, 1924.

INDEX